# ANCIENT AND MEDIEVAL THEATRE

Ronald W. Vince

# ANCIENT AND MEDIEVAL THEATRE

A Historiographical
Handbook

**GREENWOOD PRESS**
Westport, Connecticut
London, England

**Library of Congress Cataloging in Publication Data**

Vince, Ronald W.
  Ancient and medieval theatre.

  Includes bibliographies and indexes.
    1. Theater—Greece—History.   2. Theater—Rome—
History.   3. Theater—History—Medieval, 500–1500.
I. Title.
PN2131.V5   1984        792′.09        83-18330
ISBN 0-313-24107-4 (lib. bdg.)

Library of Congress Catalog Card Number: 83-18330
ISBN: 0-313-24107-4

First published in 1984

Greenwood Press
A division of Congressional Information Service, Inc.
88 Post Road West, Westport, Connecticut 06881

Printed in the United States of America

10 9 8 7 6 5 4 3 2 1

For Jane

# CONTENTS

|  | Preface | ix |
|---|---|---|
| 1. | The Origins of the Theatre | 3 |
| 2. | The Theatre of Greece | 33 |
| 3. | The Theatre of Rome | 63 |
| 4. | The Medieval Theatre | 89 |
|  | Appendix: A Review of Medieval Dramatic Texts | 131 |
|  | Index | 151 |

# PREFACE

This book purports to provide an analytical survey of the principal written and artifactual evidence for the history of the ancient and medieval theatres. But it is also concerned with theatre historians and with some classic works of theatre history. History is created by the interaction of evidence and historian, and we can therefore come to some understanding of historical writing by considering the historian's sources, methodology, assumptions, milieu, and idiosyncracies. Sources, methods, assumptions—these can be identified or inferred; a historian's quirks of personality are more difficult to ascertain. Another way of looking at the present volume, then, is to see it as a modest step towards understanding theatre historiography, the process of writing theatre history.

Clearly, it is not possible within the compass of a single volume to discuss *all* the evidence for the ancient and medieval theatres, or to list *all* the scholarship that has contributed to our understanding of them. This handbook is a compromise between theoretical historiography and a bibliography: It includes a discussion of the various kinds of evidence, with special reference to those specific sources that have proved to be of central importance; and it provides an evaluative sketch of some important reference works. In most instances the reader is referred to a source where the original evidence is reproduced.

For students of the theatre, the decision to include the classical theatres and the medieval theatre within the same volume needs no justification: On these theatres depend the subsequent theatres of Western culture. Each is viewed as having had a separate birth, and the great national theatres of the Renaissance are normally seen as the products of a fusion of classical and medieval theatrical traditions.

Until the eighteenth century, concern with the theatre of the past meant mainly concern with the theatres of Greece and Rome; but the growth of interest in the national theatres of the seventeenth century prompted a fresh examination of the vernacular drama. Claude and François Parfaict and Pierre de Beauchamps in France, Edmond Malone in England, Casiano Pellicer in Spain—these men made a significant beginning. Still, however, the medieval theatre received short shrift. It remained at best an embarrassing precursor to the real thing.

In spite of the prejudice against the medieval drama, there were indications in the last third of the eighteenth century that a true history of the theatre was being envisaged. Thomas Percy in 1765 described the seeds of tragedy and comedy in the morality play and found those of the history play in the mystery play. The influence of classical models, he argued, was limited to accelerating an indigenous process. A few years later Thomas Hawkins speculated that modern drama was not simply a revival of ancient drama but a new creation, governed by its own laws. He discerned two distinct dramatic forms at the beginning of the sixteenth century: the first derived from Greece and Rome, the second a popular, half-formed original capable of further development.

There was as yet, however, no conception of theatre history as a discipline distinct from that of literary history, and until the two could be separated there was little likelihood of the development of the history of performance or the conditions of performance. Theatre history really began in France. Charles Magnin in 1839 looked for the origins of the modern theatre in the liturgical drama of the medieval church and compared the process to that of the development of the Greek theatre from the worship of Dionysus. Louis Leclercq in 1869 examined the conditions, the methods, and the accoutrements of performance. The distinction between theatre and literature was made even more explicit in Arthur Pougin's *Dictionnaire du théâtre* (1885), from which any consideration of drama as a form of literature was rigorously excluded. Similar principles were followed by Germain Bapst in his *Essai sur l'histoire du théâtre* (1893). By the end of the nineteenth century, procedures and attitudes were in place to begin the reconciliation of the classical-neoclassical-modern sequence of theatrical development with the awkward fact of 600 years of medieval theatre that would not go away.

Without a knowledge of theatre history we proceed in our analysis and in our performance of drama at our peril. The dynamics and style of performance depend upon the relationship between performer and audience, and it is the task of the theatre historian to reconstruct and describe the theatrical forms and conventions, the audience and the playing space that originally determined the dynamic and the style. But historians concern themselves with the *why* of theatre history as well. The attempt to account for particular conditions and styles of performance, the analysis of factors—social, economic, intellectual—affecting change, the comparison of theatrical conventions, considerations of the "shape" of theatre history (linear, degenerative, progressive, cyclic, etc.)—these too are part of the historian's job of work. What elements constitute style of performance and what factors govern changes in style? However method and procedure may vary, these questions provide the ultimate focus of theatre history.

My debts to generations of scholars are documented in the bibliographical references throughout the book. I owe a debt of gratitude as well to my colleagues Laurel Braswell, Douglas Duncan, Antony Hammond, and Richard Morton, who read the work in its earlier stages and offered valuable comment; to James Brasch, Linda Hutcheon, and Joseph Sigman for their encouragement; and to Chauncey Wood, who kept the faith.

## REFERENCES

Baker, David Erskine. *Biographica Dramatica, or, A Companion to the Playhouse.* Continued to 1782 by Isaac Reed and to 1811 by Stephen Jones. 3 Vols. London, 1812.

Bapst, Germain. *Essai sur l'histoire du théâtre.* Paris, 1893.

Beauchamps, Pierre-François Godard de. *Recherches sur les théâtres de France, depuis l'anné onze cent soixants un jusqu'à présent.* 3 Vols. Paris, 1735.

Dodsley, Robert. *A Select Collection of Old English Plays.* Ed. W. C. Hazlitt. 4th ed. 15 Vols. in 7. New York, 1964 [1874–76].

Hastings, Charles. *The Theatre, Its Development in France and England, and a History of Its Greek and Latin Origins.* London, 1901.

Hawkins, Thomas. *The Origins of the English Drama.* Oxford, 1773.

Langbaine, Gerard. *An Account of the English Dramatick Poets.* Preface Arthur Freeman. New York, 1973 [1691].

Leclercq, Louis [Ludovic Cellar]. *Les Décors, les costumes et la mise en scène au XVIIe siècle 1615–1680.* Paris, 1869.

Magnin, Charles. *Les Origines du théâtre antique et du théâtre moderne.* Paris, 1869 [1839].

Malone, Edmond. "An Historical Account of the Rise and Progress of the English Stage and of the Economy and Usages of Our Ancient Theatres." In *The Plays of William Shakespeare* (London, 1803), vol. III.

Nagler, A. M. "Introduction." *A Source Book in Theatrical History.* New York, 1959.

Parfaict, Claude and François. *L'Histoire du théâtre français depuis son origine jusqu'à présent.* Paris, 1735–49.

Pellicer, Casiano. *Tratado histórico sobre el origen y progresos de la comedia y del histrionismo en España.* 2 Vols. Madrid, 1804.

Percy, Thomas. "An Essay on the Origin of the English Stage." In *Reliques of Ancient English Poetry,* ed. H. B. Wheatley (London, 1891), vol. I.

Pougin, Arthur. *Dictionnaire historique et pittoresque du théâtre.* Paris, 1885.

Vince, R. W. "Comparative Theatre Historiography." *Essays in Theatre* I (1983), 64–72.

Wellek, René. *The Rise of English Literary History.* New York, 1966.

# ANCIENT AND MEDIEVAL THEATRE

# 1

# THE ORIGINS OF THE THEATRE

Direct evidence of theatre origins is exceedingly scant even when it is not non-existent; and methodology, although often proclaimed ''scientific'' by its practitioners, begins to depend not only upon the synthesizing ability of the human imagination, but, more seriously, upon sometimes questionable assumptions concerning human behaviour and cultural development throughout the world. The interest in the origins of the theatre gained momentum just after the turn of the century. Since the period being investigated preceded the time of written drama, the object of attention was performance, which was therefore considered antecedent to the dramatic text rather than simply its *post facto* realization; and more often than not the performance in question did not make use of the spoken word at all. Drama, then, could no longer be considered simply as literature written for performance. If its origins were, as they seemed to be, non-literary, its definition had to be expanded to include non-verbal forms as well. Moreover, since performance could take place in a variety of circumstances and could serve a variety of purposes, the drama could no longer be confined to an aesthetic context. The precise area of activity encompassed by the words ''drama'' and ''theatre'' had to be redefined, ''drama'' and ''theatre'' distinguished from the ''dramatic'' and the ''theatrical.''

So long as historians confined themselves to written dramatic texts and to written and archaeological records concerning the performance of these texts, they appear to have had little interest in the primitive origins of the drama. The earliest known theatre was that of the ancient Greeks, particularly as found in Athens in the fifth century B.C., and the most valuable evidence of that theatre was the extant dramatic texts by Aeschylus, Sophocles, Euripides, and Aristophanes. These, together with Aristotle's *Poetics*, constituted the beginnings of drama and dramatic criticism in the Western world; and historians normally traced the degeneration of classical drama in the Roman theatre and its revival in the Renaissance. The drama of the Middle Ages was something of a puzzle, for unconnected with classical drama, it appeared to represent a new beginning. Nonetheless, it was generally agreed that it represented at best a crude interlude between classical and Renaissance flowerings and that its influence on the later drama of the Renaissance was minimal.

It was recognized that drama had a close connection with religion: it was performed in Athens at a festival held in honour of the god Dionysus, and in medieval Europe it flourished originally under the auspices of the Christian Church. By the end of the nineteenth century, the initial association of drama and religion was accepted as axiomatic, but the association was pursued but a little way in the direction of pre-literary theatrical forms.

In the twentieth century, however, the exploration of the connection between religious ritual and theatre has claimed the attention of scholars of various disciplinary persuasions and casts of mind. While the fact of a connection of some sort seems generally agreed, the question of its precise nature and significance seems as difficult to answer now as it ever was. And the answers postulated over the past three-quarters of a century have seldom proved satisfactory, even for a brief period of time. Instead, there has developed what we might think of as separate but equal orthodoxies, the adherents of each either oblivious or disdainful of the other. In particular, we can trace the demarcation between traditional classical scholarship and the more speculative theories based on comparative anthropology and mythology. Students of the theatre, who are usually neither classicists nor anthropologists, are therefore called upon to evaluate highly complex theories often based on unfamiliar data interpreted within the framework of another discipline. In general, it might be said that theatre historians have been more attracted by anthropological theory than by traditional classical scholarship, but there is still no theory of theatre origins that every budding theatre historian can be expected to know. The problem is normally discussed in the most general of terms and the student then referred to some of the better known works on the subject by classicists and anthropologists as well as by theatre historians. Given the necessarily highly speculative nature of such studies, the procedure is not unreasonable, but a survey of these studies may also provide us with some conception of the central issues involved and the possible value of such studies for theatre research and performance theory.

## GREEK EVIDENCE FOR GREEK ORIGINS

The theatre on which attention was lavished most was, of course, that of ancient Greece. A typical and highly respected nineteenth-century treatment of Greek theatre was Arthur E. Haigh's *Attic Theatre* (1889). Haigh's purpose was to provide a history of the Greek drama from a theatrical rather than a literary viewpoint. He points to the fresh evidence provided by the discovery of inscriptions relating to theatrical affairs, and by the archaeological excavations of several Greek theatres being undertaken; but there is no new evidence to divert his attention to the "pre-history" of the Greek theatre. Haigh is simply not interest₁ 1 in origins. "It [the Athenian drama] was developed originally out of the songs and hymns in honour of Dionysus, the god of wine," he writes. "In later times its range was widened, and its tone secularized: but it continued to be performed solely at the festivals of Dionysus" (p. 5). Again: "The first rude innovations upon the old hymns to Dionysus were mere tentative experiments by individuals, exhibited upon their own responsibility. Thespis has the credit of having introduced tragedy into Athens" (p. 7). This is all. And there is nothing that Haigh writes that could not be extrapolated from a couple of references in Aristotle's *Poetics*.

At the end of the nineteenth century, then, there was general agreement that Greek tragedy (and comedy) had developed from hymns (dithyrambs) in honour of the god Dionysus, and that satyr-drama arose from the same source and was based on evidence that was both ancient and written. While the most revered authority was Aristotle, other ancient authors of varying credibility were cited in support. In the *Poetics* Aristotle tells us: (*a*) that comedy was claimed by the Megarians and tragedy by the Dorians, both claims being based on the evidence of language (III; 1448a30–35); (*b*) that both were improvised forms, tragedy derived from the dithyramb, comedy from the phallic songs (IV; 1449a10–14); and (*c*) that back of tragedy lay the satyr-play as well (IV; 1449a20–25). So far as they concern tragedy—which has been the major focus of origin studies—these passages point not only to a non-Athenian source, but also to the dithyramb and the satyr-drama as precursors of the tragic form. Aristotle does not mention Dionysus, however, and evidence from other sources had to be brought to bear on the subject in order to forge a link between the dithyramb and the god. Passages from writers as diverse as the poet Archilochus (ca. 700 B.C.), the philosopher Plato (428–348 B.C.), and the dramatist Euripides (who referred to Dionysus as "Dithyrambos") are cited in support of the connection. Names of authors who link the dithyramb with tragedy are provided by the historian Herodotus (ca. 484-ca. 424 B.C.), the rhetorician Themistius (fourth century A.D.), and the *Suda*, a lexicon compiled about the tenth century A.D. Herodotus (I.23) refers to one Arion of Methymna as the originator of the dithyramb. The *Suda* (s.v. "Arion") credits Arion with the invention of tragedy and with the introduction of verse-speaking satyrs. Themistius cites Aristotle as authority for his contention that it was Thespis who introduced a prologue and the set speech to the choric dithyramb. (See Gerald F. Else, *The Origin and Early Form of Greek Tragedy*, p. 113.) Not only then are Arion and Thespis now identified as significant figures in the early development of tragedy, but the *Suda* manages to ring in satyrs as well.

The origins of comedy were considered similar to those of tragedy and are equally difficult to document. A standard reference book of 1897 reports: "The Greek comedy, like the Greek tragedy and satyric drama, had its origins in the festivals of Dionysus. As its name . . . implies, it arose from the unrestrained singing and jesting common in the *komos*, or merry procession of Dionysus. According to the tradition, it was the Doric inhabitants of Megara . . . who first worked up the jokes into a kind of farce'' (*Harper's Dictionary of Classical Literature and Antiquities*, s.v. ''Comoedia''). Aristotle is once again cited as the prime authority, supported by passing references in Athenaeus' *Deipnosophistae* (ca. A.D. 200) and Plutarch (fl. ca. A.D. 100). And again, we know of an early figure—Susarion—whose name appears on the Parian Marble (see Chapter 2) and who is referred to by Clement of Alexandria (ca. A.D. 200) as the man who brought the old Megarian comedy to Attica about 570 B.C. Yet once more the association was made between religious cult and drama: The ''phallic songs'' were considered to be the comic equivalent of the dithyramb. Behind dithyramb, satyr-play, tragedy, and comedy, it was argued, lay the religious cult of Dionysus.

Coming as it does from such a variety of sources from such disparate periods of time, the value of this evidence depends to a large extent on the degree to which it can be used to illuminate the testimony of Aristotle. Unfortunately, Aristotle himself is inconsistent. Moreover, there is little evidence that the philosopher was much of a historian, or even very interested in history: His historical sketches of tragedy and comedy probably derive more from his convictions concerning their natures than from knowledge of historical fact.

Certainly, not all classical scholars were satisfied with Aristotle's account, however elaborated and rationalized from other sources, or with the theory of a common origin for all Greek drama. William Ridgeway claimed to have decided as early as 1904 that the then current notions concerning origins had no basis in fact and that, at least so far as tragedy was concerned, it was necessary to ''completely remodel our views.'' He subsequently published his own theory in *The Origin of Tragedy* (1910). What is important about Ridgeway's book is not the specific theory which, elaborated five years later in *Dramas and Dramatic Dances*, was simply that Greek tragedy arose out of rituals for the heroic dead on which was superimposed the cult of Dionysus; but rather the idea that all dramatic forms need not have developed from the same source. Tragedy, he argued, having descended from these rituals, was essentially a religious rite and therefore the responsibility of the state. The satyr-play, associated with the worship of Dionysus, was grafted onto the older ritual and similarly underwritten by the state. But comedy, growing out of ''rustic buffoonery,'' had no religious function and was consequently not officially recognized until both tragedy and comedy had developed into sophisticated forms of drama.

Ridgeway altered the evidence available in only one minor respect: He drew attention to a further passage in Herodotus (V.67) which describes how the tyrant of Sicyon transferred the tragic chorus paid as a tribute to a local dead hero, Adrastus, to Dionysus. What is of more importance is that he tried to examine the parts of the evidence individually as opposed to attempting to fuse them into a single picture with Dionysus at its centre. But Ridgeway was determinedly independent as well as analytical, and his work was rejected both by main-stream classical scholars (who continued his analytical method) and by the Dionysian synthesizers.

## COMPARATIVE ANTHROPOLOGY

Traditional classical scholarship then was unlikely to provide any further insight into the origins of either the Greek theatre or theatre in general. What was needed was new evidence of a different kind and a new methodology to deal with it. The end of the nineteenth and the beginning of the twentieth centuries saw that new evidence and that new methodology in the development of the social sciences, which attempted to apply the methods of science, particularly biological science, to human behaviour and human institutions. In particular, the theory of evolution was enthusiastically embraced by the social sciences, especially cultural anthropology. Its application depended upon the assumption that surviving primitive peoples represent earlier stages in the development of modern society. Here then is the new evidence, derived from the reports of explorers, travellers, missionaries, and colonial administrators, as well as from the observations of trained anthropologists. This procedure had obvious weaknesses, as its critics have noted. It is therefore ironic that the most famous and influential work of comparative anthropology in history was written by a man who was never in the field, but who relied exclusively on materials gathered by others. *The Golden Bough* by Sir James Frazer, a classicist as well as an anthropologist, appeared in a two-volume edition in 1890; by 1915 the third edition numbered twelve volumes. Whatever social scientists now think of his method, Frazer saw himself as a pioneer in a new science. In his introduction to the second edition (1900) he wrote: ''I offer my book as a contribution to that still youthful science which seeks to trace the growth of human thought and institutions in those dark ages which lie beyond the range of history.''

We shall have occasion later to examine Frazer's more direct contribution to the theory of theatre origins. For the moment we need consider only the implications for theatre historians of the youthful science of which Frazer's work was the *magnum opus*. In the first place, it provided a means by which social and cultural phenomena could be interpreted according to a meaningful pattern, and it did so in two ways. From the theory of evolution it borrowed the idea of inevitable development from the simple to the complex and the differentiated; and, given such a sequence, it was possible to postulate a series of stages of development, whether or not it could be demonstrated that any given society had gone through all of them. In other words, the hypothesis told investigators what they *ought* to find: Evidence was used to confirm or alter or reject the hypothesis. This, of course, is the methodology of modern science, both biological and physical. (Whether the method is valid when applied to the social sciences is another matter.) In the second place, the general procedure opened the way for a very unscientific eclecticism in which, by carefully selecting evidence from the wealth of material available—some valid, some not—a theorist could support any one of several hypotheses. Finally, in that the evidence adduced for reconstructing events in a distant past was actually drawn from a much later, even a contemporary, period, history became in a sense ahistorical. Theories of theatre origins based on the methods of comparative anthropology, therefore, depended upon the assumption of the universality of cultural phenomena and development—evidence from any culture, past or contemporary, might be used to reconstruct a kind of ur-process whereby the emergence of theatre anywhere can be explained; and proceeded by a method of analogy— what is known to be true at one time and place might be assumed to be true at another time and place where evidence is lacking.

Actually the whole process proceeded according to a series of assumed identities: the development of man from animal to human; the development of society from primitive to civilized; the development of human beings from child to adult. Anthropological studies were therefore joined by studies of animal behaviour and developmental psychology, specifically those of Karl Groos. In *The Play of Animals* (1896; tr. 1898), Groos hypothesized that some animals required youthful play in order to perfect behavioral patterns necessary for survival but not instinctive. And in *The Play of Man* (1901) he extended his thesis to man, but enlarged his study to explore the basis for the pleasure we derive from play. The linking of play and drama seemed obvious: Many languages, including English, refer to a drama as a "play" and to its performance as "playing." (A later and more comprehensive study is Johann Huizinga's *Homo Ludens: A Study of the Play Element in Culture*, 1955.) All of these elements found their way into discussions of theatre's origins.

One of the earliest, and because of the unspecific and general nature of its treatment and its conclusions, ultimately one of the most influential attempts to explore the primitive beginnings of drama was Loomis Havemeyer's *The Drama of Savage Peoples* (1916). Havemeyer professed his allegiance to "the great modern doctrine of evolution" and proposed to do for drama what Frazer had done for religion—find its origins in primitive and simple forms. He found "simple stages and undeveloped forms" of all institutions among savage peoples: "What we mean to show is that the savage drama is the lineal antecedent of all modern forms, and hence that a knowledge of it is needful, in order to fill out the perspective and to afford a lapse of time sufficient to allow a conception of evolution in this social form" (p. 6). And, of course, the theory fills in where there are gaps in the sequence of evidence. Noting that there is no record of any intermediate steps between primitive dramatic ceremonies and the highly sophisticated drama of Greece or Japan, Havemeyer remains confident. "But despite this absence of a full series of transitional forms," he writes, "but little doubt should remain that there obtains, in the growth of the drama, the same development of form out of form, in a connected series, which characterizes the process of evolution elsewhere in nature and in society" (pp. 121–122). His method was simply to cite facts and observations collected by ethnologists from societies around the world in support of his contentions. The reason for this is both an assumption and a conclusion: Havemeyer assumes the universality of patterns of cultural development and concludes that no matter where his examples are taken from, the same fundamental elements always appear. The hypothesis determines the selection of data; and the data support the hypothesis.

Havemeyer assumes the virtual identity of "play" (in Groos's sense) and drama, and considers them both manifestations of the human predilection for imitation; and he finds this playful imitation in religious rites and ceremonies as well as in theatre proper. These ceremonies, acted in "his rough and awkward way," were savage man's "unconscious drama" (pp. 13–14). The development of drama from unconscious to conscious Havemeyer distinguishes into three stages: (1) the use of imitative gesture to convey meaning at a point in human cultural development when the spoken language is inadequate; (2) the use of performance in a religious context in order to facilitate communication with gods and spirits; and (3) the use of performance after the religious purpose has dropped away simply for the sake of amusement of an audience. Oddly, Havemeyer's "highest" stage of dramatic performance, which fulfills the definition of "play"—that is, something done for the sake of the doing, not for what is done—seems a hollow thing compared to the second stage. "As culture advances," he says, "the more important functions for which the drama was intended by its originators drop out, leaving only the shell" (pp. 173–174). On the other hand, Havemeyer determinedly keeps the Greek drama from becoming a shell-game by insisting that it was always religious and never purely entertainment.

Havemeyer's theory is broad enough to accommodate more specific theories of theatre origin and, with the exception of his questionable notion that gesture preceded language in human development, it retains enough seeming commonsense and coherence to remain an attractive, though often unacknowledged, underpinning to introductions to the subject of origins. In particular, the perception of a relationship between religious ceremony and theatre, and Havemeyer's perhaps unconscious preference for the phase in the development of the drama when the connection was most intimate, not only reflects an attitude common during the early years of this century but also anticipates the sometimes desperate attempts of much avant-garde theatre of our own day to make something "holy" out of the theatre, to re-invest the entertaining "shell" with significance.

Havemeyer's discussion of religious ceremonies was not restrictive: he ranged from the Hopi rain-making ceremony to the Christian mass, from totem worship to war dances to initiation ceremonies. Other writers were more specific. William Ridgeway entered the comparative lists in 1915 with *The Dramas and Dramatic Dances of Non-European Races*, partly in response to a new theory of the ritual origins of Greek tragedy and comedy derived specifically from Frazer's work. (See the section on "The Cambridge Anthropologists" below.)

While Ridgeway specifically rejects Frazer's theory that the various gods are individual embodiments of an abstract vegetation spirit, he does not reject Frazer's basic method. Previous historians, he notes, "instead of seeking for the origins of the Drama by a rigid application of the historical and inductive method have approached its study from the *a priori* standpoint of pure Aesthetics . . . [with] little regard being had to the anthropological method" (p. 1). Unlike Frazer—and Havemeyer—however, who had tended to use data abstracted from their cultural context, Ridgeway was careful to treat each culture and its drama separately. He offers the earliest and one of the few discussions of the origins of drama in western Asia, Egypt, Hindustan, Java, Burma, the Malay Peninsula, Cambodia, China, and Japan, and cites examples from contemporary primitive societies in Melanesia, Africa, and America as further support of his conclusions. Ridgeway relied on the work of experts in each area; his contribution lay in his comparative method. Wide-ranging as his investigations are, however, he took pride in the fact that he had not been seduced by the mystery of the exotic and the temptation to mythologize which he believed had misled Frazer and his followers, and which made their work so attractive to the public. Not surprisingly, his more rigorous comparative method resulted in a conclusion as sweeping and all-embracing as that of Frazer. Where the latter had suggested the origin of drama lay in the dramatization of the dying seasons, personified in various gods, Ridgeway concluded that dramatic performances arose everywhere from the worship of the heroic dead. Central to his argument was the conviction that the human mind does not normally proceed from the abstract to the particular, but from the particular to the abstract, that beneath Frazer's vegetation gods there was in each instance a real human being. There is still a religious origin for the drama, but behind the religion there is a more banal reality, for example: "Under the coffin of Adonis lies the body of some young Asiatic prince cut off in the springtime of life by the onset of a charging boar" (p. 89). Ridgeway is in a way far less speculative than Frazer or even Havemeyer, but like all comparativists he assumes, however details may vary from culture to culture, that the process of theatrical development is everywhere the same. The presentation of his evidence is intended to convince by accretion.

Havemeyer's and Ridgeway's attempts to discover a simple comprehensive origin for all drama were overshadowed at the time by the theory of ritual origin developed by the so-called Cambridge School of Anthropology in connection with the beginnings of tragedy and comedy in Greece. And the assumptions on which they based their work have been challenged by later anthropological theorists. Nevertheless, they did draw attention, along with Frazer, to the fact that religious observances and theatre often share elements of both performance and function. It seems futile to deny that religious rite is one source for theatre, although it seems likely that it is not the only possible source. In other words, there is no reason for assuming either that all theatre arose from religious rite or that ritual inevitably gives rise to theatre. Nor is there any reason for assuming that theatre evolved the same way in all cultures. The focussing of attention on a single theatre—usually that of Greece or medieval Europe—was clearly a more fruitful approach to take, although here too, as we shall see, comparative anthropology had a crucial role to play.

Given the apparent limitations of comparative anthropology, it is somewhat surprising to find the method resurrected as late as 1975 by E. T. Kirby in *Ur-Drama: The Origins of Theatre*. Kirby derides the anthropological myth of the nineteenth century, rejects the theories of Havemeyer and Ridgeway, and claims to base his study on new anthropological data and theory. The origins of the theatre have been somewhat neglected, he argues, but the time for a fresh appraisal has come:

Fine practical and conceptual field work has continued to supply vital new information which illuminates the subject directly or provides the means by which the origin and early development of forms can be reconstructed with some degree of accuracy. While certain information has been irretrievably lost, and some aspects of reconstruction must depend, as they have in the past, upon circumstantial evidence, the network of this evidence will continue to draw tighter. [p. xvi]

The information may indeed be new; but we have heard that confident tone before.

Kirby notes his indebtedness to Ridgeway's discussion of trance mediums from Burma, China, Japan, and Africa. And it is from the secondary theory advanced by Ridgeway on the basis of this discussion—that is, that the actor was originally a medium—that Kirby develops his own theory that shamanistic performance "has almost invariably been the antecedent of established theatre forms" (p. 2). The shaman performs in a trance in order to cure the sick through ritual. This performance, argues Kirby, comes to depend upon the shared participation of an audience. This leads to more elaborate curing ceremonies and trance dances, and this complex in turn develops into pure theatre, "spectacles from which the functional element has disappeared" (p. 3). We can only hope that the theatre has some function; for we are once again confronted with Havemeyer's "shell." On the other hand, Kirby raises serious and interesting doubts concerning Havemeyer's (and Aristotle's) assumptions that the desire to imitate is a universal human trait and that theatre is fundamentally a mimetic art. Ritual, he argues, is distinguished from ordinary life specifically through abstraction and stylization. Also valuable is the comparison of the techniques of the shaman and the actor.

Not so acceptable is Kirby's insistence on shamanism as the single origin of dramatic performance. His "need to prove shamanistic performance the 'origin,' " complained one reviewer, "forces discrete anthropological material into configurations which prevent us from considering it as anything but a row of items in a single argument" (Linda Walsh Jenkins, *Theatre Survey*, XIX [1978], 84–86). In short, the objections that applied to Havemeyer and Ridgeway apply with equal validity to Kirby. Contemporary theatre historians not only distrust the method and therefore the conclusions, but they also suspect that studies such as Kirby's draw attention away from the specific examples of ritualistic or ceremonial or primitive performance, and thus from the insights concerning theatre that might be derived from a disinterested comparison of these performances. Once the necessity of proving a single origin is gone, it is possible to look at Kirby's evidence and pose quite a different hypothesis, as does George R. Kernodle in another review: "I suspect that there is more evidence for considering ritual, shamanistic trance, play and games as age-old forms parallel to theatre—variant ways of knowing our relations to the gods and to our own history and destiny" (*Educational Theatre Journal*, XXVIII [1976], 435–436). And a one-volume history of the theatre by a European, Cesare Molinari's *Theatre through the Ages* (1975), offers, instead of a chapter on origins, a chapter entitled "Theatre among Primitive Peoples." "We are not attempting to make contact with the origins of the theatre as we know it," writes Molinari, "but to become acquainted with quite different theatrical forms. . . . [A modern audience] needs to realize which are the key elements of the problematic notion conjured up by the word 'theatre' " (p. 13). The time was not auspicious for Ridgeway in 1915; the time was not right for Kirby in 1975. The materials collected for the purpose of comparison remain valuable; and occasional insights or speculations do provoke further discussion. But single-origin theories have in general given way to studies of particular theatres at particular times.

## THE CAMBRIDGE ANTHROPOLOGISTS

The Cambridge School of Anthropology was so named because three of its four members—Sir James Frazer, Jane Harrison, and Francis M. Cornford—were associated with Cambridge University and because its acknowledged leader, Frazer, was indeed an anthropologist. On the other hand, all four were classical scholars, and the most articulate spokesman for the group, Gilbert Murray, was not only primarily a student of literature but an Oxonian to boot. Moreover, although the four were friends, the divergence of their interests as reflected in their published work would suggest that "school" has limited validity as a collective noun. Aside from Frazer, Harrison was primarily interested in Greek religion, Cornford in ancient philosophy, and Murray in the traditions of classical literature. Nevertheless, the latter three acknowledged the influence of Frazer and it is therefore *The Golden Bough* which must claim our initial attention.

As we have seen, Frazer was very much the product of his age: He shared its rationalism and its evolutionary ethic, but he also shared its mythological imagination in a way that puzzled his contemporaries. A recent study of *The Golden Bough* notes that "Frazer shows us the rational, evolutionary, historical, scientific temper conspiring with as well as opposing the imaginative, spiritual, irrational, myth-making impulses of mankind" (John B. Vickery, *The Literary Impact of "The Golden Bough*," p. 5). It is this interaction that makes Frazer's work a literary classic as well as a pioneer, though flawed, study in magic and religion, and that helps to raise his theories to the level of myth, the validity of which we are either persuaded of or not, irrespective of factual evidence. Certainly he shared the questionable assumptions concerning the universality of the process of social and religious development, the possibility of arranging stages of human development in chronological order, and the progress of humankind from savagery to civilization. And his methodological faults were also serious: He had no concept of cultural stratification; he assumed historical explanations of folk customs to be latter-day inventions; and he relied too heavily on amateurish accounts of primitive customs provided by tourists or missionaries who were ignorant of the relevant languages. But these assumptions and methods are questionable on the basis of rational and scientific thought. Although Frazer believed in science, he recognized that it, like religion and like magic, was "nothing but [a theory] of thought," that he was engaged in a speculative hypothesis, the value of which was as dependent on his imagination as on fact. In the conclusion to *The Golden Bough*, Frazer refers to the sound of the church bells of Rome being heard on the shores of Lake Nemi. It was objected "by a distinguished scholar" that this was a physical impossibility. Frazer's answer to the objection, printed in his introduction to the second edition, is as significant for understanding the man and his work as anything he wrote. Citing a similar defense offered by Walter Scott to a similar objection to a passage in *Old Mortality*, Frazer writes: "In the same spirit I make bold to say that by the Lake of Nemi I love to hear, if it be only in imagination, the distant chiming of the bells of Rome, and I would fain believe that their airy music may ring in the ears of my readers after it has ceased to vibrate in my own."

Frazer's theories are actually relatively straightforward. He believed that the evolution of societies proceeded through three stages: (1) the stage of the hunt, in which magic was the dominant mode of knowledge; (2) the pastoral stage, in which religion replaced magic; and (3) the agricultural stage, which is dominated by science. He argued that primitive deities were primarily vegetation gods, and that Christianity derives from fertility cults in which the dying and reviving vegetation-god is central. Finally, he hypothesized that myths are the dramatic or narrative records of ritual performances, and that they therefore retain the imprint of these rites. The central "ur-myth" which ties *The Golden Bough* together is that of the dying and reviving vegetation-god, linked with the rhythm of nature and variously personified in the figures of Tammuz, Adonis, Attis, Hyacinth, Osiris, and—most significant of all for the study of the Greek theatre—Dionysus.

Jane Harrison was more interested in Greek religion than in Greek theatre, and she brought Frazer's insights to bear on the Greek religious experience, using clues from Australian aboriginal rites, African voodoo, and American Indian rituals to elucidate a religion and a theology that she saw as essentially primitive. Behind the dithyramb was the *drōmenon*, a rite of group initiation, a thing "re-done" or "pre-done." And it was at this level that she implies a

connection between religion and theatre. The thing done is neither religious nor
theatrical. The thing re-done as a mimetic act begins to be both: "In all religion, as in all art, there is this element of make-believe, not the attempt to
deceive, but a desire to *re*-live, to *re*-present" (*Themis*, p. 43). While this comment is interesting, *Themis* is significant for another reason. Buried in this erudite and difficult book on Greek religion is Gilbert Murray's "Excursus on the
Ritual Forms Preserved in Greek Tragedy" (pp. 341–363), destined to become
the cornerstone of the ritual origin theory.

Murray did not begin in a vacuum; nor did he see himself as breaking new
ground, except insofar as he developed the relationship between the idea of
Dionysus as vegetation-god and Greek tragedy and comedy. His assumptions
as he sets them out are as follows:

1. Tragedy is in origin a *Sacer Ludus*, a ritual dance, representing normally the *Aition*
   or the supposed historical cause of some current ritual practice.
2. The dance was originally or centrally that of Dionysus, performed at his feast, in his
   theatre.
3. Dionysus was the *Eniautos-Daimon* or vegetation-god, who, like Adonis and Osiris,
   represented the cyclic death and rebirth of the world, the tribe's lands, and the tribe
   itself.
4. Tragedy and comedy represent different stages in the life of this vegetation-god or
   "Year-Spirit"; tragedy leads to his death and *threnos* (lamentation); comedy to his
   marriage feast and *komos* (celebration).

Murray's debt to Frazer is clear; and he acknowledges the work of others, particularly that of Albrecht Dieterich, who in 1907 had argued in a similar vein.
He admits that the extant examples of Greek tragedy contain many non-Dio-
nysiac elements, derived from the epic, from hero cults and from other ceremonies, but he insists that the original imprint is discoverable: "While the content has strayed far from Dionysus, the forms of tragedy retain clear traces of
the original drama of the Death and Rebirth of the Year Spirit" (p. 342).

The pattern of the underlying myth, reflected in the dramatic texts, Murray
postulates thus: (*a*) *Agon*—the struggle between Summer and Winter, Light and
Dark, the Year Spirit and his enemy; (*b*) *Pathos*—the death of the god (Adonis,
Osiris, Dionysus, etc.), the *sparagmos* or tearing apart; (*c*) *Messenger*—who
announces the death of the god; (*d*) *Threnos* or lamentation; (*e*) *Theophany*—
the discovery or recognition of the reborn god, his resurrection, apotheosis,
ephiphany; together with an accompanying *peripeteia* from sorrow to joy. The
bulk of the "Excursus" is then devoted to analyses of three tragedies by Euripides—*Andromache*, *Hippolytus*, and especially the *Bacchae*, "a most instruc-
tive instance of the formation of drama out of ritual" (p. 346). By the end of
his essay, in fact, Murray has shifted his focus from origins to dramatic criticism.

Murray was a sensitive and perceptive literary critic, and the best of his criticism depends very little on the validity of his theory of the ritual origins of tragedy. But that his interests were primarily critical is borne out by his subsequent career, and particularly by his fascinating study of Hamlet and Orestes, delivered as the Annual Shakespeare Lecture before the British Academy in 1914. (See *The Classical Tradition in Poetry*, pp. 180–210.)

In *The Origin of Attic Comedy* (1914; rpt. 1961), Francis Cornford attempts to explain the origins of Old Comedy on the basis of the same ritual propounded by Murray for tragedy. The forms inherited from ritual drama in honour of Dionysus, Cornford argues, are traceable in the "constant features" of Aristophanes' plays, and the content of this ritual drama can therefore be reconstructed. Cornford is explicit about the source for his theory. "This hypothesis," he writes, "was . . . forced upon me by the facts; but very probably it would never have occurred to me, if I had not had in my mind Murray's theory of the 'ritual forms' in Tragedy. My debt to him is, therefore, great" (p. xxxi). Cornford notes that Attic comedy begins with a struggle or *agon* and ends with a marriage (or a sexual union) and an attendant celebration or *komos*. The comedy developed two regular incidents in addition—the scene of sacrifice and the scene of feasting—but the ritual pattern of agon, pathos, and resurrection governs the structure of the comic drama. Perhaps because he developed his thesis over an entire book and thus provided more scope for attack, perhaps because he was a less sensitive reader of texts than Murray while retaining his enthusiasm, perhaps because he wrote about comedy rather than tragedy, Cornford has not exerted the degree of influence his friend did, and his theories have been more easily dismissed. Even those who agree in general with the theory are hesitant about Cornford's application of it. "It is one thing to prove that Greek comedy in general derives from a primitive ritual pattern," writes Theodore Gaster in the Foreword to the 1961 reprint of Cornford's book; "quite another to identify specific features of the plays of Aristophanes as relics of that pattern."

The Cambridge Anthropologists postulated a ritual pattern and claimed to have discovered traces of it in the extant texts of the Greek dramatists. The traces are not so obvious as to provide in themselves the outline of the ritual—as Cornford noted—and therefore the theory is dependent upon evidence drawn from a variety of cultures and folk customs. The method is still common among students of comparative religions. (One of them, as we shall see, might be considered to be a junior scholar of the Cambridge School.) But the absence of specifically *Greek* evidence concerning the ritual in question, and the lack of any evidence by which the development of Greek drama from ritual can be traced has led classical scholars almost from the beginning to reject the theory—at least so far as its details are concerned. Perhaps the severest criticism of all is that Murray's and Cornford's readings of the plays are faulty. Else's description of Murray's attempt to apply the theory to the extant plays as "a tissue of *non-sequiturs* and *petitiones principii*" (*The Origin and Early Form of Greek Tragedy*, p. 28) is perhaps harsh, but it is an opinion with which many would agree; for instance, A. W. Pickard-Cambridge: "It is only possible to find the

Forms in the extant plays if their order . . . can be changed to almost any extent, and the very broadest meaning given to the terms themselves" (*Dithyramb, Tragedy and Comedy*, p. 192). The most fundamental objection remains, nevertheless, that there is no evidence of the ritual described by Murray as ever having existed in Greece, and it was in Greece and Greece alone that tragedy emerged.

Nevertheless, there is little doubt that the ritual theory of theatre origin formulated and promulgated by the Cambridge School of Anthropology, however sceptically received by classicists, made a deep and lasting impact on students of the drama. Gerald F. Else points out in *The Origin and Early Form of Greek Tragedy* (1965; rpt. 1972) that the theory is not held, at least in any strict sense, by any leading classical scholar, and he expresses considerable concern that it was accepted without question by Francis Fergusson in *The Idea of a Theatre* (1949), "one of the most penetrating and influential books written on the drama in our time." Else interprets this as evidence of "intellectual lag between one field and another" and clearly in his own book tries, for the benefit of all concerned, to set the record straight. On the other hand, it is difficult to reconcile "the misreadings and misinterpretations" based on the uncritical acceptance of a discredited theory with the "penetrating" nature of Fergusson's study. Either the theory provides a valid frame of reference for critical commentary or Fergusson is a good critic in spite of the theory. There is yet another possibility: However inaccurate as a record of the historical origins of the theatre, the ritual theory appeals on a metaphorical level to unconscious patterns and longings in our own psyches and we find drama considered in its terms a richer and more satisfying experience than it might otherwise be. The point is worth making here, not only because of the theory's staying power, but because the real emphasis of the studies carried out by the Cambridge School of Anthropology was not anthropological at all, but literary. In fact, it did nothing more, so far as origins are concerned, than to elaborate and confirm on the basis of theories proposed in *The Golden Bough* the idea, current at the turn of the century, of a common origin for all Greek drama. Its real contribution was to interpret plays in the light of these theories.

## THE EGYPTIAN CONNECTION

As part of his argument that tragedy originated in a kind of passion-play with the ubiquitous vegetation-god as its protagonist, Murray cited several passages in Herodotus that identified Dionysus with Osiris, and that purported to give accounts of the ritual of Osiris in Egypt and to describe a festival of Osiris analogous to that of Dionysus in Greece. (See Herodotus, *Histories*, II, 42, 48, 61, 132, 144, 170.) Since 1912, a good deal has been discovered and written about this Egyptian connection, and the same seasonal pattern discussed by Murray and Cornford has been postulated as underlying religious practices, not only in Egypt but throughout the Near East among the Mesopotamians, Canaanites, and Hittites 1,000 years before Aeschylus. Theodore H. Gaster in *Thespis: Ritual, Myth, and Drama in the Ancient Near East* (1950) traces the now-familiar seasonal pattern in several mythological texts from the ancient Near East, the most important of which—from the point of view of theatre history— being the "dramatic" texts from Egypt.

Gaster's relationship with the Cambridge School is easily documented. He is the editor of *The New Golden Bough* (1959), a one-volume redaction of Frazer's work; he contributed an introduction to the 1961 reprint of Cornford's *Origin of Attic Comedy*, and Gilbert Murray did the same for *Thespis*. And the relationship is more than perfunctory: Gaster continued the method and the interests of the master, and shared with Murray and Cornford the conviction of the ritual origins of drama. In his comparative analysis—on the psychological rather than the historical level, he explains—of Near Eastern texts, Gaster believes he has provided support for their theories. The seasonal pattern described by Gaster bears a marked resemblance to that described by Murray: (*a*) the king, as representative of the topocosmic spirit, is deposed or slain; (*b*) a temporary king is appointed; (*c*) the king is ceremonially purified in some manner; (*d*) the king engages an antagonist in mock combat, undergoes a sacred marriage, and either he is ceremonially instated or a successor is inducted; and (*e*) the pattern concludes with an appropriate celebration. Again, then, we have a "persistent formal cause" of drama. Gaster's description of the process by which ritual becomes drama has a sophisticated ring to it, but it also echoes Frazer and Harrison and Murray. The community rites, says Gaster, centre on a representative individual, a king, who

does on the punctual plane [what] the god does on the durative. Accordingly, all the ceremonies performed by the king are transmuted, through the medium of myth, into deeds done by the god. This transmutation in turn gives rise to the idea that the king and the other performers of the seasonal rites are merely impersonating acts originally performed by the gods, and the tendency develops to represent what is really a parallel situation on the durative plane as something that happened primordially—the archetype of what may be periodically repeated with the same effect. Presentation then becomes representation; the ritual turns into drama.[pp. 17–18]

Gaster is clearly thinking of drama as literature, and although he notes that the Hittite *Snaring of the Dragon* and the *Canaanite Poem of the Gracious Gods* "seem certainly" to have been the spoken accompaniment of ritual acts, most of his discussion concerns texts having little or no association with performance or theatre.

The exceptions to this are the Egyptian materials, which are at least arguably dramatic although their "performance" remained ritualistic and therefore continues to beg the question concerning the relationship between ritual and theatre. (Gaster skirts the difficulty by referring to "ritual and drama.") These Egyptian texts are, nevertheless, very suggestive.

1. *Ramesseum Drama*. This coronation drama, inscribed on papyrus, was discovered in
   1896 in the precincts of the *Ramesseum* at Thebes. The papyrus was written in the
   reign of Sesostris I (ca. 1970 B.C.), but the scholar who published the text estimates
   that the contents go back as far as 3300 B.C. The "play" consists of an account in
   forty-six "scenes" of the ceremonies performed at the installation of a new king.
   Kurt Sethe published the text in *Dramatische Texte zu Altaegyptischen Mysterienspielen* (1928); and Gaster provides an English translation based on Sethe's text in
   *Thespis* (pp. 378–399).

2. *Memphite Drama*. This text is inscribed on a slab of black granite now in the British
   Museum. The slab was set up by one King Shabaka about 711 B.C., but the inscription itself dates between 3300 and 2500 B.C. The drama depicts the contest of Horus
   and Set, the triumph of Horus, and the death and resurrection of Osiris. (See Sethe's
   *Dramatische Texte* and Gaster, pp. 401–405.)

3. *Edfu Drama*. This was found, along with illustrative reliefs, on a wall of the temple
   at Edfu and evidently represents the text of a drama performed annually at a spring
   festival. (For an English translation see A. M. Blackman and H. W. Fairman, *Journal of Egyptian Archaeology*, 28 [1942], 32–38; 29 [1943], 2–36; and 30 [1944],
   5–22; also Fairman's *Triumph of Horus*, 1974.)

There is one further bit of evidence from Egypt attesting to dramatic activity
of some sort. It consists of a short description of the ceremonies performed in
connection with the festival of Osiris by one Ikhernofret, who participated in it
at Abydos about 1870 B.C. The description comprises lines 17–24 of a limestone stele, now in the Königliches Museum in Berlin. An English translation
is provided by Gaster (pp. 67–68).

The difficulties of interpreting this Egyptian material are formidable, and its
significance uncertain. So far as we know, Egypt never developed a theatre that
was not bound to ritual and worship; and the relationship between Egyptian ritual and Greek drama depends on highly speculative extrapolation from Herodotus' tenuous testimony. Gaster demonstrated the presence of Murray's seasonal pattern in myth and mythic literature two millenia before its articulation
in Greek drama, but in itself this tells little about drama's origins. In the first
place, the identification of drama with the *agon* or struggle allows too much
non-theatrical literature to qualify as "dramatic," and at the same time ex-
cludes performances that do not feature conflict. In the second place, while Gaster
assumes that there is no meaningful or useful distinction to be made between
ritual and theatre, most historians of the theatre would disagree, arguing that
their different purposes and effects are of crucial importance.

## OTHER THEORIES OF THE ORIGINS OF THE GREEK
## THEATRE

What we might consider the orthodox view of the origin of Greek theatre is
provided by A. W. Pickard-Cambridge in *Dithyramb, Tragedy and Comedy*
(1927; rev. 1962), the standard survey of the subject and its evidence. The

problem so far as tragedy is concerned is to reconcile the passages in Aristotle that locate the origins of tragedy in both the dithyramb and the satyr-play. The nineteenth-century answer had been to postulate a dithyramb of satyrs, the invention of Arion, as the source of tragedy. But a further problem presents itself: Tragedy deals mainly in heroic myth, but it was presented at the Festival of Dionysus. Moreover, there is the question of how the element of sorrow and lament entered a form derived from the joyful ribaldry of the satyr-play. Pickard-Cambridge, specifically discounting vase-paintings and non-Greek dramatic rituals and ceremonies, takes as his major evidence only written records. He acknowledges that this evidence is late and fragmentary, but argues that it is the product of scholars "of great industry, ability, and discernment" and can be disregarded only at great risk. A hypothesis formed on the basis of such evidence, "though it may not be proved, is likely to be nearer the truth than one based on *a priori* assumptions and indifferent to the literary evidence" (pp. vii-ix). He postulates that there were two types of performance associated with the worship of Dionysus: the serious dithyramb, developed as a literary form by Arion at Corinth (whence Aristotle's reference to "certain Dorians"), and the dance of satyrs or Selini, brought by the tragic poet Pratina to Athens where, at the end of the sixth century, it became partially assimilated with tragedy (performed as the fourth play of a tragic tetralogy). The threnodic element derived from the dramatic or semi-dramatic choral performances—much as described by Ridgeway—which provided Thespis with his opportunity to invent an actor and bring his "plays" to Athens where they were "grafted" onto the spring Dionysiac festival:

This village drama met and mingled in Athens with another outcome of the solemn side of Dionysiac ritual, the lyrics which were composed to the music in the *tragikos tropos* invented by Arion, and were in vogue also at Sicyon and perhaps at other places; and by its union with these, and under the influence of contemporary Greek lyric poetry generally, tragedy became elevated into a supremely noble form of literature, as we see it in Aeschylus. [p. 219]

Pickard-Cambridge similarly denies comedy a specifically Dionysiac origin, but since written records are even more fragmentary for comedy than they are for tragedy, he is forced to rely on vase-paintings to support his contention that it derived from animal masquerades and from Megaran farce, "vulgar and probably indecent" (p. 277). In its Attic form, comedy originated at best in a synthesis of archaic rituals.

Once again, then, we find the tendency to analyze the evidence in terms of its parts, leading to the idea that the various forms of the Greek drama arose independently of one another and became associated with Dionysiac festivals only after they had attained the forms pretty much as we know them. Moreover, the forms themselves are made out to be the product of various elements coming together. Such conclusions, based on a methodical sifting of literary remains and records from antiquity, must ultimately founder on the same scarcity of evidence that undermines the comparative theories of origins.

What is of more interest are the different attitudes of mind exhibited by Pickard-Cambridge and, say, Murray. For the former, the scarcity of evidence limits the conclusions that can be drawn; for the latter, as for his mentor Frazer, it presents a challenge to the speculative imagination. Pickard-Cambridge determines the relevance of evidence on the basis of connections made or implied in the evidence itself; Murray allows his own mental processes to provide connections and relationships between pieces of evidence, so that evidence and hypothesis are derived one from the other. Such attitudes of mind are probably irreconcilable in their extreme form, but a kind of compromise is put forward by T.B.L. Webster in *Fifty Years . . . of Classical Scholarship* (ed. M. Platnauer, 1954; rev. 1968), who points out that "origin" is being used in two different ways, that Murray's theory gives a "persistent formal cause rather than an origin" and that the sequence of prosperity, suffering and renewed prosperity "is the nerve of all Greek tragedies (as also of much Dionysiac ritual and of the Eleusinian mysteries)" (pp. 98–99).

Most classical scholars, however, have not been so tolerant of ethnological theories of the origins of tragedy and comedy as has Webster. Murray and Cornford have hardly been mentioned in studies since the publication of Pickard-Cambridge's *Dithyramb, Tragedy and Comedy*, as scholars have persisted in looking at specifically Greek material for the origins of a specifically Greek theatre. C. del Grande in *Tragodia* (1952) harkens back to Ridgeway when he argues that the origins of tragedy lie in lyric derived from a cult of heroes and later inserted into the cult of Dionysus. Similarly, H. Patzer in *Die Anfange der Griechischen Tragodie* (1962) views the tragic choruses for Adrastus at Sicyon (described by Herodotus and cited by Ridgeway) as a kind of lyric tragedy, transformed by Arion into a mimetic performance on the model of the satyr chorus. It is worth mentioning these two studies in particular in order to illustrate the limited permutations and combinations possible when dealing with a severely limited amount of inconclusive evidence. Except in relatively minor matters, del Grande and Patzer are in general agreement with William Ridgeway in his *Origin of Tragedy* of 1910.

The tradition of classical scholarship, represented by Ridgeway and Pickard-Cambridge, begun near the turn of the present century in reaction to the nineteenth-century assumption that all Greek theatrical forms derived from a common source and spurred by an antipathy to the methods of the Cambridge School of Anthropology, acquired a most eloquent and persuasive spokesman in Gerald F. Else, whose *Origin and Early Form of Greek Tragedy* appeared in 1965. Else rejects the notion of ritual origins completely and argues instead that Greek tragedy was the conscious creation of two men, Thespis and Aeschylus. The content of most Greek tragedy is heroic myth of non-Athenian origin. "The conclusion," writes Else, "is obvious: tragedy did not begin as cult drama, Dionysiac or otherwise, and its mythical material normally had nothing to do with Athens'' (p. 63). The beginnings of tragedy are therefore removed from the misty and mysterious world of cult and ritual and are relocated in the conscious acts of rational men. Thespis is held to have invented *tragoidia*, the expression by the actor of "epic content, drawn from heroic myth, in Solonian form (iambic verses) combined with choral songs" (p. 63)—and in so doing brought together the epic hero, impersonation, and iambic verse. And what was presented was the hero's *pathos*, his suffering at a moment of disaster or failure. Thespis, then, invented "tragedy," but it was not yet tragic *drama*. This was the contribution of Aeschylus, who attempted to explain the Thespian *pathos* causally and so was led to project "outward, forward, and upward from the *pathos*, in the three dimensions of space, time, and relationship to God" (p. 83). This expansion brought about a series of technical and dramaturgical changes, including the increase in the number of actors, the development of the *agon* or conflict, the closer focussing on the hero and his tragic choice, and so on. But it was with Aeschylus' creative act that tragic drama was born.

Else's theory is rational, narrowly focussed, and assumes that conscious human decision determines cultural and artistic change. Familiar human attributes are called upon as explanations for change, not "elusive, quasi-natural, energies." (The phrase is Albin Lesky's in *Greek Tragedy*, p. 28.) For example, the suggestion in the *Poetics* that tragedy was linked to the satyr-drama Else dismisses as pro-Dorian propaganda. Tragedy and comedy had quite different origins, he continues, and the satyr-drama was introduced to tragic competition in response to a public protest against a steady diet of death and disaster. As he says, "Athenians were not so different from other people in wanting to laugh occasionally" (p. 25).

There are two further studies of the origins of Greek theatre that merit attention. Both self-consciously apply methods derived from other disciplines to the problem. The first of these, *The Origin of the Greek Tragic Form* (1938) by August C. Mahr, is based on several assumptions: that the Thespian actor was added to the choric dithyramb; that conflict is a necessary ingredient of the drama; that Greek art in general was determined by a sense of the finite; and that this art consequently reveals a clearly defined, even tactual structure. Mahr therefore applies the methods of art criticism to his study of the development of the visible scene. He argues that with the introduction of the actor, primary attention shifted from the centre of the choric dancing space (orchestra) to a point on the circumference of the circle, and that this shift helped to determine the new shape of the performance. Since conflict is a dramatic necessity, "the dramatic action was inevitably bound to develop between [the] chorus and the one actor, [and therefore] situations could only be dramatized on the basis of a *single kinetic pattern, the approach of an individual to a group*" (p. 54). And the hero's intention is to overcome a resistance. Mahr suggests that the special relevance of this particular action to the worship of Dionysus is due to the fact that the god had to struggle to overcome resistance to his worship: "His epiphany, therefore, is accompanied by a continuous struggle against this resistance. All the plays that present such a structure end with the ultimate triumph of the god or of that spirit which he embodies'' (p. 57). Mahr's theory is ingenious, even if unconvincing. It seems to have had no impact whatever on classical studies or on more general theories of the theatre's origins. It might be conceded, neverthless, that the idea would not conflict with Else's notion of the Thespian origin of the *tragoidia*; and Mahr's emphasis on the visible scene suggests a relationship between dramatic form and theatrical space which has been too little explored. But Mahr assumes too much, and he avoids the question of impersonation entirely: How did Thespis come to invent the actor in the first place?

The second study is more recent: *Festival, Comedy and Tragedy: The Greek Origins of Theatre* by Francisco R. Adrados, a student of linguistics and author of *Linguistica Estructural* (1969), was first published in 1972 in Spanish and was translated into English in 1975. While Adrados rejects the specifically Dionysiac origin of Greek theatre, he equally rejects Else's hypothesis: "Theatre is an omnipresent phenomenon, the roots of which are always in lyric rituals, of mimetic type, and we cannot separate Greek theatre from Greek rituals in order to interpret it as the result of a literary synthesis of two literary, nonmimetic forms'' (p. 7). Adrados' own objective is "to demonstrate in detail how the passage from the agricultural cults (not always heroic) to the various theatrical forms became possible'' (p. 6). In order to do this, he utilizes linguistic method to analyze the extant dramatic texts in terms of their "elementary units," which he describes as "passages of similar content in similar form," the literary equivalent of morphemes or words:

The hypothesis I develop is that the ultimate nucleus of the elementary units derives from the rituals of the agricultural religion—not solely Dionysian. There is then a phenomenon of transformation by which ritual becomes Theatre. The elementary units fuse into typical sequence, which evolve and differentiate into various types. These types, marked by differences in the way the units are organized, are the three genres of Theatre: Tragedy, Comedy and Satyric Drama. [p. vii]

The method is clearly analogous to the process by which lost languages are reconstructed from the data preserved in their later descendants. Adrados proceeds to identify and analyze the elementary units, not only of dramatic texts, but of ancient rituals as reconstructed from archaeological and historical records. Although initially he confines himself to Greek material, Adrados does note parallels between the elementary units of Greek theatre and ritual and the theatre and ritual of other peoples in order to verify his conclusions. But he makes no effort to speculate on the origin of the common features. In brief, the procedure is this: (1) analysis of the elementary units in order to identify the most ancient; (2) verification of the results in terms of ancient Greek rituals; (3) reconstruction of the history of the dramatic genres as they underwent differentiation, polarization, etc.; and (4) noting of parallels from outside Greece and outside the theatre. The elementary units that figure at the centre of this procedure are as follows: hymns, supplications, prayers; *agones*; sacrifices; *anagnorismoi*; blessings, curses, thanksgivings, *threnoi*; and nuptial and triumphant *komoi*.

Adrados' conclusions include the postulate that all Greek theatre arose from the *komos*, "a chorus that moves, to perform a cult action, with a procession and dance" (p.16); but obviously the cults and their attendant rituals could otherwise differ. The differentiation of genre he explains thus. He argues that tragedy and satyric drama arose from *komoi* "in which heroes were celebrated and in which certain actors called *tragoidoi* came to specialize" (p. 16). Comedy, he suggests, is a later creation, derived from different rituals than were tragedy and satyr-play, and modelled on the tragic form. In the final analysis, Adrados hypothesizes an undifferentiated ur-form of dramatic ritual that began generic differentiation even before it developed into theatre. This is a sophisticated study, but nevertheless we are once again back with ritual origins and a common source for all Greek dramatic forms.

## ORIGINS OF MEDIEVAL THEATRE

The drama that appeared in Europe in various forms between the tenth and the fifteenth centuries was mainly religious, and coming as it did after a period during which theatre and dramatic activity seem to have been nearly totally eclipsed, this drama represented for early theatre historians—as indeed it represents for many today—a second birth of the theatre, this time in Christian rather than Dionysian worship. The analogy with Greece was made explicit as early as 1838 when Charles Magnin in his *Origines du théâtre . . . moderne* proclaimed that the new theatre had been established "absolument de la même manière" as the Greek. And the investigations of comparative anthropology, which saw such close connections between religious ritual and theatre, prompted the expansion of the analogy into a universal principle. Religion, writes Gustave Cohen, "est elle-même génératrice de drama et que tout culte prent volontiers et spontanément l'aspect dramatique et théâtral" (*Le Théâtre en France au moyen-âge*, I, 5). There has been little agreement, nonetheless, on the precise process by which the Christian religion gave birth to a new theatre.

The case is complicated by other factors (to which we will turn later), but the seed of modern drama is held to be either in the so-called *tropes*, elaborations on the chanted liturgy associated mainly with the Benedictine monasteries of St. Gall in Switzerland and St. Martial at Limoges in France, or in the Mass itself. The most pertinent evidence is as follows:

1. The Roman Liturgy, including the Mass and the Canonical Office: Historical perspective and knowledge are essential here, and the student of the theatre is necessarily dependent upon more specialized scholarship. Karl Young provides a brief introduction to and a description of the medieval liturgy in *The Drama of the Me-*

*dieval Church* (I, 15–75), but a better guide is Dom Gregory Dix's *The Shape of the Liturgy.*

2. *Peregrinatio Etheriae*: Generally considered to be the work of a fourth-century Galician woman concerning her travels to the Holy Land, this document describes in some detail the ritual of the early Christian Church. The manuscript was discovered in the 1880s in Arezzo, Italy, and is printed in L. Duchesne, *Christian Worship: Its Origin and Evolution* (pp. 490–523).

3. Tropes and Sequences: The most convenient collection is that of Young in *The Drama of the Church.* Of particular importance is the *Quem Quaeritis* trope, the simplest form of which is found in a tenth-century manuscript from the monastery of St. Gall. The oldest text, however, is found at the monastery of St. Martial at Limoges. Two men are associated with these early tropes and sequences, both of them from St. Gall. Notker Balbulus (ca. 840–912), in a letter to Liutward, Bishop of Vercelli, prefixed to his *Liber Sequentiarum*, notes how he devised a text for the wordless melodies of the *Alleluia* (*Patrologia Latina*, cxxxi, 1003–1004; quoted by Young, I, 183–184). And a man known only as Tutilo, a contemporary of Notker, is mentioned by Notker's pupil Ekkehard IV in his history of the abbey, *Casus Sancti Galli*, as the most celebrated writer of tropes.

4. *Regularis Concordia*: About the year 960, three newly appointed English bishops, former Benedictine abbots, met in Winchester to settle disputes concerning liturgical reforms. The result was the *Concordia*, in which Bishop Ethelwold of Winchester provided instructions for the correct conduct of the *Quem Quaeritis* trope at Matins, one of the eight *Horae* of the Canonical Office. This document exists in three manuscripts held by the British Library (Cotton Ms. Tiberius A. III, Cotton Ms. Faustina B. III, Ms. Harley 552), and a fragmentary manuscript in the Bodleian Library, Oxford (Ms. Junius, 52). The Latin text has been edited by Dom Thomas Symons (1953).

5. Amalarius of Metz, *Liber officialis*: This work, which went through three editions between 821 and 835, offers an allegorical interpretation of the Mass. The third book, *De Ecclesiasticus officius*, is particularly important. (It is printed in *Patrologia Latina*, cv, 815–1360.)

6. Honorius of Autun, *Gemma Animae* (ca. 1100): Honorius compares the mass to drama. (See *Patrologia Latina*, clxxii, 570.)

The tropes were first identified as one of the origins of the modern theatre in 1886 by Léon Gautier, who in his *Histoire de la poésie liturgique* noted that he was tempted to believe that they represented *the* origin. Gautier saw the tropes as local additions to the Mass, neither recognized nor approved by Rome, and not as an inevitable outgrowth of the medieval liturgy. Karl Young takes a similar tack. He defined a trope as "a verbal amplification of a passage in an authorized liturgy," designed to adorn, enforce the meaning, and enlarge the emotional appeal of the liturgy (I, 178), but he insists that the dramatic potentialities of the trope—specifically the *Quem Quaeritis*—were realized only when it was removed from the Mass and placed at the close of Matins, between the last responsory and the *Te Deum*: "In this new position it achieved a generous amount of literary freedom, and developed into an authentic Easter play. To this we may refer henceforth as the *Visitatio Sepulchri*" (I, 231). Young denies that the Mass itself was theatre, or that it gave rise to theatre, on the grounds that it lacked the essential element of theatre—impersonation. O. B. Hardison, in *Christian Rite and Christian Drama*, on the other hand, argues that impersonation is a modern concept, and that in the ninth century the boundary between religious ritual and drama did not exist, that religious ritual *was* the drama of the early Middle Ages. In support of his contention he points specifically to Amalarius' allegorical interpretation of the Mass and to Honorius' description and understanding of the Mass as a "living dramatic form" (p. 41).

Such differences of opinion tend to resolve themselves into questions of definition. As we have seen throughout this chapter, the relationship between ritual and theatre is problematic. Is ritual a form of theatre? Is theatre a special kind of ritual? Is there a distinction to be made at all? If there is, how do we go about making it? One possible answer is to maintain, as Young and many others do, that there is indeed a difference, and to argue that dramatic art rests on impersonation and imitation, that a priestly performer never pretends to be anything other than what he is. A related idea would have it that ritual becomes theatre at that moment when the audience sees the person imitated before it sees the person doing the imitating, when the character moves into the foreground in front of the actor. This, for example, is Glynne Wickham's view in *The Medieval Theatre* (1974). Another answer would be to cite the purpose of the performance as the criterion for definition; theatre emerges from ritual when an aesthetic-moral purpose replaces a religious-utilitarian purpose. It can also be argued, of course, that there is no meaningful or useful differentiation to be made between ritual and theatre.

Hardison would in general agree with this last statement, but he stops short of insisting that all ritual is theatre: It is the Mass specifically that is "a rememorative drama depicting the life, ministry, crucifixion and resurrection of Christ" (p. 44). If this description seems an echo of something we have heard before, it is not accidental. Hardison notes the similarities that the Mass has to dramatic rituals "which are apparently universal in primitive societies and which are widespread among the various mystery cults that flourished in the West between the first and the fifth centuries" (p. 43). Moreover, he goes on in his discussion of *Gemma Animae* to point out that Honorius uses the vocabulary of dramatic criticism in attributing to the "drama" enacted in the Mass a plot based on a conflict between a champion and an antagonist, a plot with a rising action, a dramatic reversal, and a kind of catharsis. The vocabulary may be Aristotelian, but the plot, as described by both Honorius and Hardison, is another version of Murray's vegetation-myth. And the vocabulary and the description both should alert us to the literary nature of Hardison's conception of drama. The pattern, not the performance, is crucial.

The introduction of comparative anthropology or ethnology, nonetheless, opens the door to a radical departure from the theory of the liturgical origins of the medieval theatre, by begging the question of the relationship between the tenth-century Mass—which was after all a highly sophisticated expression of a highly sophisticated religion—and the more primitive manifestations of the Year Spirit in the European folk-play. It has been argued that the structure of the liturgical drama was derived from the folk-play, and that the important concept of impersonation was introduced into the Church service by the descendants of the Roman mimes, professional singer-actors whose varied and usually ribald performances the Church had attempted unsuccessfully to curb throughout the early Middle Ages. The theory, in effect, recasts the Church's role as foster-mother rather than mother of the new theatre, which now finds its true origin in pagan rite.

Initial interest in folk customs and drama was largely a phenomenon of the nineteenth century, but early stage historians found it difficult if not impossible to determine any positive influence it may have had on the medieval religious theatre. E. K. Chambers, for example, devotes fully one-half of *The Mediaeval Stage* to minstrelsy and folk-drama; but in the midst of his 419 pages devoted to the subject he feels compelled to declare that "modern drama arose, by a fairly well defined line of evolution, from a three-fold source, the ecclesiastical liturgy, the farce of the mimes, the classical revivals of humanism. Folk drama contributed but the tiniest rill to the mighty stream" (I, 182). Actually, European scholars have been more receptive to this so-called Aryan theory than have English and American scholars.

One of these Europeans is the Dutch theatre historian Benjamin Hunningher who, in the somewhat misleadingly entitled *The Origin of the Theatre* (1955; tr. 1961), points out that the liturgical origin theory does not account for the fact that it took almost 1,000 years for theatre to suddenly emerge from the liturgy in the tenth century. And he further argues that there was little similarity between primitive rites and tenth-century Christian worship. He maintains that impersonation is as foreign to the tropes as it is to the Mass. So far as the *Quem Quaeritis* trope is concerned, he asks why it alone developed into theatre. In short, Hunningher denies the possibility that the Christian Church did create or could have created drama in a way analogous to primitive or ancient rites. He theorizes instead that the church assimilated pagan rites and adopted dramatic forms established outside its precincts.

Central to Hunningher's thesis is the assumption of the validity of the Frazer-Murray-Gaster vegetation-god myth as the underpinning of all theatre. He notes, for instance, that the pattern of the dying and reviving god, together with evidence of theatre, ritual marriage, and fertility drama, can be traced in Icelandic literature, and he theorizes that ritual drama was as well known among the pre-Christian Europeans as among primitive peoples elsewhere. The function of the mimes in bringing this patterned ritual to theatrical life is even more crucial to the rebirth of dramatic art. The literature of late antiquity and of the Church Fathers is filled with references to *mimi*, *histriones*, and *ioculatores*, and Hun-

ningher cites ninth-century rulings against the practice in support of his contention that mimes actually gave religious performances with clerical approval and
connivance (pp. 69ff.). His most telling piece of evidence, however, is a troparium from St. Martial at Limoges, now in the Bibliothèque Nationale in Paris
(Lat. 1118), which is illuminated with miniatures that he says portray mimes
acting and dancing. The figures may actually depict dancing *joculatores* which
traditionally appeared with King David, as in the *Psalterium Aureum* of St. Gall,
rather than mimes. But neither interpretation of the pictorial evidence is completely persuasive.

The most important evidence for the existence of the pre-Christian drama
postulated by Hunningher are the folk plays of Europe which have survived in
written form—most of them dating from the eighteenth century—or, more rarely,
in continued local performances. To this we can add occasional eyewitness accounts from earlier centuries. The Cambridge Anthropologists pointed to the
ritual background of the folk drama; and the ritual noted was, of course, connected to the ubiquitous vegetation-god. For example, in *The Classical Tradition in Poetry* (1927), Murray writes:

Ritual was connected with the cult of what is sometimes called a Year-Daemon, or a
Vegetation God, or a Life Spirit, which everywhere forms the heart of Mediterranean
religion; and . . . we can find a sort of degraded survival of the original form of the
drama in the Mummers' Play, which still survives among the peasantry of Europe. [pp.
46–47]

The pattern of ritual combat, death, and resurrection that makes up the original
form alluded to by Murray is accepted as the dominant pattern of the Mummers' Play by most scholars. Its presence in the Mass is explained on analogi-
cal grounds by Hardison, and as an importation from pagan ritual-drama by
Hunningher. Something of a wrinkle is added by Kirby who, pointing to the
Cure rather than to the Combat as the essential feature of the play, finds its
origin in the same shamanism he found behind all the world's theatre. But the
corrupt and sorry condition of the texts of the folk drama makes the existence
and role of an extra-Christian ritual drama a matter of speculation and opinion,
just as the ambiguous references to mimes and the miniatures of the Limoges
troparium are insufficient to gauge the role of the mimes with any accuracy.

Theories of the origins of the medieval theatre can depend upon no piece of
conclusive evidence, and theorists have developed no fresh techniques or methodologies for dealing with what evidence there is. It seems, however, that the
shadow of the Cambridge Anthropologists looms larger in the world of modern
medieval scholarship than in that of modern classical scholarship. Frazer and
Murray were accused of viewing primitive myth through the prism of Christianity. Their theory of ritual origin has in turn become a glass for viewing the
beginnings of Christian drama.

## CONCLUSION

The questions raised by nearly a century of exploring theatrical origins figure more prominently than the details of the highly speculative answers postulated. Does all theatre derive from a common source in religious ritual? Is theatre a universal phenomenon, rooted in man's psychic and social nature, or is it the product of specific cultures and specific circumstances? Is humankind theatrical by nature? What role, if any, does the conscious artist play in the historical development of the theatre? Is the process of change in theatrical form governed by evolutionary laws? These are not idle questions, for the answers we provide help to determine our attitude towards the theatre, not only in times past but, more importantly, in our own time. And ironically, our present attitudes can in turn help to determine our answers to questions concerning the origins of the theatre. Ultimately, our hypotheses about the origins of institutions both reflect and inform our perceptions of them in our own time; and in turn our hypotheses and perceptions interact to produce new theoretical conceptions concerning the nature of those institutions. It is doubtless safe to hazard, for instance, that what we treat as theatre in the last quarter of the twentieth century is far more embracing than it was at the end of the nineteenth century. And it has been in large measure the attempts to discover the origins of the theatre that have expanded our notions of theatre and, by forcing us to more precise definitions, increased our capacity to appreciate non-classical and non-literary theatrical forms.

Much of the impetus to an expanded view has come not so much from the theories of origins themselves as from the evidence adduced to support the theories. In particular, the investigations of cultural anthropology, of mythology, of religion, of folklore, undertaken on a comparative basis, have provided new data, which the speculations and theories of the origin hunters have rendered meaningful to the student of dramatic and theatrical history. So long as the attention of theatre scholars was confined by the aesthetics of the literary drama, it is unlikely that such phenomena as American Indian ceremonials, happenings, or street theatre—however important to the participants or to students of folklore, anthropology, sociology, or politics—would ever have been admitted to discussions of theatre or theatre history.

But the expanded conceptions of theatre prompted by this new information and by scholarly speculation are not unconfined. The same theories that encouraged a broader view of theatre and the theatrical also called for more precise definitions of terms and clearer distinctions between theatrical and non-theatrical performance. Three areas in particular have been of concern to those interested in specifying the limits of theatre history and research: the relationship between ritual and theatre, the idea of impersonation as a prerequisite for drama, and the question of the mimetic basis of theatrical art. While final agreement on these matters has not been reached, it is possible to outline briefly a few of the issues.

The difficulties of distinguishing clearly between ritual and theatre have been apparent throughout the present chapter, and some of the possible responses to the problem have already been summarized. But it is important to consider the question, for upon the answer depend some very practical as well as theoretical considerations. A scholar who wishes to concern himself with theatre history, or a student who wishes to study the theatre, must decide what it is that constitutes his field and what its limits and foci are. Moreover, the question ought to be answered in terms of a coherent discourse developed within but not confined by a critically derived theory. It serves little purpose to skirt the issue as, in effect, O. B. Hardison does when he cites the testimony of Honorius as evidence that the medieval Mass was drama. Honorius' likening of the Mass to drama is no more authoritative in arriving at a definition of drama than any other comment might be, and it must be subjected to the same critical scrutiny as any other comment. Honorius' comparison is authoritative in what it tells us about Honorius, but it has no special validity in what it tells us about theatre.

On the other hand, Hardison's assertion that impersonation is a modern concept, and therefore not a necessary constituent of drama, forces us to reconsider what we mean by impersonation and, indeed, to rethink our assumptions about the mimetic nature of theatre in general. We normally view a dramatic production with a kind of double vision, observing and more or less registering the theatrical representation provided by the actor, his accoutrements, and the theatrical setting, while simultaneously having our interest directed to the characters and actions being represented or imitated. Among Western audiences and critics, at least, there is the further assumption that the more accurate the imitation, the more vividly is the action presented. However much theatrical convention may be acknowledged as a necessary, even interesting, language, we have found it difficult to break beyond the critical point of view defined by such terms as "verisimilitude," "realism," and "believability."

The search for the origins of the theatre among "primitive" theatrical and quasi-theatrical forms has drawn attention to the importance of the theatrical representation itself, not as an imitation of something else, but *sui generis*, as a sign of itself. And it becomes therefore at least theoretically possible for a performance to be considered as form presenting itself, rather than as an imitation of something in the "real" world. The idea is implied in Jane Harrison's discussion of the *drōmenon*, although she assumes the mimetic nature of the thing pre- or re-done. And it is made explicit by E. T. Kirby, who notes that for drama to be effective it must, like ritual, be distinguished from the "real" world, and that consequently theatre is rooted in stylization and abstraction rather than in realistic imitation. It is worth noting that Kirby's contention has a parallel in the concept of defamiliarization or foregrounding central to semiotic theory. Theatre, it is argued, forces our attention to the material components of performance in order to lengthen and intensify the perception which is an aesthetic end in itself. The upshot of this kind of rethinking is that theories of drama now concern themselves with performance as well as with Aristotelian notions of dramaturgy.

It is perhaps fitting that a discussion of dramatic theory conclude a consideration of so speculative a field of theatre research as the search for origins. While it cannot be affirmed that the search has been entirely successful, it also cannot be said that the effort has been in vain. We can no longer remain satisfied with our culturally confined conceptions of what is and what is not theatre, and we are therefore creating a new and expanded context for new theatre as well as for a reconsideration of the old.

## REFERENCES

Aristotle..*Aristotle's Theory of Poetry and Fine Art*. Ed. and tr. S. H. Butcher. 4th ed. New York, 1951.

Adrados, Francisco R. *Festival, Comedy and Tragedy: The Greek Origins of Theatre*. Leiden, 1975.

Amalarius of Metz. *De ecclesiasticus officiis*. In *Patrologiae Cursus Completus: Patrologia Latina*, ed. J. P. Migne (Paris, 1844–64), vol. CV.

Blackman, A. M., and H. W. Fairman. "The Myth of Horus II: The Triumph of Horus over His Enemies: A Sacred Drama." *Journal of Egyptian Archaeology* XXVIII (1942), 32–38; XXIX (1943), 2–36; XXX (1944), 5–22.

Chambers, E. K. *The Mediaeval Stage*. 2 Vols. Oxford, 1903.

Cohen, Gustave. *Le Théâtre en France au moyen-âge*. 2 Vols. Paris, 1928.

Cornford, Francis Macdonald. *The Origin of Attic Comedy*. Ed. Theodore H. Gaster. Garden City, New York, 1961 [1914].

Dieterich, Albrecht. "Die Entstehung der Tragodie." *Archiv für Religionswissenschaft* XI (1908), 163–96.

Dix, Gregory. *The Shape of the Liturgy*. 2d ed. Westminster, 1949.

Duchesne, L. *Christian Worship: Its Origin and Evolution*. Tr. M. L. McClure. London, 1923.

Ekkehart IV. *Casus Sancti Galli*. Ed. G. Meyer von Knonau. St. Gall, 1877.

Else, Gerald F. *Aristotle's Poetics: The Argument*. Canbridge, Mass., 1957.

————. *The Origin and Early Form of Greek Tragedy*. New York, 1972 [1965].

Fairman, H. W., ed. *Triumph of Horus*. London, 1974.

Fergusson, Francis. *The Idea of a Theatre*. Princeton, 1949.

Frazer, James George. *The Golden Bough: A Study in Magic and Religion*. Abridged ed. New York, 1922.

Gaster, Theodore H. *Thespis: Ritual, Myth, and Drama in the Ancient Near East*. Garden City, New York, 1950.

Gautier, Léon. *Histoire de la poésie liturgique au moyen âge*. Paris, 1886.

Grande, C. del. *Tragodia: Essenza a genesi della tragedia*. Naples, 1952.

Groos, Karl. *The Play of Animals*. New York, 1898 [1896].

————. *The Play of Man*. Tr. Elizabeth L. Baldwin. London and New York, 1901.

Haigh, Arthur E. *Attic Theatre*. Oxford, 1889.

Hardison, O. B. *Christian Rite and Christian Drama in the Middle Ages*. Baltimore, 1965.

*Harper's Dictionary of Classical Literature and Antiquities.* Ed. Harry Thurston Peck. 2d ed. New York, 1965 [1897].

Harrison, Jane Ellen. *Epilegomena to the Study of Greek Religion* [and] *Themis: A Study of the Social Origins of Greek Religion.* New York, 1962.

Havemeyer, Loomis. *The Drama of Savage Peoples.* New York and London, 1916.

Herodotus. *The Histories.* Tr. Aubrey de Sélincourt. Rev. A. R. Burn. Harmondsworth, 1972.

Honorius of Autun. *Gemma Animae.* In *Patrologiae Cursus Completus: Patrologia Latina*, ed. J. P. Migne (Paris, 1844–64), vol. CLXXII.

Huizinga, Johann. *Homo Ludens: A Study of the Play Element in Culture.* Boston, 1955.

Hunningher, Benjamin. *The Origin of the Theatre.* New York, 1961.

Jenkins, Linda Walsh. Review of E. T. Kirby, *Ur-Drama* in *Theatre Survey* XIX (1978), 84–86.

Kernodle, George R. Review of E. T. Kirby, *Ur-Drama* in *Educational Theatre Journal* XXVII (1976), 435–436.

Kirby, Ernest Theodore. "Dionysus: A Study of the Bacchae and the Origins of Drama." Carnegie-Mellon University Dissertation, 1970.

———. *Ur-Drama: The Origins of Theatre.* New York, 1975.

Lesky, Albin. *Greek Tragedy.* Tr. H. A. Frankfort. 2d ed. London and New York, 1967.

Magnin, Charles. *Les Origines du théâtre antique et du théâtre moderne.* Paris, 1868. [Originally *Les Origines du théâtre moderne*, 1838.]

Mahr, August C. *The Origin of the Greek Tragic Form: A Study of the Early Theatre in Attica.* New York, 1938.

Molinari, Cesare. *Theatre through the Ages.* Tr. Colin Homer. London, 1975.

Murray, Gilbert. *The Classical Tradition in Poetry.* New York, 1957 [1927].

———. "Excursus on the Ritual Forms Preserved in Greek Tragedy." In Jane Harrison, *Themis: A Study of the Social Origins of Greek Religion* (New York, 1962).

Patzer, H. *Die Anfange der Griechischen Tragodie.* Weisbaden, 1962.

Pickard-Cambridge, A. W. *Dithyramb, Tragedy and Comedy.* 2nd ed. Rev. T.B.L. Webster. Oxford, 1962 [1972].

Platnauer, M., ed. *Fifty Years (and Twelve) of Classical Scholarship.* Oxford, 1968.

Ridgeway, William. *The Dramas and Dramatic Dances of Non-European Races.* Cambridge, 1915.

———. *The Origin of Tragedy with Special Reference to the Greek Tragedians.* Cambridge, 1910.

Sethe, Kurt. *Dramatische Texte au Altaegyptischen Mysterienspielen.* 2 Vols. Leipzig, 1928.

*Suda.* Ed. Ada Adler. 5 Vols. Leipzig, 1928–38.

Symons, Thomas, ed. *The Monastic Agreement of the Monks and Nuns of the English Nation: Regularis Concordia.* New York, 1953.

Vickery, John B. *The Literary Impact of "The Golden Bough."* Princeton, 1973.

Wickham, Glynne. *The Medieval Theatre.* London, 1974.

Young, Karl. *The Drama of the Medieval Church.* 2 Vols. Oxford, 1933.

# 2

# THE THEATRE OF GREECE

## SCHOLARSHIP

The study of ancient Greek literature and antiquities has been going on for a very long time, and students of the drama who are not at the same time classical scholars may be forgiven if they find the mass of material, interpretation, commentary, and opinion concerning the theatre of the Greeks somewhat intimidating. Nor is the intimidating nature of the material likely to be decreased by the fact that a large portion of the research, particularly in the nineteenth and early twentieth centuries, was carried out by German scholars—a hurdle indeed for those whose German is likely to be as rusty as their Greek is non-existent. Nevertheless, the Greek theatre is the foundation of Western theatre, and it is therefore necessary to come to some understanding of the available evidence concerning it and the processes by which the evidence has been painstakingly assembled, sifted, interpreted, and misinterpreted over the past one hundred years. There is no reason why even the non-classicist cannot be informed sufficiently to avoid falling victim to misleading or faulty scholarship. While it will be necessary in the following sketch of Greek theatre studies to refer to some German works, the international tradition of classical scholarship, coupled with the increasing prominence of studies published in English, has made it possible to trace the effects of new evidence and changing methodologies by referring mainly to works written in English.

Until relatively late in the nineteenth century, the study of the Greek theatre was characterized by three things: (1) a reliance on written records, especially those in Greek and Latin; (2) an assumption that all such evidence, whatever its source or date, was of equal value for determining theatrical conditions in fifth-century Athens; and (3) the belief that the scholar's task was to reconcile evidence when it was contradictory, not to question or reject it. The preference for written records is understandable, in that serious and systematic archaeological work on ancient theatres, on pictorial monuments concerning the drama, and on public inscriptions relevant to theatrical activities did not get under way until the latter half of the last century. The indiscriminate use of written source is another matter: Reverence for the "classics" and an all too human desire to accept the questionable as evidence in the absence of any other has sometimes led scholars pretty far afield. For example, one of the most commonly cited sources, the *Suda*, is a lexicon that was not completed until the end of the tenth century A.D.; and testimony concerning the origins of tragedy has been found in a twelfth-century commentary on the second-century rhetorician Hermogenes. Such sources may have their value, but they clearly cannot be taken as authoritative.

What is even more serious was that the texts of the plays, which might have some claim to special relevance, were not treated as having any special authority when it came to staging. Indeed, there is little evidence that in general scholars who were primarily philologists had much interest in the dramatic texts as theatrical as opposed to literary documents. When it came to the actual revival of a Greek play on the stage, therefore, even Ulrich von Wilamowitz-Moellendorff, possibly the greatest Hellenist of his time, treated the plays of Aeschylus as though there were no relationship between the resources of the Greek theatre and the requirements of the dramatic texts. He staged the Greek playwright's plays as he would have staged a Victorian play. Thus to the three elements characterizing the study of the Greek theatre we can add a fourth: the assumption that the Greek theatre, like the Victorian, was illusionistic, differing in detail perhaps but dedicated to the same aesthetic principle.

A good example of mid-nineteenth-century scholarship in English is John William Donaldson's *The Theatre of the Greeks*, which in 1860 was in its seventh edition. Donaldson's treatment of the subject was basically theatrical rather than literary, and he was not entirely unaware of the fresh evidence provided by figured monumental sources, such as vases, terracotta figurines, and mural paintings. (F. Wieseler's *Theatergebaüde und Denkmäler des Bühnenwesens* had appeared in 1851.) But the bulk of his evidence, nevertheless, consists of commentaries by ancient writers, particularly Aristotle, Vitruvius, and Julius Pollux. Donaldson trusts his written documents: He seldom discusses their reliability, and he almost never indicates the date of their composition. Indeed, one of the most disquieting features of *The Theatre of the Greeks* is the author's unhistorical attitude towards chronology. A thousand years of history are treated as a single historical moment. One example will suffice. In order to arrive at a description of the "great stone theatres, in which the perfect Greek dramas were represented," Donaldson confidently refers to the Theatre at Aspendos in Turkey, designed by the architect Zenon and built during the time of Marcus Aurelius (A.D. 161–180), as a model which "enables us to restore, with very slight risk of error, all the details of the proscenium and orchestra which were presented to the eyes of a Greek audience'' (pp. 220–221). He goes on to admit that "the minor arrangements of the stage'' must be gleaned from ancient descriptions, by which he means Vitruvius' *De Re Architectura* (ca. 15 B.C.) and Pollux's *Onomastikon* (ca. A.D. 180). The discrepancies between what was built at Aspendos and what Vitruvius described are explained away: "Vitruvius makes certain distinctions between the Greek and Roman theatres, [but] it does not follow that all theatres built in Greek cities during the Roman period departed from the ancient model, which, after all, was the point of departure for the Roman architects themselves'' (p. 222). The fact that Vitruvius wrote four centuries after the death of the youngest of the Greek tragedians whose plays have come down to us, and the fact that the theatre at Aspendos was built over 500 years after Aeschylus and Sophocles and Euripides presented their plays at the Theatre of Dionysus in Athens, are not mentioned.

Donaldson nevertheless was simply typical of his time. His attitude and method continued in the work of both German and English scholars: Albert Müller's *Lehrbuch der Griechischen Bühnenalterthumer* appeared in 1886, A. E. Haigh's *The Attic Theatre* in 1889. The latter was the first treatment of the Greek theatre in English since Donaldson, and Haigh is at pains to note that the discovery of inscriptions relating to theatrical affairs, and the archaeological excavations of ancient theatres, had in the meantime revolutionized the subject:

The materials have . . . to be collected from the most multifarious sources—from casual remarks in ancient authors, from incidental references in the Greek dramas, from obscure and often contradictory notices in the scholiasts and grammarians, from old inscriptions, and the ruins of Greek theatres, from vases, statuettes, wall-paintings, and other works of art. [p. vi].

The revolution in the subject did not, however, extend to Haigh's method in treating his evidence, old or new. He commends Müller's book as "auspicious for the industry, learning, and sound judgment displayed in its compilation'' and follows the German's example in preferring written evidence from late antiquity over both play texts and archaeological and pictorial evidence. Certainly he relies much less on the evidence of vases, paintings, and statuary than his Preface would indicate. Given this preference however—which, incidentally, was continued through the third edition of 1907, revised and partially rewritten by A. W. Pickard-Cambridge—Haigh does weigh contradictory evidence with some care and caution when trying to arrive at a reasonable conclusion, and in this sense represents a marked improvement over Donaldson's less discriminating method.

The turn of the century was marked by several important publications that militated against the blind acceptance of written authority so far as the Greek theatre was concerned, and that helped as well to initiate a never-ending debate between the believers in ancient scholarship and the supporters of pictorial and archaeological evidence. The most important of these were *Das Griechische*

*Theater*, by Wilhelm Dörpfeld and Emil Reisch (1896), which presented the results of the excavations of Greek theatres undertaken in the 1880s by Dörpfeld and others; and A. Wilhelm's *Urkunden dramatischer Aufführungen in Athen* (1906), which printed the inscriptions on stones relating to the theatre in Athens. The accumulation of pictorial monuments, especially vase-paintings, was reflected in J. H. Huddilston's *Greek Tragedy in the Light of the Vase-Paintings* (1898). The new, non-literary evidence called much of the older written testimony into question and encouraged a more sceptical attitude towards it on the part of theatre historians. As early as 1904, for instance, in *Plutarch as a Source of Information on the Greek Theatre*, Roy C. Flickinger concluded that Plutarch tended invariably to "modernize" his comments on the ancient theatre.

The same author's *The Greek Theater and Its Drama* (1918), comprehensive and rigorously argued, is of a different order from the studies of Donaldson or even Haigh. The emphasis is still on written evidence, but Flickinger makes use of the vase-paintings in his discussion of the satyr-drama, and of Dörpfeld's excavations and conclusions in his discussion of theatre architecture; and he is more inclined than his predecessors to cite evidence from play texts. Finally, he includes a chapter on theatrical records, in which he discusses mainly the inscriptions transcribed, restored, and printed by Wilhelm in 1906. In short, Flickinger's critical survey of evidence, theory, problems, and scholarship (including that of the prolific Germans) made *The Greek Theater and Its Drama* a useful handbook, still respectfully cited by theatre historians. In spite of Flickinger's obvious willingness to consider all available evidence, the thrust of his work is philological and literary in that there is an unspoken assumption that written records, however scrupulously they must be scrutinized, present the basic picture, which the evidence from archaeological and pictorial monuments can only modify and clarify.

In the meantime, the case for pictorial monuments as evidence for theatre history was being championed by Margarete Bieber whose *Die Denkmäler zum Theaterwesen im Altertum* appeared in 1920. "In this book," she later explained, "I attempted to demonstrate how indispensable are the hitherto neglected figured monumental sources, like vases, terracottas and mural paintings, which are objective and contemporary, in contrast to the literary sources which are for the most part subjective opinions of individuals, and often of late writers." And she followed in 1939 with *The History of the Greek and Roman Theater* (from which the preceding quotation is taken), in which she constructed a history of the theatre in the ancient world based primarily on the monuments.

Conservative classical scholars remained unconvinced of the value of such evidence. In *Dithyramb, Tragedy and Comedy* (1927; rev. 1962), A. W. Pickard-Cambridge expressed scepticism concerning pictorial evidence, noting that "the painters of vases may have been exercising their imagination, and . . . the greatest caution is needed in accepting the evidence of vase-paintings as

proof of the existence or the characteristics of particular rituals or performances'' (p. x). As for the literary authorities on whom classical scholarship
had so long depended, Pickard-Cambridge was willing to acknowledge their
fragmentary and uncertain nature, but rose to their defense as fellow scholars:

Nevertheless, the tradition which filtered into such notices [in scholia and lexicons] was,
at least in part, the work of scholars of great industry, ability, and discernment, and it
is dangerous to disregard definite statements made by scholiasts, lexicographers, and
writers on literary and social history (such as Athenaeus), unless the supposed error can
itself be accounted for and good reasons found for setting the disputed statement aside.
[p. ix]

The appeal of scholar to scholar is obviously not diminished by time. Nevertheless, Pickard-Cambridge was a scholar of the highest ability and integrity,
and he did not allow his doubts about vase-paintings or his preference for written record to create an imbalance in the three volumes on the Greek theatre that
constitute his legacy to theatre history.

In *Dithyramb, Tragedy and Comedy*, Pickard-Cambridge compiles and discusses the evidence concerning the origins and early history of the Greek drama.
In *The Theatre of Dionysus* (1946), he does the same thing for the theatre where
the great plays of ancient Greece were first performed, incorporating not only
the archaeological evidence described in Dörpfeld and Reisch's *Das Griechische Theater*, but also the information contained in two later records of archaeological digging, Heinrich Bulle's *Untersuchungen an Griechischen Theatern* (1928) and Ernst Fiechter's *Das Dionysos-Theater in Athen* (1935–36). *The
Dramatic Festivals of Athens* (1953; rev. 1968), conceived as a companion volume to *The Theatre of Dionysus*, is devoted to discussion of the evidence concerning not only the dramatic festivals, but actors, costumes, and audience as
well. All three books have become standard reference works for students of the
Greek theatre.

In spite of Pickard-Cambridge's caution about their relevance to the classical
stage, pictorial monuments have been given more and more weight as evidence
since Bieber's *Greek and Roman Theater*. But even more important, dramatic
texts have gradually been subjected to more sophisticated analyses in order to
determine the stage requirements for their production, as well as dramaturgical
method. T.B.L. Webster, for example, in *Greek Theatre Production* (1956; rev.
1970), places considerable weight on the evidence of monumental material, much
of which, he argues, ''can be accepted at its face value as illustration of actors
as they appeared in theatres where the artist had seen them perform'' (p. xvi).
He allows that vase-pictures are not photographs of stage performances, but insists that ''it would be foolish to reject them because they are the records of an
intelligent artist rather than of a stupid camera. They must be interpreted, and
the rules of interpretation are no different from those used in understanding the
scenes on the many thousands of other Greek vases that have survived'' (p.

xvii). At the same time, Webster insists that the seeming demands of the play text must be interpreted in terms of the nature of a Greek dramatic text. He argues that the playwrights wrote for the reader as well as for an audience, and had therefore to create an imaginary as well as a stage world, and the two worlds might not coincide. Certainly a verbal description need not be accompanied by an equivalent scenic representation; indeed, a detailed description may indicate that spectacle was neither required nor even possible.

Not all scholars since 1970 would agree with Webster's estimate of the value of vase-paintings, but most seem to have come to similar conclusions concerning the importance of dramatic texts. Both C. W. Dearden, *The Stage of Aristophanes* (1976), and David Bain, *Actors and Audience: A Study of Asides and Related Conventions in Greek Drama* (1977), are dependent primarily on play texts as guides for their discussions, as is Oliver Taplin in *The Stagecraft of Aeschylus* (1977) and *Greek Tragedy in Action* (1978). Taplin in particular is emphatic about the value of play texts, which he considers ''the paramount evidence for their own staging'': ''Not only should any reconstruction base itself on the texts but any conclusion must on no account be incompatible with the texts. No other evidence available to us can be allowed to count against the evidence of the plays themselves'' (*Stagecraft of Aeschylus*, p. 434). And he is equally emphatic about the limitations of the scholarship of later antiquity: Its testimony can be corroborative only and ought never to be accorded any contrary weight.

Taplin indeed represents a new breed of scholar-critic who is able to take advantage of a century of painstaking and laborious research on the ancient Greek theatre to explore questions of dramatic theory and criticism. He argues not only that the stage action of a Greek tragedy is recoverable from the text and from the comparative study of conventional dramatic methods, but that such action is integral to the playwright's conception and the play's meaning. ''The *words*— which are, after all, almost all we have—contain and explain the visual dimension: there could be no play and no meaning without them. . . . Visual meaning is inextricable from verbal meaning; the two are part and parcel of each other. They are the vehicles of the dramatist's meaning'' (*Greek Tragedy in Action*, p. 5). Rather than using dramatic texts in order to help determine the physical characteristics of the Athenian theatre, Taplin is concerned with what he calls ''the dramatized visible event,'' with what was acted out in a particular instance, with the patterns and sequences of stage movement, in order to derive a play's total meaning and significance. He views his books as critical studies of plays in action, dependent upon but not identical with theatre history.

To sum up: Study of the Greek theatre during the twentieth century has shifted away from a reliance on the scholarship of late antiquity and has looked to the archaeological remains of theatres, to pictorial monuments, to inscriptions, and above all to the play texts themselves in order to reconstruct the original conditions of performance. This change in emphasis has been accompanied by a more sceptical attitude towards all evidence and an insistence on a rigorous estimate of its reliability. Finally, there has been a reaction against what appeared at times to be simple antiquarianism in favor of a fresh examination of ancient dramaturgy and the theatrical masterworks that were its product.

## DRAMATIC TEXTS

The study of classical texts and their transmission is a highly complex and technical art, the details of which do not directly concern us. But some of the conclusions of such study concerning the texts of tragedy and comedy that have come down to us are of some import when those texts are used as evidence for theatre history. Only one complete Greek play—Menander's *Dyskolos*—has reached us directly from antiquity, and it was produced in the third century A.D., more than 500 years after it was written. The remainder of the extant Greek drama derives from manuscripts copied after A.D. 1000. Under these circumstances, it is especially important to know not only how the plays were treated at the time of their original performance, but by what process the extant copies came into being. If play texts are to be used as evidence for anything, we must ascertain their nature as accurately as possible and delineate their scope and limits as precisely as possible.

It is generally assumed that after their initial production plays were circulated in manuscript, written on rolls of papyrus. If contemporary stone inscriptions can be taken as a guide, it appears that the texts lacked word division, had only rudimentary punctuation, no helpful accentuation (which was not introduced until the Hellenistic period 200 years later), and treated choric songs as prose rather than verse. There is evidence too that actors may have added or deleted lines to suit themselves, and that copyists may have misinterpreted the texts—although the extent of the consequent corruption ought not to be overestimated. Alexandrian scholars detected many of the actors' alterations, especially in Euripides; and *The Lives of the Ten Orators (X. Oratorum Vitae)* a first-century work attributed to Plutarch, records that the Athenian politician Lycurgus (ca. 390 B.C.–324 B.C.) ordered copies of the plays of Aeschylus, Sophocles, and Euripides to be deposited in public archives and forbade deviations from these official texts in performance. It was evidently these official copies that were acquired by the famous library at Alexandria, where serious editorial work was begun. Traces of the work of the most famous of the Alexandrian editors, Aristophanes of Byzantium (ca. 257–180 B.C.), can still be found in extant commentaries on the manuscripts. The comedies of Aristophanes the playwright were also edited and annotated by the Alexandrians, and once again traces of this work survive in the extant commentaries or *scholia*.

Other factors helped to determine which plays were destined to come down to us. We know, for example, that the three great Attic tragedians produced a total of approximately 300 plays: We possess the texts of only thirty-three. The narrowing of ancient references to these thirty-three after the third century A.D. indicates that the loss of the others is most likely attributable to events that took place during the second or third century. The most commonly accepted explanation, formulated in 1889 by the German scholar von Wilamowitz, is that, as scholarship declined, tragedies became too difficult for a general readership and became therefore an exclusively academic concern. The bulk of the tragedies that survived, then, did so because they were selected as school texts. When scholars once again turned their attention to dramatic texts at Byzantium in the ninth century, only these school texts were available for study. The early Byzantine copyists and editors were evidently competent and conscientious, but after A.D. 1200 the standard of scholarship declined markedly. As a result, manuscripts that can be dated before 1200 are considerably more reliable than those of later date.

Texts of the Greek tragedies reached the West by various routes. Only one copy of the school edition of Aeschylus, containing seven plays—*Suppliants, Persians, Seven against Thebes, Prometheus, Agamemnon, Choephorae,* and *Eumenides*—reached Byzantium. Of the Byzantine copies based on this edition, only one survives. Transcribed about 1000, it was brought to Italy in 1424 by Giovanni Aurispa and was ultimately deposited in the Biblioteca Medicea-Laurenziana in Florence, catalogued as 32.9. There is a further Byzantine manuscript from the thirteenth century, containing *Prometheus, Seven against Thebes,* and *The Persians,* and two more manuscripts from the fourteenth century that contain all seven plays. As important as Medicea-Laurenziana 32.9 is, it is not necessarily the source for all other Aeschylean manuscripts. The Byzantine triad indicates a common model, which we assume goes back to the original school selection.

Sophocles' seven plays, transcribed in the eleventh century, are also bound in Medicea-Laurenziana 32.9. Included are *Ajax, Antigone, Electra, Oedipus the King, Trachiniae, Philoctetes,* and *Oedipus Colonus.* Again, the Byzantines appear to have made a further selection of three plays (*Ajax, Electra, Oedipus the King*), which are represented in seventy of the ninety-five manuscripts produced between the eleventh and the sixteenth centuries. It was long assumed that all extant manuscripts derive from a single school copy that survived into the Middle Ages, but scholars are no longer sure. Euripides' nineteen extant plays are the result of two main lines of transmission. The first, evidently another school selection, consists of nine plays: *Hecuba, Orestes, Phoenician Women, Andromache, Hippolytus, Medea, Alcestis, Trojan Women,* and *Rhesus.* To these was added from an independent line of transmission *Bacchae.* The second, perhaps a part of a complete edition of Euripides arranged in alphabetical order, also included *Hecuba,* and adds nine new titles: *Helen, Electra, Heracles, Heracleidae, Cyclops, Ion, Suppliant Women, Iphigenia in Taurus,* and *Iphigenia at Aulis.* The earliest manuscript dates from the twelfth century. The most important of the extant manuscripts date from the twelfth and thirteenth centuries and are found in the Biblioteca Nazionale Marciana in Venice (471), the Bibliothèque Nationale in Paris (2712, 2713), the Biblioteca Apostolica Vaticana (909)—all in the first line of transmission—and in the

Biblioteca Medicea-Laurenziana (32.2), which represents the second line of transmission.

Our knowledge of the transmission of Aristophanes' texts is equally hazy, in some respects more so. The fact that his eleven plays are the only examples of Old Comedy to have come down to us is evidence either of a fortunate accident or of the esteem in which Aristophanes was held. We must assume that his comedies underwent the same vicissitudes as did Athenian tragic texts, but there are not the same indications of occasional care that we find in the case of the tragedians. Nevertheless, even though we can assume the usual corruption from miscopying and loss from misadventure of one sort or another, eleven out of forty comedies survived to be edited at Byzantium in the ninth century. They are: *The Acharnians, The Knights, The Clouds, The Wasps, The Peace, The Birds, Lysistrata, Thesmophoriazusae, The Frogs, Ecclesiazusae,* and *Plutus.* The only medieval manuscript to contain all eleven plays is that held by the Biblioteca Classense (Ravenna gr. 429), which is dated ca. 1000. Another manuscript in the Biblioteca Nazionale Marciana (Marciana gr. 474) contains seven plays and dates from the twelfth century. These are the only copies to antedate the sack of Constantinople in 1204; all other manuscripts have been dated between 1261 and the fall of the city in 1453.

In some ways, the story of Menander and his plays is the most interesting of all. Until the twentieth century, Menander was known by reputation, by fragments of his plays quoted by ancient authorities, and by the comedies of Plautus and Terence, which were ostensibly based on the Greek writer's work. Down to the fourth or fifth century, Menander had evidently been extremely popular, his plays a standard part of Western literature. But his reputation as well as copies of his plays evaporated over the next several centuries, and by the eleventh century he and his work had all but disappeared. Just prior to the turn of the twentieth century, a papyrus fragment containing eighty lines of *Georgus* was discovered; and in 1905 a papyrus codex (book as opposed to roll) containing substantial portions of three plays and smaller parts of others was found in Egypt. This so-called *Cairo Codex* was badly mutilated and its reconstruction has not proceeded without controversy. At any rate, we now had a total of about 4,000 lines by Menander.

But the most exciting discovery was yet to come. In 1957, in the library of Dr. Martin Bodmer at Le Grand Cologny near Geneva, Switzerland, was found a complete play by Menander, including hypothesis, didascalia, and dramatis personae. While the circumstances of its original discovery are unknown, it has been determined that the *Dyskolos* papyrus dates from the latter half of the third century A.D., and is therefore the earliest text of a Greek play that has come down to us. Scholars are divided as to its reliability, although most believe that beneath superficial blemishes the text is reasonably sound. The standard text is that of Hugh Lloyd-Jones (1960), but a most useful bilingual edition is provided by Warren E. Blake (1966).

Enough fragments of Greek drama survive to fill several volumes, but they are for the most part so brief and disconnected that they can tell us very little about the lost plays and practically nothing at all about their staging. They do, nevertheless, help us place the extant drama in some perspective, and the number of known plays and playwrights otherwise lost to us ought to make us grateful for the handful of masterpieces that have survived. The principal collections are by A. Nauck (2d ed. 1889; rev. 1964), T. Kock (1880), J. Demianczuk (1912), G. Kaibel (1899), and Colin Austin (1973). The Greekless reader can find some consolation in J. M. Edmonds' *The Fragments of Attic Comedy* (1957–61), and in the first volume of D. L. Page's *Greek Literary Papyri* (1942).

Finally, we can thank the sands of Egypt for the preservation of several mime texts, dating from the second century A.D. Seven more or less complete texts and fragments of seven others by the Greek mime writer Herodas were discovered in 1890 and edited the following year by F. G. Kenyon. A more recent edition is that of I. C. Cunningham (1971), and a translation by Walter Headlam appeared in 1922. A further discovery of a papyrus containing two dramatic pieces was made in 1897: The texts were printed in *The Oxyrhynchus Papryi* III (1903). The verso mime can be found in English translation in William Beare's *The Roman Stage* (pp. 314–319).

Some of the peculiarities of fifth- and fourth-century manuscripts—the lack of word division, the paucity of punctuation, the writing of verse as prose— were remedied by Alexandrian and Byzantine scholarship. In particular, Aristophanes of Byzantium is credited with improving the system of punctuation and inventing a system of accentuation, both very helpful in reading a text that still lacked word-division. Of even more significance for dramatic texts was the haphazard manner in which speeches were assigned to characters (who were often not named), and the imprecise method of indicating a change of speaker (— at the beginning of a line, : within a line). This method—or lack of it— continued to bedevil manuscript copies of plays through the Middle Ages. Indeed, editors and commentators seem to have felt themselves free to reassign speeches arbitrarily. Readers were left to fill in much of the detail themselves; for example, the names and numbers of characters, who spoke what and to whom, and which characters were present in a given scene. Moreover, the extant texts contain few stage directions, and readers were left to reconstruct movements and gestures as well.

The task of sorting out these difficulties has fallen to modern textual scholars, and for the most part their labours have proved as fruitful as they were arduous. Nevertheless, theatre historians are aware that modern editions of Greek plays are synthetic reconstructions of texts whose relationship to an original performance remains ultimately enigmatic. Moreover, as potentially troublesome as the texts are, the implications for theatre history of the state of the manuscripts on which they are based are equally serious. For the evidence indicates that the initially circulated copy of a play was nothing more than a bare record of the words spoken: It did not include the kind of helpful detail that we might expect in a text intended to be read. This is an important consideration;

for the interpretation of a text can be influenced by the question of whether or not the poet wrote for a reader as well as for an audience. In other words, does the text of a play represent a literary or a playhouse document? Because Greek plays were in general intended for a single performance and because Aristophanes appears to have composed his comedies for an audience familiar with the written text of the tragedies he caricatures (as in *The Frogs*, for example), older scholarship assumed that the circulated texts were prepared with the reader in mind. It was further assumed that the text *required* no stage spectacle to complete the imaginative dramatic picture provided to the mind's eye. Oddly, this assumption fired scholars to imagine all kinds of stage business quite unwarranted by the text. Stage action, not tied to the text by any necessity, was not bound by it either. Later scholarship has tended to the view that play-reading did not enter significantly into the playwright's intentions. As a result, text and performance are considered as inextricably linked, performance complementing and interpreting the lines, words putting meaning into the action.

We have noted that explicit stage directions in Greek drama are rare. Fourteen examples are cited by Peter Arnott in *Greek Scenic Conventions in the Fifth Century B.C.* (1962), but Taplin points out that only four of them may go back to the dramatists themselves; the rest are the work of later editors (*Stagecraft of Aeschylus*, p. 15n). Whether fourteen or four, it is obvious that determining staging requirements and stage action on the basis of play texts must proceed conservatively, preferring the simple to the complex, the essential to the possible. And the investigator must rely heavily on implicit stage directions in the characters' speeches. In *Agamemnon*, for instance, the Chorus' inquiry of Clytemnestra as to the reason for her appearance is the only indication of her presence on stage during the *parados*; her silence serves to indicate that she deliberately ignores the Elders of Argos; and the beginning of the first choric ode signals her departure into the palace. Or in *Oedipus the King* the entrance of the protagonist is announced by the servant who has just described his blinding ("you will see"), and confirmed by the Chorus' line that immediately follows ("dreadful to see").

Initially, at least, such a method produces negative conclusions. Pickard-Cambridge, for example, in *The Theatre of Dionysus in Athens*, through an analysis of the extant Greek tragedies, concludes that a raised stage would have been an impediment to the acting of Aeschylus' plays and was not necessary for the performance of those of Sophocles and Euripides (pp. 30–74). His conclusions concerning the use of the *ekkeklema* (a device for revealing tableaux), though more tentative, are equally negative: "It amounts to this—that there is no play in which its use can be considered necessary, and some in which it is definitely improbable . . .; that in several plays it *could* have been used . . . but that the scenes could quite well have been acted without it" (p. 115). More positive results emerge when the method is turned to dramatic criticism. Taplin provides an example. At the conclusion of *Agamemnon*, Clytemnestra tells the Chorus to go home, and they evidently leave, silently rather than singing. This unusual stage instruction has been ignored by many scholars, but if Taplin is right it was intended to be noticed: "The silent exit of the chorus reinforces the meaning of the exit of the rulers into the palace . . .; Aegisthus and Clytemnestra are, for the moment, victorious" (*Stagecraft of Aeschylus*, p. 232).

## ARCHAEOLOGICAL REMAINS OF THEATRES

In 1860 J. W. Donaldson confidently referred to archaeological remains of theatres in support of his picture of the "great stone theatres in which the perfect Greek dramas were represented (*Theatre of the Greeks*, p. 220)." In 1978, a classical archaeologist cautions us when considering the *Theatre of Dionysus in Athens* "to bear in mind that almost nothing of this was there when for example, Aeschylus produced the *Oresteia* in 458 B.C.; the question now is whether there was much more even when Aristophanes produced the *Frogs* in 405 B.C." (R. E. Wycherly, *The Stones of Athens*, p. 206). This difference in perception is principally the result of over one hundred years of archaeological excavation, but it also owes something to changing assumptions underlying the interpretation of what has been found. Donaldson assumed all ancient theatres—Greek or Roman—to have been essentially identical and happily cited a late Roman theatre as evidence for what the Theatre of Dionysus was like in the fifth century B.C. No one in the twentieth century is likely to proceed on so erroneous an assumption, but classical archaeology has been devilled by its own assumptions, equally misleading. In the Preface to *The Theatre of Dionysus in Athens*, Pickard-Cambridge lists some of these assumptions or "mere superstitions" as he calls them:

1. that the chronological order of architectural change can be inferred from the logical;
2. that work from the classical age was perfect and therefore that imperfect work indicates a later date;
3. that stone structures must previously have existed in wood;
4. that all art and architecture is "derived" from something earlier.

Still, these assumptions have been challenged and corrected, and archaeological history continues, like all history, to modify itself.

The site of the Theatre of Dionysus was not discovered until 1765, and excavations did not begin until 1862. In the intervening years the Turks built a fortification-wall across it, using stones from the theatre. Excavations were begun again in 1877, but it was not until Dörpfeld began his work in 1886 that the theatre was subjected to a serious and sustained examination. Further work was done in the 1920s by Heinrich Bulle and again during the years 1927–29 and 1933 by Ernst Fiechter. Unlike laboratory experiments, field work in archaeology cannot be repeated, and we are still dependent upon the data published as a result of these men's excavations. Pickard-Cambridge's *The Theatre of Dionysus in Athens*, the standard work on the subject in English, depends heavily on the work of these archaeologists. And sketches and drawings of the theatre published by Dörpfeld and Fiechter continue to illustrate standard textbooks in theatre history. Unfortunately, the methods employed, especially during the nineteenth century when the crucial initial digging was done, left something to be desired from the point of view of the modern archaeologist. As a result, while the main sequence of structural changes in the theatre is reasonably clear, there has been considerable difficulty in dating the alterations with any precision. In general, however, informed opinion has tended to down-date the more elaborate additions to the theatre to the fourth century and later.

Investigation of the Theatre of Dionysus has determined the following chronological distinctions in the most significant remains:

1. The oldest remains consist of six limestone blocks, arranged in a slight curve covering approximately four meters, on the south side of the Acropolis. (Dörpfeld reports a seventh, but it has disappeared.) These are taken to be the remains of a retaining wall for a terrace, necessary to make a flat surface suitable for an orchestra. It is assumed that the slope itself initially served as the auditorium, and that wooden seats may have been provided sometime near the beginning of the fifth century B.C. But these assumptions depend upon literary rather than archaeological evidence.

2. Next in time are four foundations of large blocks of red conglomerate stone: one about twenty-three meters long on the east side of the present orchestra; another about thirty-two meters long on the west side; and the foundations of two straight walls approximately sixty meters long south of the present skene ruins. The more northerly of the latter two foundations is provided with a series of slots cut into the blocks in the central section. The assumption is that the foundations are those of the first permanent skene, and that the slots provided support for wooden uprights and structures which were used for scenic purposes.

3. Later are the remains of the stone auditorium, the skene, and paraskene.

4. Later still is the foundation of the proskenium.

5. Last of all are the "improvements" of the Romans: the paved orchestra, now a slightly elongated semi-circle about twenty-one meters in diameter, with an extended north-south radius of fifteen meters; and the stone barrier between orchestra and auditorium.

While the sequence is relatively clear, the dating of the innovations, particularly those of the second phase, is crucial. Pickard-Cambridge believed them to have been the result of a comprehensive reconstruction of the theatre which was completed by 443 B.C. Thus the bulk of extant Greek drama would have been acted before a permanent skene; only Aeschylus would have had to make do with the primitive conditions of the first phase. Pickard-Cambridge relegated the third phase to the fourth century and the remaining changes to Hellenistic and later times. More recent work by Greek archaeologists, however, suggests that the foundations for the supporting walls and the skene must be down-dated into the fourth century, to the time of Lycurgus (338–326 B.C.). The principal evidence is the red conglomerate stone, which was not used to any extent before the fourth century. Now it appears that all of the plays of Sophocles, Euripides, and Aristophanes, as well as those of Aeschylus, were performed under the circumstances of the first phase. And these circumstances indicate a simplicity of staging quite at variance with the elaborate spectacles imagined by nineteenth-century scholars.

There are many other extant Greek theatres, of course, and archaeologists have excavated more than sixty-five of them, dating from the mid-fifth century B.C. to about 150 B.C., although few of them have received the attention of the Theatre of Dionysus at Athens. An extensive study of the theatre at Priene (ca. 330 B.C.) was published by A. Von Gerkan in 1921, and a brief survey of facts relating to forty-eight Greek theatres can be found in P. E. Arias' *Il Teatro Greco Fuori di Atene* (1934). But, as usual, the history of the development of theatre architecture is difficult to trace with any precision; and the overall picture has been clouded by the "superstitions" lamented by Pickard-Cambridge. Certainly, found as they are spread over mainland Greece, the Aegean, Asia Minor, and Italy and ranging in their origins over three hundred years, the extant Greek theatres offer evidence difficult to generalize on. And the difficulty is compounded if, as is often the case, they underwent extensive remodelling at the hands of the Romans as well as deterioration under the vicissitudes of time. Nevertheless, it is reasonably certain that the orchestra was the original feature of the Greek theatre, that the auditorium was the next development in the fifth century, and that the skene and its elaborations were the products of the fourth century B.C. and later. It is even arguable that these three features did not form a single architectural unit until the end of the fourth century B.C.

By far the best known of the Greek theatres outside Athens, and the one whose photograph graces every handbook and textbook, is that at Epidaurus. This theatre, built in the fourth century B.C. and the best preserved of all ancient Greek theatres, features a circular orchestra, architectural symmetry, and near perfect acoustics. It is regularly used by the Greek National Theatre. Few visitors to Epidaurus have come away unimpressed with this confirmation of classical Greek perfection.

Unfortunately, when this idea of architectural perfection is associated with the Athenian theatre—as it too often is, in scholarly works as well as in introductory textbooks—we run the risk of distorting archaeological evidence and misunderstanding the nature of the theatrical experience in fifth-century B.C. Athens. There is little doubt that the Theatre of Dionysus was the most important theatre in Greece, perhaps in the whole history of the theatre; there is little doubt as well that the Greek drama acted there represents one of humankind's greatest artistic achievements. But there is also little doubt that architecturally the Theatre of Dionysus was asymmetrical—almost rough and ready—compared to Epidaurus. In fact, so far as early Greek theatres are concerned, Epidaurus' perfectly circular orchestra may have been the exception rather than the norm. In 1947 C. Anti suggested a trapezoidal shape for the ancient orchestra (*Teatri Greci Arcaici*), and since that time archaeological excavations of the theatre at the sanctuary of Poseidon on the Isthmus of Corinth indicate that there at least the orchestra was rectilinear. (See Elizabeth R. Gebhard, *The Theater at Isthmia*.) For the theatre historian such things are worth remembering: The glory lay in the text and its performance, not in the physical theatre.

## INSCRIPTIONS

The Greeks wrote on stone as well as on papyrus, and the inscriptions so preserved, covering approximately a 1,000-year period from the sixth century B.C. to the fourth century A.D., are a treasure-trove of information concerning nearly every aspect of Greek life and culture. Making up as they do authentic, first-hand, contemporary, and detailed records of events, inscriptions have from very early times served as important sources for historians. They were used as early as the fifth century B.C. by the Greek historian Herodotus. By the third and second centuries B.C., serious attempts had been made to collect inscriptions, a practice picked up again in the fifteenth century and continued on a rather hit-and-miss basis through the seventeenth and eighteenth centuries. It was not until the nineteenth century, however, that systematic efforts were made to collect and publish Greek inscriptions. The mammoth task was undertaken by August Boeckh in 1825 and continued by others to 1877. The result was the *Corpus Inscriptionum Graecarum*. But even before this great work was completed, the finding of new inscriptions, particularly at the site of the Athenian *agora* or meeting-place, prompted the Berlin Academy to begin publishing the *Inscriptiones Graecae* (1873-), intended to include all the Greek inscriptions of Europe. Since the original materials were often found in Egypt and Asia Minor as well as in Greece, other collections of non-European Greek inscriptions have also been made. So far as theatre history is concerned, however, the *Inscriptiones Graecae* (*IG*) remains the most frequently cited collection. (The student should be warned, however, that some volumes have gone into second editions, and the numbering of the inscriptions has consequently been altered; for example, *IG* ii 977 = *IG* ii² 2325.)

While the great bulk of inscriptions deal with non-theatrical matters, many do refer to events of some interest to the theatre historian, and a few are of crucial importance. In the former category we can place the famous Parian Marble (Marmor Parium), an inscribed marble stele discovered on the island of Paros, commemorating a variety of political, religious, and especially literary events ostensibly dating from the time of the legendary King Cecrops (1580 B.C.) to the archonship of Diognetus at Athens (263 B.C.). A total of 107 items is to be found on the two fragments that survive: The first, discovered in 1627 and now in the Ashmolean Museum in Oxford, contains eighty items; the second, found in 1897 and preserved in the museum on Paros, contains another twenty-seven items. A convenient edition is that of Felix Jacoby, *Das Marmor Parium* (1904). Included on the marble are references to the establishment of festivals. It is the Parian Marble, for instance, that tells us that the first tragic contest, won by Thespis, took place in 534 B.C.; that the first contests of *choroi andron*, or men's choruses, occurred about 509 B.C.; and that the dramatist Anaxandrides recorded his first Dionysiac victory in 376 B.C. Some of the information can be substantiated from other sources, a fact that argues for the reliability of the unique notices (such as that concerning Thespis in 534).

But by far the most important inscriptions so far as the performance of lyric choruses and plays is concerned are those that record the victors in the Athenian dramatic festivals (*IG* ii$^2$ 2318–2325). These, together with some few others relating to the Athenian dramatic festivals, were collected, discussed, and published along with photographs of the pertinent stone fragments by Adolf Wilhelm in *Urkunden Dramatischer Aufführungen in Athen* (1905). (A transcript of the inscriptions bearing on the Dionysia and Lenaea is also included in Pickard-Cambridge, *Dramatic Festivals of Athens*, as an appendix to the second chapter.) The inscriptions, the few statements on the Parian Marble, and the statements of Alexandrian scholars in the "Arguments" prefixed to many plays provide interlocking and corroborating evidence concerning Athenian official records.

The stone fragments containing these records have been sorted out by date of initial cutting as well as by content. The first series of inscriptions (*IG* ii$^2$ 2318; *IG* ii 971), referred to as *Fasti* (calendar or register), was possibly originally cut between 346 and 330 B.C. and was added to year by year until about 320 B.C. The Fasti record the names of the various victors at the Dionysia each year, but because parts at the beginning are missing it is uncertain with what year they began: The first extant entry refers to 472 B.C. For each year the relevant inscription notes the archon's name, the victorious boys' chorus and choregos, the victorious men's chorus and choregos, the victorious comic poet and choregos, and the victorious tragic poet and choregos. The last extant entry is for the year 328 B.C. The Fasti were cut on the face of a wall, perhaps in a parados of the theatre, composed of four rows of blocks almost two meters high. The text was arranged in sixteen vertical columns of forty-one lines each.

Two other series of inscriptions—the so-called Didascaliae and the Victors-Lists—date from approximately 278 B.C. Most of these fragments were found on the south side of the Acropolis. The main inscriptions of the Didascaliae (*IG* ii$^2$ 2319–2322; *IG* ii 972–975) were arranged under four categories: (*a*) tragedies at the Dionysia, (*b*) comedies at the Dionysia, (*c*) comedies at the Lenaea, and (*d*) tragedies at the Lenaea. In each instance we find the archon's name, the names of the playwrights in order of success, the names of their plays, the names of the actors, and the names of the winning actor. A further inscription (*IG* ii$^2$ 2325; *IG* ii 977), engraved on the same building as the Didascaliae, records for both the Dionysia and the Lenaea the total number of victories won by poets and actors in tragedy and comedy—eight lists in all. Here we learn, for example, that Aeschylus took first place thirteen times and Sophocles eighteen times.

Classical scholars agree that the Fasti, the Didascaliae, and the Victors-Lists do not derive directly from the official record kept on an annual basis by the archons. Rather they are based principally on a lost book by Aristotle, the *Didascaliae* (335–321 B.C.), a record of lyric and dramatic performances drawn from official records. Aristotle's work was probably the authority for performances up to 334 B.C.; his record would have simply been brought up to date for subsequent periods by later recorders. Nevertheless, taken together these lists provide a remarkably accurate chronology of plays and performances in the fifth century B.C.

## MONUMENTS

We have seen that one of the major changes in the study of Greek theatre history in this century has been the new emphasis on the evidence provided by painting and statuary. The interpretation of this evidence has presented difficulties, which arise from the fact that each art has its own conventions and these conventions need bear no discernible relationship to those of another art. Details of the interpretation may vary, then, and there is agreement that such evidence must be carefully weighed and cautiously used, but no theatre historian has been able to ignore pictorial evidence, particularly that derived from vases.

### Vase-Paintings

Vase-paintings whose subjects relate to drama and the theatre number many hundreds, but they can be classified as evidence for theatre history as follows: those whose subject matter is similar to or identical with the subject matter of known plays; those that depict a performance of some kind (which may of course correspond in content to a known play); and those whose subject matter is the theatre itself. The first group contains the largest number of examples, but it is the third and smallest group that is of special value. Nevertheless, it is unlikely that many vase-paintings, however "theatrical" they seem, represent scenes as they were acted on the stage. The figures normally do not wear masks, and in those instances where it has been possible to identify the extant play from which the representation was drawn, it is common to find that the painter has presented an episode from the story that the playwright did not include in his scenario. And difficulties are compounded by the fact that, while the plays date from the fifth century B.C., most of the vases ostensibly depicting scenes from them date from the fourth century and later.

In *Illustrations of Greek Drama*, a very useful selection of the surviving monuments, A. D. Trendall and T.B.L. Webster divide the illustrations into five groups: (1) Pre-dramatic monuments, (2) Satyr-plays, (3) Tragedy, (4) Old

and Middle Comedy, Phlyakes, and (5) New Comedy. (More complete cata-
logues are provided by T.B.L. Webster in Supplements to the *Bulletin of the
Institute of Classical Studies*, Nos. 9, 11, 14.) In date the monuments range
from about 700 B.C. to about A.D. 300. While many of them are from Athens,
a far greater number originated in other parts of mainland Greece, the Greek
islands, Sicily and Italy, Asia, and Africa. Such geographical variety, and such
an extended chronology, are obvious warnings to the historian to proceed with
caution, especially if he or she wishes to apply the evidence of the monuments
to fifth-century B.C. Athens.

Some vase-paintings have been singled out as particularly valuable evidence
for staging, although there is no universal agreement on their interpretation.
Among those whose subject matter is the theatre itself we find (*a*) the Oenochoe Fragments from the Athenian Agora and a bell-krater and pelike, all from
the fifth century (Pickard-Cambridge, *Dramatic Festivals of Athens*, figs. 32–
34); (*b*) the Pronomos vase of about 400 B.C. (Trendall and Webster, II.l); and
(*c*) fragments of a Gnathia vase from Taranto, from the same date (*Dramatic
Festivals*, fig. 54). These all seem to be portraying actors in the process of
dressing for their parts. The well-known Andromeda vase (Trendall and Webster, III.3, 10) has also been regarded as providing information on stage costume; but in this instance, while Euripides' lost *Andromeda* may have inspired
the painting, the scene as represented does not constitute a stage scene, but rather
a gathering of plot strands into a stylized pictorial narrative.

A Campanian vase now in the Louvre (Trendall and Webster, III.3, 31), dating from about 330–320 B.C. and based on Euripides' *Iphigenia in Taurus*, has
been taken as evidence that even in the fourth century B.C. plays were still being
acted in front of the skene, between the paraskenia on the ground floor of the
orchestra. It is true that the temple before which the characters stand is given
the effect of a stage background, but again it is not clear whether the painter
wished to do any more than suggest a theatrical performance. The theatre of
his mind's eye may have been far removed from contemporary stage practice.

A number of vases, mostly from southern Italy and mostly from the fourth
century B.C., feature a *prothyron* or porch of either four or six columns (Pickard-Cambridge, *Theatre of Dionysus in Athens*, figs. 9–23; Trendall and Webster, III.l, 10; 3, 29; 3, 30; 4, 2; 5, 4). These have been taken as evidence that
in plays that took place before a temple or palace, this *prothyron* was placed in
front of the central entrance. Pickard-Cambridge, however, points out that the
structure also appears on vases having no connection with the theatre, and that
consequently it may represent a convention of vase-painting rather than of the
theatre. Obviously, though, we may not rule out the possibility that the convention derived from stage practice.

Aside from a series of black-figured vases depicting padded dancers, dol-
phin-riders, and ostrich-riders from the seventh and sixth centuries B.C. (Trendall and Webster, I.1–15), comedy as a subject for vase-painting is confined to
sixteen Attic and Corinthian vases dated from about 420 B.C. to about 375 B.C.

(Trendall and Webster, IV.1–6) and to a group of vases from southern Italy depicting scenes from the local farce or phlyax (Trendall and Webster, IV.10–37). (Trendall's *Phlyax Vases*, 2d ed., Supplement No. 19 of the *Bulletin of the Institute of Classical Studies*, contains a complete catalogue of both the Greek and the Italian vases, together with numerous photographic illustrations.) The phlyax vases, numbering 185, first appeared at the end of the fifth century B.C., although the majority of them are from the fourth century. Approximately one-quarter of them include the depiction of a temporary low stage, and there seems no good reason for doubting that in these vases especially we have fairly reliable evidence concerning the staging, the characters, and the costumes associated with this local form of comedy. Whether or not this evidence can legitimately be applied to the performance of Attic comedy is another matter. One of the extant Attic vases of about 420 B.C. (Trendall and Webster, IV.1) features a picture of a comic performance that includes a stage much like that depicted on some of the phlyax vases. On the basis of this evidence and on some other less obvious similarities, it is sometimes argued that some of the scenes on the phlyax vases are direct reflections of fourth-century B.C. Attic comedies; and further, that the fifth-century Athenian B.C. theatre had both a raised stage and steps in the phlyax manner. (This last view is expressed by Peter Arnott in *Greek Scenic Conventions in the Fifth Century B.C.*) While few scholars are inclined to press the point this far, there does seem to be agreement on the possibility of some link between Athenian comedy and the phlyakes. Costume seems to be the most likely point of linkage.

### Reliefs, Mosaics, Wall-Paintings

Other pictorial monuments frequently cited as evidence concerning costumes and masks include stone and marble reliefs, mosaics, and wall-paintings. Few examples, however, are from a date prior to Hellenistic times. Among them are (1) the Peiraeus relief from Athens (ca. 400 B.C.) depicting three actors before Dionysus (Pickard-Cambridge, *Dramatic Festivals of Athens*, fig. 51); (2) a marble relief in the Epigraphical Museum in Athens (ca. 340 B.C.) in honour of a choregos, decorated with five masks and possibly representing comedy (Trendall and Webster, IV. 8a); and (3) an Attic relief of about 380 B.C. of a comic poet holding one mask, while another mask hangs on the wall (Trendall and Webster, IV.7a). New Comedy is particularly well represented in later reliefs and mosaics. The famous relief showing Menander in his studio studying a mask while two other masks rest upon the table before him (Pickard-Cambridge, *Dramatic Festivals of Athens*, fig. 109) dates from the Hellenistic period, as does the Naples relief depicting a scene from New Comedy (fig. 110). New Comedy masks are also a feature of three mosaic floors in a house built in the second century B.C. on the island of Delos (Trendall and Webster, IV.8c). Scenes from New Comedy are the subject of other mosaics from Pompeii, signed by Dioskourides of Samos about 100 B.C. (Trendall and Webster, V.1, 3) and from Mytilene about A.D. 300 (Trendall and Webster, IV.2, 4).

The wall-paintings that have attracted the most attention are those discovered at Pompeii and Herculaneum, but whether these numerous and elaborate house decorations can tell us anything about the ancient Greek theatre is questionable. Some of them are undoubtedly theatrical in content, in that they show actors studying roles or preparing for performances; and there are other scenes that appear to be based on Greek drama, set against an architectural background, although there is no indication that these settings derive from stage presentation. Even if something can be gleaned from these paintings concerning dramatic costume, it is very likely more relevant to the Roman stage than to the Greek. And there is an even greater possibility that they present a largely conventionalized picture of theatre and drama that need have borne no relationship to actual theatre production. Objections can also be made to several wall-paintings at Boscoreale near Pompeii, which have been interpreted as representing tragic, comic, and satyric stage scenery (Bieber, *Greek and Roman Theater*, figs. 471–74), after the manner described by Vitruvius in *Ten Books of Architecture* (V.vi.9). Indeed, in VII.v.2 Vitruvius specifically mentions the practice of depicting the façades of scenes in large rooms. Unfortunately, it is not clear whether the architect had first-hand knowledge of Greek theatre practice, whether he was attributing Roman practice to the Greeks, or whether the three scenes existed only in theory.

### Statuettes

Terracotta statuettes found in many parts of Greece and Italy, assumed to represent comic stage figures, have served as evidence for the characters and the costumes of ancient Greek comedy. Margarete Bieber, for example, provides over sixty illustrations of them in *The History of the Greek and Roman Theater* and, on the basis of both "content" and date, more or less confidently allots them to Old or Middle Comedy. On the other hand, while the similarity of the faces to masks depicted on some vases indicates a connection with stage comedy, individual statuettes can remain problematic. And dating is difficult. Terracottas were copied and widely dispersed, and both the date and the place of production of the original can well be a mystery. It has been possible to determine, however, that some of them at least originated in the first half of the fourth century B.C. It is therefore possible that they could represent figures from Old Comedy, and Bieber so considers them. A more conservative scholar such as Pickard-Cambridge is more inclined to caution that the terracotta figurines are more safely treated as parallel to the dramatic figures of Middle and New Comedy. In short, it is difficult not to see these statuettes as originally inspired by stage-figures, and a comparison of them with the extant remains of Old, Middle, and New Comedy can not only help us to sort them out, but can also tell us a great deal about the performance of the plays. Is it not possible too, that, while Old and New Comedy are clearly distinguishable on a literary basis, they may have shared some details of mask and costume, or at least that the dividing line between them, so far as performance was concerned, may not have been as sharply drawn as we have assumed?

## WRITTEN SOURCES

Written materials form the backbone of classical studies, and written records of the Greek drama were long unquestioned as valid evidence for theatre history. This attitude has changed somewhat and such sources are now used very cautiously. Nevertheless they do exist, and they can provide corroboration of fact even when they cannot be used to establish fact. The problem is that the classical drama of Greece has made a magnet of fifth-century B.C. Athens, while the bulk of the written references to the theatre date from a much later period. It is wise, therefore, to bear in mind that these references vary in kind and quality. Some purport to refer to the fifth-century B.C. Athenian theatre, others to theatre contemporary with the writer, and still others constitute only incidental references. Too, the nature and purpose of the text should be noted: Is it a work of fiction or of fact? of imagination or of history? We must remember that for many ancient writers imagination and history were not to be separated. We must note the author: Was he likely to know what he purports to know? The consistency of the document is also important; for if one part can be shown to be wrong, the rest is automatically suspect. And finally, the information must be tested against other, independent sources, preferably non-written sources. Only by such cautious appraisal can we begin to distinguish the nonsensical from the valid, the irrelevant from the material.

Some of the well-known later Greek and Latin authors who were at one time thought to provide evidence for the fifth-century B.C. Greek theatre include Lucian of Samasota (fl. A.D. 150), Horace (65 B.C.–8 B.C.), and Quintilian (ca. A.D. 38–100); but their late dates and the nature of their writings clearly make them relevant principally to their own times, and we will reserve discussion of them until the next chapter.

### Plutarch and Pausanias

The biographer and moralist Plutarch (ca. A.D. 46–100), on the other hand, presents a greater challenge to interpretation. Throughout the *Moralia* and the *Lives* he on occasion refers to things theatrical, and while his interests are mainly ethical, he gives the appearance—particularly in the *Lives*—of providing historical fact as well. It is to Plutarch, for instance, that we owe the story of Solon's confrontation with Thespis ("Life of Solon"). What muddies the evidence, however, is Plutarch's predilection for making his accounts more vivid by modernizing them and adding details from contemporary life. So far as the physical theatre is concerned, he always assumes the theatre of his own day. More a preserver of anecdotes concerning the theatre and dramatists than a historian, Plutarch provides possible hints rather than answers, and demands careful interpretation and verification.

In contrast, the overall accuracy of Pausanias of Lydia (fl. A.D. 150), a Greek traveller and geographer, is attested by topographical observation and archaeological excavation. His *Descriptions of Greece*, in ten ancient books (5 modern vols.), sketches the history, topography, customs, religious and historical remains, and artistic monuments of various Greek cities and has provided an invaluable guide for archaeologists and classical scholars. As useful as he is, nonetheless, Pausanias can tell us relatively little directly about performance in the Greek theatre of the fifth century B.C.

### Aristotle

The ancient writer on the theatre commanding the most respect and in the best position to provide accurate information is something of a disappointment. Aristotle (384–322 B.C.) is believed to have devoted a considerable amount of time and effort to the compilation of Athenian theatrical records, but the only evidence of his *Didascaliae* are the inscriptions held to have been based on his work. And the *Poetics*, undoubtedly the most significant and influential critical document in history, is not itself a work of theatre history. Aristotle had no real interest in history, and he preferred the literary over the theatrical dimension of drama. He was, nevertheless, writing within one hundred years of the initial production of the drama he was analyzing, and what he tells us should be treated with respect. We saw in Chapter 1 the way in which his comments on the origins of tragedy and comedy have figured centrally in the discussions of theatre origins, although in the final analysis he must be considered a theorist on the matter like everybody else. His sketch of the history of tragedy (IV.11–15), although we learn from it that Aeschylus introduced a second actor and Sophocles a third actor as well as scene-painting, is based on the philosopher's conception of the nature of poetry rather than on historical research. Aristotle's indifference to the historical process by which change occurs is evident from his idea of a natural form towards which tragedy had inevitably moved: "Tragedy advanced by slow degrees, each new element that showed itself was in turn developed. Having passed through many changes, it found its natural form, and there it stopped" (IV.12). The final (and perfect) form of tragedy was Aristotle's real concern, not its history. His discussion of comedy (V.2) is even briefer. Aside from some references to plays and playwrights otherwise unknown, Aristotle tells us very little more about the history of the Greek theatre and even less about the resources of the fifth-century B.C. stage.

### Vitruvius and Pollux

Apparently more rewarding sources of information—or at least deemed more rewarding by most classical scholars until the present century—are to be found in the *De Re Architectura*, a treatise in Latin on architecture and building construction by Vitruvius Pollio, probably written between 16 and 13 B.C.; and in the *Onomastikon* of Julius Pollux (second century A.D.), a compendium of miscellaneous information derived from various sources. Vitruvius' work, rediscovered in 1414 and published in 1486, has not only served classical scholars, but provided a model for Renaissance architecture as well. Pollux's work has perished in its original form. The extant manuscripts derive from four mutilated and interpolated copies of an epitome or summary owned by Arethas (ca. 860-ca. 935), Archbishop of Caesarea in Cappodocia. Neither of these sources can be considered even remotely contemporaneous with the classical Greek theatre, although there is more reason to trust Vitruvius than Pollux. On the other hand, both writers give evidence of having had access to earlier scholarship, some of it now lost. In the Introduction to Book VII, Vitruvius refers to a multitude of earlier Greek architects and architectural treatises, including Agatharcus' lost work on scene-painting in the time of Aeschylus, and he specifically attests his dependence upon them: "Hence, as I saw that such beginnings on their part formed an introduction suited to the nature of my own purpose, I set out to draw from them, and to go somewhat further" [section 11]. Pollux mentions Juba of Mauretania, and he may have used Aristophanes of Byzantium and his contemporary Eratosthenes, both Alexandrian scholars of the third century B.C. But even assuming the reliability of their sources, the uses to which Vitruvius and Pollux put the information must also be taken into account if we are to interpret and evaluate their testimony justly.

Vitruvius sets out his purpose in the Preface to Book I. Addressing his remarks to Augustus, he writes:

I began to write this work for you, because I saw that you have built and are now building extensively, and that in future also you will take care that our public and private buildings shall be worthy to go down to posterity by the side of your other splendid achievements. I have drawn up definite rules to enable you, by observing them, to have personal knowledge of the quality both of existing buildings and of those which are yet to be considered. For in the following books I have disclosed all the principles of the art [section 3].

One point in particular needs emphasizing. Vitruvius was intent on prescribing rules and principles for the guidance of contemporary and future builders of public edifices. He had no interest in the history of architecture beyond providing him with examples to illustrate the principles he advocated; certainly he had no interest in non-existent structures. He was interested in prescribing an ideal, not in describing past imperfections. The point is underscored by his observation that "whoever is willing to follow these directions will be able to construct perfectly correct theatres" (V.vii.2).

Vitruvius discusses both "Roman" and "Greek" theatres (V.iii-viii), their acoustics, their plans, their *scaenae*, including the use of *periaktoi*, "triangular pieces of machinery which revolve, each having three decorated faces" (V.vi.8), and the three kinds of scenes—tragic, comic, and satyric. His discussion has caused confusion on two counts. First, he constantly compares Greek and Roman practice and terminology, carefully noting differences and similarities. As a result, it has often been assumed that where he notes similarities, Greek and

Roman theatres were indeed identical (in the use of *periaktoi*, for instance). Second, Vitruvius' use of the designations "Greek" and "Roman" has been taken as historical rather than descriptive, and his "Greek" theatre in particular was associated with the theatre of the great tragedians. Vitruvius' descriptions of theatres, however—Roman and Greek—do not correspond exactly with any extant theatre. Indeed, his mathematically precise plans for a Greek theatre were a greater appeal to later scholarship's faith in Greek perfection than an indication of the shape of the Athenian theatre in the fifth century B.C. Both types of theatre described by Vitruvius were in fact being built in his time (although not exactly according to his directions). They are now referred to as the Roman and Graeco-Roman. But any attempt to force the wide variety of theatres built in the ancient world into Vitruvius' two categories is bound to distort reality.

Pollux too writes of the stage, the *scaenae*, and especially the machinery of the ancient theatre (*periaktoi, ekkeklema, mechané*); and in some respects, at least, he appears to agree with Vitruvius. Both note the *periaktoi* (although Pollux's explanation of their use is a bit confusing), and both indicate that actors performed in a place separate from other performers or the chorus. The actors occupied the *skene*, according to Pollux; and the chorus, the orchestra. Vitruvius notes that the actors performed on the *logeion*, while other artists used the entire orchestra. Although both *skene* and *logeion* have been interpreted to mean "stage," there is considerable doubt that *skene* necessarily meant anything of the kind, and Pollux's statement cannot therefore be verified by Vitruvius and thereby taken as evidence of the general veracity of his other comments. Pollux's description may indeed be accurate, but it is impossible to tell to what period any of the details refer. The arrangement of the *Onomastikon* is topical and the book is primarily a thesaurus of terms; consequently, the material Pollux presents is classified without any regard for date. Once again, the writing of history was not the writer's object, and he is far more likely in general to reflect contemporary rather than past stage practice.

The same qualifications must be made concerning Pollux's catalogue of theatrical masks. This descriptive list of approximately seventy-five masks has been matched and compared with characters from the extant plays of both Greece and Rome, and with the various statuettes and pictorial monuments that seem to represent masks. Whatever Pollux may be able to tell us about tragic masks, his continued references to the *onkos* indicate that he had contemporary practice in mind; and his list of comic masks relates specifically to New Comedy. In short, Pollux's chief value lies in reference to the performance mainly of New Comedy in late Hellenistic and Imperial Roman times. And even here his descriptions are suggestive rather than definitive.

### Scholarship

Ancient scholarship has come down to us in various forms—lexicons, *scholia*, various kinds of compendia and encyclopedia—and it is wise to be aware of the scholarly activities and the lines of descent behind any document which appears to offer information on the theatre. We have had occasion previously to consider the contributions of the scholars at Alexandria. It is these men who laid the foundations of classical scholarship on which succeeding generations both drew and built. Very little evidence of their enormous industry and painstaking labours survives in its original forms, but careful cross-checking and sifting of later materials has enabled modern scholars to trace a reasonably clear pattern of their influence on each other and on later scholarship. We can assume, for instance, that the lost *Chronological Register of the Athenian Dramatic Poets*, compiled by the Alexandrian cataloguer and poet Callimachus (ca. 305-ca. 240 B.C.), was used by his colleagues and successors at the famous library. And a work in twelve books on ancient comedy by Callimachus' pupil Eratosthenes (ca. 275–194 B.C.), which discussed the production of plays as well as literary, lexical, historical, and antiquarian matters, was used by Aristophanes of Byzantium (ca. 257-ca. 180 B.C.), and later by Didymus (63 B.C.-A.D. 10). Aristophanes wrote on character-types in Greek comedy, and compiled a treatise on Menander. None of this work survives, but his *hypotheses* or introductions to various plays of Aristophanes the comic poet and the Greek tragedians, based in part on Aristotle's *Didascaliae*, are extant in an abbreviated form (edited by A. Nauck, 1848). Didymus, nicknamed *chalcenterus*— "brass-bowelled"—because of his incredible industry, belonged to the Alexandrian school founded by Aristarchus of Samothrace (ca. 216-ca. 144 B.C.), whose lost works include commentaries on Aeschylus, Sophocles, and Aristophanes. Didymus himself wrote commentaries on Aristophanes and Menander as well as on the three tragedians, but his importance lies mainly in his compilations and discussions of the work of earlier scholars. As a transmitter of knowledge he is responsible for much of the material in extant scholia and lexicons. In particular, much of the oldest scholia on Sophocles, Euripides, and Aristophanes derive from Didymus.

Didymus was also the compiler of an early lexicon which, although now lost, was used as a source by other lexicographers. While there are of course some gaps in the sequence, the tradition of lexicon writing can be traced through to the tenth century A.D. Didymus' pupil Apion contributed a lexicon in the first century A.D., of which fragments remain. And during the same century Pamphilus of Alexandria compiled a great lexicon in forty-five books, which absorbed many earlier and more specialized collections. Diogenianus of Heraclea used an abridged version of Pamphilus' work by one Vestinus, in order to compile an alphabetically arranged epitome or summary, which was in turn used as a source by the fifth-century A.D. lexicographer Hesychius of Alexandria. Hesychius' lexicon, which the author says was based on works by Aristarchus and Apion among others as well, is known only from a badly mutilated manuscript from the fifteenth century (Biblioteca Nazionale Marciana gr. 622), which has come down to us with the notes and emendations made by its editor, Marcus Musurus, when he prepared it for publication in 1514. Fragments of other lexica based on Didymus and Pamphilus by Dionysius Aelius and Pausanias (sec-

ond century A.D.) also exist, as do bits and pieces of the lexicon in turn based
on their work, that of Phrynichus Arabius of Bithynia (fl. A.D. 16l–192). But
all three survive principally in the lexicon of Photius (ca. 810–891), who also
utilized Diogenianus' lexicon and the lexicon of Plato compiled by Timaeus in
the fourth century A.D. Photius, generally considered to have been the best of
the Byzantine scholars of the ninth century, had the first complete copy of his
lexicon discovered in a Macedonian library in 1959. Finally, towards the end
of the tenth century was compiled what is known as the *Suda* (meaning ''for-
tress'' but sometimes mistakenly taken to be the name of the lexicographer),
the result of collaboration among various Byzantine scholars. While some of its
sources can be traced, the great value of this dictionary-encyclopedia lies in the
fact that it preserves, albeit imperfectly, information derived from works now
lost and unknown.

With the *Suda* we are in fact moving beyond lexica and into the area of encyclopedia and collections, and there are a variety of works dating from the
second century A.D. and later that provide a vast miscellany of more or less
trustworthy information on a wide variety of things Greek and Roman. The most
important are the following:

1. Aulus Gellius (ca. A.D. 123–ca. 165) in *Noctes Atticae* discusses in twenty books
   law, grammar, antiquities, history, biography, and literary criticism; and preserves
   extracts from some 225 Greek and Roman writers.

2. Athenaeus of Naucratis (fl. ca. A.D. 200) probably drew upon lexica such as that of
   Pamphilus for his *Deipnosophistae*, in which the participants of the literary banquet
   range over a wide variety of topics and in the process preserve a good deal of information. Of particular interest are the sizeable extracts from Middle and New
   Comedy otherwise not known.

3. Diogenes Laertius (third century A.D.), author of *The Lives of the Philosophers*, is
   interesting insofar as he preserves a kind of compendium of ancient philosophy; but
   he is useful for our purposes insofar as he provides a collection of more or less
   classified quotations and excerpts from ancient writers.

4. Photius' *Bibliotheca* or *Myriobiblion* (before A.D. 858) is a badly arranged account
   of 280 prose works on romance, philosophy, science, medicine, lexicography, history, and especially theology. Once again, we are confronted with an ill-assorted
   storehouse of information and extracts, from which it has been possible to glean
   various theatrical references.

One final form of ancient scholarship must be considered. We have seen that
some of the work of ancient scholars formed the basis of certain *scholia* on
ancient playwrights. These consist of notes preserved in the margins of texts,
which explain or comment on the language or subject matter, or more rarely
on the performance, of specific passages. A scholium normally includes a *lemma*,
a word or phrase repeated from the text, and an interpretation of it. Scholia are
usually differentiated from a gloss, which provides occasional explanations of

individual words, and a commentary, which is a continuous exposition transmitted as a separate work. Most scholia are redactions of ancient, usually lost, commentaries, and it is sometimes possible to trace their sources. But we do not know the identity of the scholiasts, and we do not know the date at which the practice of compiling, selecting, and entering scholarly material in the margin of a text began. The word is first found in the first century B.C., but the writing of scholia seems unlikely to have been practised much before the codex or book replaced the scroll between the second and fourth centuries A.D. Moreover, there must have accumulated enough scholarship and commentary to make its availability in summary form a convenience. The fourth or fifth century is regarded as the date of this activity, although scholia in any quantity are not common until the ninth century. The extant scholia clearly suffered from mistaken copying and scholarly stupidity, but there is an occasional grain among the chaff. Once again, the interdependence of scholarly activity is attested by the fact that, while the scholia on the Greek dramatists derive ultimately from Didymus (with the probability of several intermediate stages), the scholia themselves provided some material for the *Suda*.

## CONCLUSION

It is not difficult to see from this survey of evidence that our picture of the Greek theatre and theatre production will necessarily be a shifting and changing one. The bulk of the evidence that is likely to exist is available to us, some of it relatively reliable, some of it difficult to interpret, some of it highly questionable. The relative weight of the various kinds and pieces of evidence cannot be universally agreed upon and consequently the interpretations of the total picture are bound to vary. Nevertheless, so long as each picture is viewed as a hypothesis, subject to modification as our point of view is challenged, extended, or altered, we have at least a framework within which to attempt to understand and recreate for ourselves a theatre whose very existence depends upon our minds and imaginations.

## REFERENCES

Arias, Paolo Enrico. *Il Teatro Greco Fuori di Atene*. Florence, 1934.

Aristotle. *Aristotle's Theory of Poetry and Fine Art*. Ed. and tr. S. H. Butcher. 4th ed. New York, 1951.

Arnott, Peter. *Greek Scenic Conventions in the Fifth Century B.C.* Oxford, 1962.

Anti, C. *Teatri Greci Arcaici*. Padua, 1947.

Athenaeus. *Deipnosophistae*. Tr. C. B. Gulick. 7 Vols. Cambridge, Mass., and London, 1927–41.

Austin, Colin, ed. *Comicorum Graecorum Fragmenta in Papyris Reperta*. Berlin and New York, 1973.

Bain, David. *Actors and Audience: A Study of Asides and Related Conventions in Greek Drama*. Oxford, 1977.

Beare, W. *The Roman Stage*. 3rd ed. London, 1964.

Bieber, Margarete. *Die Denkmäler zum Theaterwesen Altertum*. Berlin, 1920.

———. *The History of the Greek and Roman Theater*. Princeton, 1939; rev. 1961.

Blake, Warren E., ed. and tr. *Menander's Dyscolus*. American Philosophical Association, 1966.

Bulle, Heinrich. *Untersuchungen an griechischen Theatern*. Munich, 1928.

*Corpus Inscriptionum Graecarum*. 4 Vols. Berlin, 1828–77.

Dawe, R. G. *The Collation and Investigation of the Manuscripts of Aeschylus*. Cambridge, 1964.

Dearden, C. W. *The Stage of Aristophanes*. London, 1976.

Demianczuk, Jan, ed. *Supplementarum Comicum*. Cracow, 1912.

Diogenes Laertius. *Lives and Opinions of the Eminent Philosophers*. Tr. R. D. Hicks. 2 Vols. Cambridge, Mass., and London, 1925.

Dörpfeld, Wilhelm, and Emil Reisch. *Das Griechische Theater*. Athens, 1896.

Donaldson, John William. *The Theatre of the Greeks*. 7th ed. London, 1860.

Dover, K. J. *Aristophanic Comedy*. Berkeley and Los Angeles, 1972.

Edmonds, J. M. *The Fragments of Attic Comedy*. 3 Vols. Leiden, 1957–61.

Else, Gerald F. *Aristotle's Poetics: The Argument*. Cambridge, 1957.

Fiechter, Ernst. *Das Dionysos-Theater in Athen. Antikegriechische Theaterbauten*, vols. 5–7. Stuttgart and Cologne, 1935–36.

Flickinger, Roy C. *The Greek Theater and Its Drama*. 4th ed. Chicago, 1936 [1918].

———. *Plutarch as a Source of Information on the Greek Theater*. Chicago, 1904.

Gebhard, Elizabeth R. *The Theater at Isthmia*. Chicago, 1973.

Gellius, Aulus. *Noctes Atticae*. Tr. J. C. Rolfe. 3 Vols. Cambridge, Mass., and London, 1927–28.

Gerkan, Arnim von. *Das Theater von Priene*. Munich, 1921.

Ghiron-Bistagne, Paulette. *Recherches sur les acteurs dans la Grèce Antique*. Paris, 1976.

Haigh, Arthur E. *Attic Theatre*. Oxford, 1889.

Handley, E. W., ed. *The Dyskolos of Menander*. London, 1965.

Harsh, Philip Whaley. *A Handbook of Classical Drama*. Stanford, 1944.

Herodas. *The Mimes and Fragments*. Tr. Walter Headlam. Ed. A. D. Knox. Cambridge, 1922.

———. *Mimiambi*. Ed. I. C. Cunningham. Oxford, 1971.

Huddilston, J. H. *Greek Tragedy in the Light of the Vase-Paintings*. London, 1898.

*Inscriptiones Graecae*. Berlin, 1873–1915.

Jacoby, Felix. *Das Marmor Parium*. Berlin, 1904.

Kaibel, Georg, ed. *Comicorum Graecorum Fragmenta*. Berlin, 1889.

Kock, T., ed. *Comicorum Atticorum Fragmenta*. Berlin, 1880.

Lesky, Albin. *Greek Tragedy*. Tr. H. A. Frankfort. 2d ed. London and New York, 1967.

———. *A History of Greek Literature*. Tr. James Willis and Cornelis de Heer. New York, 1966.

Lloyd-Jones, Hugh, ed. *Dyskolos*. Oxford, 1960.

Müller, Albert. *Lehrbuch der Griechischen Bühnenalterthumer*. Freiburg, 1886.

Nauck, A., ed. *Aristophanis Byzantini Grammatici Alexandrini Fragmenta*. Halle, 1848.

———. *Tragicorum Graecorum Fragmenta*. 2d ed. Supp. B. Snell. Leipzig, 1964.

Pack, Roger A. *The Greek and Latin Literary Texts from Graeco-Roman Egypt*. Ann Arbor, 1965.

Page, D. L. *Actor Interpolations in Greek Tragedy*. Oxford, 1934.

———. *Greek Literary Papyri*. 2 Vols. Cambridge, Mass., and London, 1942.

Pausanias. *Descriptions of Greece*. Tr. W.H.S. Jones, H. A. Ormerod, and R. Wicherly. 5 Vols. Cambridge, Mass., and London, 1918.

Photius. *Bibliothèque*. Tr. (French) R. Henri. 4 Vols. Paris, 1959–65.

Pickard-Cambridge, A. W. *Dithyramb, Tragedy and Comedy*. Oxford, 1927.

———. *Dithyramb, Tragedy and Comedy*. 2nd ed. Rev. T.B.L. Webster. Oxford, 1962.

———. *The Dramatic Festivals of Athens*. Rev. John Gould and D. M. Lewis. Oxford, 1968 [1953].

———. *The Theatre of Dionysus in Athens*. Oxford, 1946.

Platnauer, M., ed. *Fifty Years (And Twelve) of Classical Scholarship*. Oxford, 1968.

Plutarch. *X. Oratorum Vitae*. In *Plutarchi Chaeronensis Varia Scripte* (Leipzig, 1929), V, 129–176.

——— *Lives*. Tr. B. Perrin. 11 Vols. Cambridge, Mass., and London, 1915–76.

———. *Moralia*. Tr. F. C. Babbitt, et al. 14 of 16 Vols. Cambridge, Mass., and London, 1915–76.

Pollux. *Onomasticon*. Ed. Immanuel Bekker. Berlin, 1846.

Reynolds, L. D., and N. G. Wilson. *Scribes and Scholars: A Guide to the Transmission of Greek and Latin Literature*. 2d ed. Oxford, 1974.

Sandbuch, F. H., ed. *Menandri Reliquiae Selectae*. Oxford, 1972.

Séchan, L. *Etudes sur la Tragédie grecque*. 2d ed. Paris, 1967.

Sifakis, G. M. *Parabasis and Animal Choruses: A Contribution to the History of Attic Comedy*. London, 1971.

———. *Studies in the Hellenistic Theatre*. London, 1966.

*Suda*. Ed. Ada Adler. 5 Vols. Leipzig, 1928–38.

Taplin, Oliver. *Greek Tragedy in Action*. London, 1978.

———. *The Stagecraft of Aeschylus: The Dramatic Use of Exits and Entrances in Greek Tragedy*. Oxford, 1977.

Trendall, A. D. *Catalogue of Phlyax Vases*. 2d ed. *Bulletin of the Institute of Classical Studies*, Supplement No. 19. London, 1967.

Trendall, A. D., and T.B.L. Webster. *Illustrations of Greek Drama*. London, 1971.

Turyn, A. *The Byzantine Manuscript Tradition of the Tragedies of Euripides*. Urbana, 1957.

Vitruvius. *The Ten Books of Architecture*. Tr. Morris Hicky Morgan. New York, 1960 [1914].

Webster, T.B.L. *Greek Theatre Production*. 2d ed. London, 1970.

———. *Hellenistic Poetry and Art*. New York, 1964.

———. *Monuments Illustrating New Comedy. Bulletin of the Institute of Classical Studies*, Supplement No. 11. London, 1961.

———. *Monuments Illustrating Old and Middle Comedy. Bulletin of the Institute of Classical Studies*, Supplement No. 9. London, 1960.

———. *Monuments Illustrating Tragedy and Satyr Play. Bulletin of the Institute of Classical Studies*, Supplement No. 14. London, 1962.

Wieseler, Friedrich. *Theatergebaüde und Denkmäler des Bühnenwesens bei den Griechen und Römern*. Göttingen, 1851.

Wilhelm, A. *Urkunden Dramatischer Aufführungen in Athen*. Amsterdam, 1965 [1906].

Wycherly, R. E. *The Stones of Athens*. Princeton, 1978.

# 3

# THE THEATRE OF ROME

Because of the close association in the minds of many scholars between the theatre and dramatic literature, the history of the Roman theatre has often been seen as a continuation of the history of the Greek theatre. The extant Roman drama consists of twenty comedies by Plautus (ca. 254–184 B.C.), and a further six by Terence (ca. ·195–159 B.C.), together with nine tragedies by Seneca (4 B.C.-A.D. 65). One further comedy, the fifth-century *Querolus*, at one time attributed to Plautus, and a tragedy, the anonymous *Octavia*, once thought to be by Seneca, complete the corpus. All of these plays are based on Greek models, particularly the plays of Menander and Euripides, as indeed was all Roman drama of the so-called Golden Age (ca. 240–140 B.C.). The remains of ancient theatres, some Greek, some Graeco-Roman, some Roman, together with Vitruvius' pairing of the Greek and Roman theatres architecturally in *De Re Architectura*, seemed also to proclaim the continuum of the ancient theatre. Too, we are the inheritors of a tradition that esteemed both cultures as "classical," and that tended to stress similarities and suppress differences. A classicist is by definition still a student of both civilizations.

There are, of course, good reasons for linking Rome with Greece. The Romans consciously adopted elements from Greek religion and literature; they thought of themselves as successors of the Greeks; and, as the Roman Empire grew, it encompassed an eastern half that was Greek in language as well as in culture. But to over-emphasize the connection, at least so far as the theatre is concerned, is to lay too heavy a stress on what was in fact a relatively short-lived phenomenon, and to distort the nature and significance of that phenomenon itself. The Romans borrowed from the Greeks, but they borrowed from others as well, and they grafted their borrowings on their own traditions. The character of the literary theatre of the Golden Age can best be determined by considering it in the context of the various theatrical activities that preceded, influenced, and succeeded it.

This at least has been the view of theatre historians since about 1950. In that year appeared W. Beare's *The Roman Stage* which, in its third edition (1964), remains the standard book on the pre-Augustan theatre. And in 1952 appeared George E. Duckworth's *The Nature of Roman Comedy*, the most thoroughgoing discussion of that topic. As we might expect, both Beare and Duckworth begin with the fact that a corpus of dramatic literature, however pitifully small, has come down to us. But both writers assume as well the importance of the theatrical dimension. Duckworth: "It is highly important for all readers of ancient comedy to visualize as fully as possible the presentation of the plays on the stage" (p. xiii). And Beare: "It is agreed by all that we should try to read them [the texts] as plays and to picture them as performed on the Roman stage" (p. 8). But of most importance is the willingness of Beare and Duckworth to discuss Roman theatre in terms of its Italian origins and as popular entertainment, a salutary corrective to the long-held assumption of the totally derivative character of Roman drama and to its analysis in exclusively literary terms. Consequently, we find our attention directed to such peripheral or sub-literary dramatic and theatrical forms as the Fescennine verses, the dramatic *satura*, the *fabula atellana*, the mime, and the pantomime.

Nevertheless, there is little doubt that, for students of the drama, the literary remains of the Roman drama are of the greatest importance. During the Renaissance, it was the Roman drama that provided the principal models for new playwrights, and Plautus and Terence lay back of the plays of Ariosto, Molière, and Jonson. The essentially literary nature of this influence is underscored by the fact that Seneca—very likely not performed in his own time—provided the Renaissance with models for tragedy, and again the influence was far-reaching, informing plays by Giraldi, Cinthio, Garnier, Kyd, and even Shakespeare. This literary drama of Rome, however, had a specific beginning and a pretty clearly identifiable ending, and it is convenient to divide the history of the Roman theatre into three periods:

1. Theatrical activity before Livius Andronicus, identified by Livy (VII.ii) as a writer of *argumento fabulam*, a play with a plot, which he first introduced to Rome in 264 B.C.

2. The literary theatre of Plautus and Terence, beginning with Livius Andronicus in 264 and ending with the performance of Varius Rufus' *Thyestes* (now lost) at the victory games following the battle of Actium in 31 B.C.

3. The theatrical activities of the Empire, from 27 B.C. to the fall of the Western Empire in A.D. 476.

Although the treatment of Roman theatrical history during this century has paralleled in some ways that accorded the history of the Greek theatre, a measure of the difference in their treatment can be estimated by the fact that the Roman theatre often has not received attention in its own right, but rather has been discussed in terms of the light it could throw on Greece. Evidence that was relevant to Republican or even Imperial Rome has been used to explain a theatre that had flourished several hundred years earlier. And even in those instances where the connection had some validity, the direction of the inquiry and the assumptions on which it was based have prevented a just estimation of the Roman contribution. The plays of Terence and Plautus, for example, can tell us a great deal about Greek New Comedy, which before the discovery of the *Dyskolos* papyrus in 1957 was available to us only in fragments; but the intimacy of the connection between the Roman playwrights and, say, Menander is a matter of assumption as much as of verifiable fact. Even so astute a scholar as Roy Flickinger unquestioningly accepted the evidence of Roman plays for the Greek drama:

Inasmuch as the comedies of Plautus and Terence are but translations and adaptations of Greek originals, and since Seneca's tragedies are constructed upon the Greek model, I have not hesitated to cite these Latin plays whenever they seemed to afford better illustrations than purely Greek productions. [*The Greek Theater and Its Drama*, p. xx].

This easy assumption has, of course, been challenged, and there has been considerable discussion among classical scholars concerning the originality of the Roman playwrights and their specific relationship to the Greek models they supposedly followed.

Terence in particular not only acknowledged his debt to Greek originals but boasted of it. On the other hand, it is abundantly clear that he deliberately departed from them. He was accused of doing so in his own time, of spoiling the Greek plays: The word used was *contaminatio*. And his replies to the accusation in the prologues to *Andria* and the *Heautontimorumenos* (*The Self Tormentor*)—in which he indicates that he used two plays by Menander to fashion the *Andria*, that there is precedent for the procedure, and that he intends to go on with the practice—have been turned against him and by extension against Plautus as well. It is sometimes held that not only is Latin comedy derivative and therefore unoriginal, but any original touches added by the Roman playwrights made their new plays inferior to the Greek originals. Any perceived flaws are attributed to the Romans, not to the Greeks. This is in essence the original charge of *contaminatio*, now allied to the hypothesis of Greek perfection. To reconstruct the New Comedy of Greece on this basis, that is, to delete the infelicities from Plautus and Terence and call the residue Greek, seems highly questionable. It is now believed that the Roman playwrights were far abler than scholars previously thought and that their comedies deserve attention in their own right. While the influence of Greek New Comedy was obviously crucial, Roman comedy is best considered in terms of its Italian and Roman environment, and Plautus and Terence must be allowed their own contributions to its form.

The evidence available for reconstructing Roman theatrical conditions during

the Golden Age is similar in many respects to that available for the study of
the Greek theatre. And the methods and assumptions of theatre historians vary
in much the same way as they did when the subject was the Greek theatre. We
have a limited number of play texts, the remains of numerous Roman theatres,
pictorial monuments, and a variety of written sources. Beare's description of
the standard method for writing the history of the Roman theatre has a familiar
ring: ". . . we depend on scattered references in ancient writers of various periods. . . . Evidence was supposed to be 'good' if found in such authors as
Cicero or Livy; but often it was cited from post-classical authors, separated by
centuries from events or customs which they claimed to describe" (p. 2). Beare
nevertheless normally prefers written over pictorial evidence, the value of which
he remains as sceptical of as was the equally cautious Pickard-Cambridge, and
for much the same reason: "Pictorial art has its own resources and its own limitations, which are not the resources and limitations of stage-production" (p.
6). Far less sceptical about the value of art as evidence is, of course, Margarete
Bieber, whose *History of the Greek and Roman Theatre* depends on such evidence, as does T.B.L. Webster's *Hellenistic Poetry and Art* (1964), the final
chapter of which deals with the Greek influence in Italy.

But pictorial or written, extra-textual evidence can ultimately only corrobo-
rate the evidence of the play texts themselves. The necessity, if not the infal-
libility, of relying on the texts has long been recognized. Mary Johnston explored details of staging implied in them in *Exits and Entrances in Roman Comedy*
(1933). And the bulk of Duckworth's commentary is based on the extant plays
themselves. Still, we must be cautious. "On few things do scholars differ more,"
writes Beare, "than on the deductions about stage practice which they draw
from the study of dramatic texts" (pp. 8–9).

When we turn to the traditions of the non-literary or "popular" theatre, we
find not only that a connection exists here as well between Greek and Roman
practice, but also that there is every likelihood that it was through this tradition
that theatrical activity persisted in an unbroken line through the Middle Ages
to the seventeenth century. So long as attention was centered on the literary
masterpieces of fifth-century Athens and the lesser but considerable drama of
Plautus and Terence, much of the available evidence for a popular theatre was
allowed to speak less on its own behalf than as an illuminating commentary on
the literary theatre. The Dorian mimes were considered mainly in terms of the
possible origins of Aristophanic comedy; the phlyakes vases in terms of the
Athenian stage; the *fabula atellana* in terms of its influence on Plautus and Terence; and the mime and pantomime as "degenerate" forms of the literary drama.
Studies of the Greek and Roman mime had, of course, been done by various
continental scholars, as had investigations of the later commedia dell'arte, but
the possibility of a coherent history of the popular entertainments and entertainers was not realized in English until the publication in 1931 of Allardyce
Nicoll's *Masks, Mimes, and Miracles*.

Unconfined by considerations of a particular culture, language, or national-

ity, or even by the self-imposed limits of an established discipline, Nicoll viewed
theatrical phenomena in a broader perspective than did the more specialized
classicists, even as he made use of their findings. He paid particular attention
to pictorial evidence as a basis for his discussion. He saw the commedia dell'arte
of the seventeenth century as the culmination of a continuous development in a
popular theatre that had begun in the pre-Periclean era, and his book is designed to investigate this development in broad outline. "There seems here,"
he writes,

ample material on which to base the theory that from the days of ancient Megara to
those of Republican Rome there existed a very clear and definite theatrical tradition of
a "popular" sort. The literary drama continues its own career, but here is essentially
the actors' theatre of antiquity—a thing passed down from generation to generation,
changing its name and its medium, but preserving fundamentally the outlines which had
been established in dim days before history began. . . . [p. 79]

Nicoll goes on to trace this tradition through the Middle Ages and into the Renaissance. The importance of *Masks, Mimes, and Miracles* does not lie in its
original scholarship, as the author himself admits. It lies rather in two shifts in
perspective in re-examining the known facts. First, Nicoll treats the popular theatre
as having a life and tradition of its own, independent of the literary drama.
Second, he traces the tradition beyond the normal confines of classical scholarship. Indeed, it might well be argued that these modest steps, undertaken by
others besides Nicoll of course, form the basis for the development of theatre
history as a discipline.

## DRAMATIC TEXTS

So far as dramatic texts are concerned, we are interested primarily in the
twenty-six comedies of Plautus and Terence performed during the late third and
early second centuries B.C. (Seneca's tragedies present a special problem.) Our
earliest manuscripts date from the fourth and fifth centuries A.D., and the early
history of their transmission is murky. The original scripts which were performed at the *ludi scaenici* seem to have been intended strictly for the actors,
and if we are to believe Terence's contention in the *Eunuchus* that he was not
aware that Menander's *Kolax* had been adapted for a Roman performance,
they seem not to have circulated as reading texts. There is evidence in the extant manuscripts as well that the texts may have sometimes been altered for
revivals. Evidence of such alterations appears especially at the beginning and
the end of a manuscript. The idea of reworking the texts in this manner (*retractatio*) ought not to be overly emphasized, however; there is no good reason
for assuming that the texts as we have them differ markedly from those originally performed. What is of more significance is that our manuscripts are derived from actors' and producers' copies: We are dealing with a theatrical rather

than a literary textual tradition. The prologues, too, which accompany all of Terence's plays and most of Plautus', belong to a period when the Roman theatre was active and before the texts had been preserved and edited as literature. They are, therefore, like the texts themselves, of particular value for the study of theatrical conditions of the second century B.C.

Plautus appears to have been an exceedingly popular playwright and there was a tendency for his name to be attached to a multitude of plays for which he was not responsible. Aulus Gellius, in *Noctes Atticae* (III.3), informs us that at one time 130 plays were ascribed to Plautus and that these were examined by Marcus Varro (116–27 B.C.), possibly the greatest scholar and antiquary of his time, who attested to the authenticity of twenty-one of them. These *fabulae Varronianae* are probably to be identified with the twenty plays and a fragment of a twenty-first that survive in the extant manuscripts. Of these, by far the most important is the Ambrosian Palimpsest, written in the fourth or fifth century A.D. and now preserved in the Biblioteca Ambrosiana in Milan (S.P.9/13–20). The manuscript originally contained the twenty-one Varronian plays, but many leaves have been lost and many pages can no longer be deciphered. What makes the reading of the manuscript particularly difficult is that in the seventh or eighth century the original text was erased and replaced with parts of the Books of Kings and Chronicles. The palimpsest was discovered in 1815, and the Plautine undertext was deciphered, transcribed, and published in 1889 by Wilhelm Studemond, who paid the price of his eyesight. Prior to this discovery, the only known Plautine manuscripts dated from the tenth, eleventh, and twelfth centuries. These "Palatine" manuscripts descended from a lost eighth-century original, which was in turn a copy of a fifth-century manuscript. Early printed editions of Plautus were based on these late copies; but modern study is based on the much earlier Ambrosian Palimpsest.

In general Terence seems to have received more scholarly attention in antiquity than Plautus, and to have suffered less at the hands of producers and actors. Probus of Beirut (A.D. 20–105) is reputed to have edited Terence's plays, and the grammarian Helenius Acron to have written a commentary on them in the late second century A.D. Of more importance is the fourth-century commentary by Aelius Donatus, an incomplete version of which is extant. Terence is also the only Republican poet annotated with *scholia*; and in one manuscript the plays are preceded by *didascaliae*, which inform us of the time and occasion of performance, together with the names of the producer and the composer of the music. We possess one manuscript from the fourth or fifth century, the Codex Bembinus, now housed in the Vatican Library (Lat.3226); more than twenty manuscripts dating from between the ninth and the twelfth centuries; and over four hundred more from the fourteenth and fifteenth centuries. In addition, in the late 1950s approximately 110 lines of the *Andria* were discovered in a papyrus fragment from the fourth or fifth century. The Codex Bembinus not only carries the authority of the earliest extant manuscript, but it also contains the important *didascaliae* and the most significant *scholia*. (The scholia have been edited by J. F. Mountford, 1934.)

The medieval manuscripts probably derive from a fourth- or fifth-century copy, the work of the otherwise unknown Calliopius. There are, however, two families within this "Calliopian recension," one of which is distinguished by being illustrated with miniatures, mostly in colour, evidently depicting scenes from the plays. Of the thirteen manuscripts so illustrated, the four most important are as follows: (1) Vaticanus 3868, (2) Parisinus 7899, (3) Ambrosianus H75 inf., and (4) Bodleianus, Auct. F. 2, 13. The most convenient collection and discussion of these illustrations is found in Leslie Webber Jones and C. R. Morey, *The Miniatures of the Manuscripts of Terence Prior to the Thirteenth Century* (1931). The value of these miniatures as evidence of staging depends upon whether they are copies of illustrations deriving from Terence's own time or whether they originated in Calliopius' fifth-century edition. Scholarly opinion tends to the latter view, and the pictures are consequently treated cautiously as evidence for stage production: "If the illustrations originated in the fifth century A.D., as the best evidence indicates, they can hardly depend on actual stage productions but they perhaps vaguely reflect earlier traditions about the costumes and masks of the *palliata*" (Duckworth, *The Nature of Roman Comedy*, p. 88).

Seneca, whose plays were written 200 years after Terence's death, presents a problem for the theatre historian. There is no denying his influence on the writing of tragedy in the Renaissance, but in this respect he belongs to the Renaissance, for there is considerable doubt whether his plays were ever performed in antiquity. The question is not easy to decide on the basis of the internal evidence of the plays. Beare (pp. 224–234, 351–354) maintains that the texts give evidence that Seneca did not envisage a stage production, that he ignored stage conventions and even stage possibilities in his disposition of character and stage action. Duckworth (p. 71) similarly maintains that there is no positive evidence that Seneca's plays were performed, but notes that they *do* conform to the necessary technical requirements and that they therefore were written "with an eye to presentation." External evidence can also be used to support either contention. Beare insists that it would have been unthinkable for the aristocratic Seneca to present plays to a public he despised. Margarete Bieber on the other hand cites one of Seneca's letters (*Epist.*, I.xi.7), in which he comments on the methods of actors, as proof of the playwright's interest in performance and points to a Pompeian wall-painting in support of her contention that killings did indeed take place on the stage and that Seneca's plays could well have been performed (*Greek and Roman Theatre*, pp. 230–234). The dilemma is this: If we assume that Seneca's tragedies were indeed performed, then the staging that they seem to require was somehow provided by Roman theatres in the first century A.D. If we assume that these theatres lacked the facilities for the performance demanded by the texts, we must conclude that the plays were not performed. In any event, the oldest complete manuscript that we have, the Codex Etruscus (Biblioteca Medicea-Laurenziana 37.13), dates from the eleventh century, although excerpts from the plays are to be found in the *Florilegium Thuancum* (Paris lat. 8071) from the ninth century. A number

of manuscripts survive from the thirteenth century, the two principal represen-
tatives of which are at Cambridge (Corpus Christi College 406) and Paris (Bibliothèque Nationale, lat. 8260).

In addition to the complete plays of Plautus and Terence and Seneca, we also
have a Virgilian *cento* or patchwork of a *Medea*, prepared by Hosidius Geta in
the second century A.D. (edited and translated by J. J. Mooney, 1919), and the
fifth-century *Querolus*, extant in a ninth-century manuscript (Vatican lat. 4929)
and in others at Leiden and Paris. As we found in Greece, there also exist a
number of fragments of the Roman drama, which help us to trace its history
from Livius Andronicus to the end of the Republic. Major collections include
those by M. Bonaria (1965), O. Ribbeck (3d eds., 1897, 1898). E. H. Warmington, *Remains of Old Latin* (1935–36) provides specimens in English translation.

## INSCRIPTIONS

Like the Greeks, the Romans used inscriptions to record a variety of events
both public and private, dealing with military life, legal relationships, trade,
municipal government, public works, religious cults, and official decrees. Such
inscriptions are usually classified as *tutuli*, those relating to individuals connected with the object bearing the inscription, and *acta*, public or private documents of an official or legal nature. Since most of the inscriptions date from
the early Empire, they are of little use so far as the period of literary drama is
concerned; but they can provide some information concerning later games and
performers. The collection and publication of Roman inscriptions began as early
as the ninth century, but it was not undertaken on a systematic basis until the
nineteenth century. The first volume of the *Corpus Inscriptionum Latinarum*
(*CIL*) appeared in 1863, and new supplements continue to be published as new
discoveries are made. Current discoveries are published in *Ephemeris Epi-
graphica*. A useful collection of the most significant inscriptions is provided in
H. Dessau's *Inscriptiones Latinae Selectae* (*ILS*), published between 1892 and
1916. There are no Roman inscriptions comparable in importance to the Athenian Victor-Lists and *Fasti*, but those relating to the *ludi* are of interest (*ILS*,
5051–5316), as are the epitaphs of various mimes. An epitaph of A.D. 169, for
instance, in honour of a mime-director named L. Acilius Pontinus Eutyches (*CIL*,
xiv, 2408), not only offers a eulogy on the dead man but goes on to list the
sixty members of his acting troupe. And the existence of his female counterparts is attested by the death records of actress-managers (*CIL*, vi, 10107, 10106).

## MONUMENTS

Our earlier estimation of the value of vase-paintings, reliefs, wall-paintings,
and statuary for the study of the Greek theatre remains valid for the study of
the Roman theatre as well. In point of fact, some of the monuments commonly

cited as illustrations of Greek staging are also noted by historians for the Roman theatre; although there is usually more reason for doing so in that their late dates strengthen the possibility of their relevance to the later theatre. In particular, we are revisiting familiar territory as we consider once again the phlyax vases from southern Italy and the wall-paintings from Pompeii and Herculaneum.

## Phlyax Vases

While there is no known direct connection between the phlyax farces and the development of drama at Rome, a literary form of the phlyax-play by Rhinthon was being performed in the third century B.C. in Tarentum, the possible birthplace of Rome's first playwright, Livius Andronicus. On such tenuous connections does history depend. T.B.L. Webster is eager to establish the identity of practice between Athens and southern Italy in order to argue a chain of influence from Athens to southern Italy to Rome. He therefore emphasizes the parallel between vase-paintings from Italy and Attic terracottas and comedy, and points to scenes from Euripides depicted before a stage background on fourth-century Apulian vases (*Monuments Illustrating Tragedy and Satyr Play*, fig. 73) as evidence that plays were at this time imported into Italy from Athens (*Hellenistic Poetry and Art*, pp. 253–254). Even if Webster is correct, the evidence of the vases indicates a method of staging quite at odds with anything we know of Athenian practice, and there is no indication that Roman staging during the Republic necessarily followed the phlyax method either, although facilities of such an obviously temporary nature were clearly not beyond Roman conception and execution.

## Pompeii and Herculaneum

The wall-paintings at Pompeii and Herculaneum are similarly inconclusive evidence for stage practice. Often only the content of the scene is depicted, and the stage setting merely conventionally indicated. Too, the paintings may simply have been copies of famous pictures and consequently of no immediate relevance to the living theatre at all. Even the otherwise enthusiastic Margarete Bieber hesitates to weigh such evidence very heavily. Several of the wall-paintings from Pompeii (Bieber, figs. 775–778) depict a *scaenae frons* before which actors and athletes are performing and are therefore of particular significance for the study of the Roman theatre building.

## Etruscan Tomb Paintings

The Roman historian Livy (VII.ii) testifies to the influence of Etruscan theatricals on the Roman theatre, and art remains from various Etruscan cities constitute some of the main evidence for estimating the nature and extent of that influence. Most of the tomb-paintings, which date from the sixth and fifth centuries B.C., have been discovered in the ancient cities of Tarquinii, Vulci, Volsinii, and Clusium. Tarquinii especially proved a rich repository: At least fifty paintings have been preserved. Most of these murals portray scenes of banqueting, dancing, and athletics. For the theatre historian their importance lies in the association of the typically Greek theatrical arts of flute-playing and dancing with the less obviously theatrical activities of wrestling and chariot-racing. Later paintings of fighting and dying gladiators (ca. 300 B.C.) are sometimes assumed to have taken their inspiration from earlier Etruscan paintings, but whether or not this is true or whether we can point to Etruria as the source of the cruder of Roman dramatic entertainments is a debatable question. Frederick Poulsen's *Etruscan Tomb Paintings* (1922) is a useful introduction to the subject.

## Funeral Monuments

The performance of tragedy in the first century B.C. can be illustrated from several monuments (Bieber, figs. 588–591). A terracotta relief of P. Numitorius Hilarus seems to represent a scene from a tragedy, perhaps Accius' *Astyanax*, and is usually taken as a depiction of a performance at Numitorius' funeral. A wall-painting discovered in a columbarium in the Villa Dorai Pamphili similarly contains a tragic scene, as do a marble tablet painting and a tomb-painting from Ostra. All of these pictures, which have been dated about mid-first century B.C., suggest that Roman tragedy adopted Greek costume and masks, but greatly exaggerated the *onkos*, the *cothurnus*, and the expression of the mask. The first two examples also indicate that tragedies were performed at funerals.

Funeral plays are also attested by wall-paintings from a grave in the necropolis of Cyrene dating from the second century A.D. (Bieber, fig. 787) and by a marble relief depicting a performance at the funeral of Flavius Valerianus (Bieber, fig. 788), probably from the third century A.D. Both monuments represent various kinds of performers—actors, singers, musicians—but the arrangement of the figures suggests a concert or a recital rather than a mimetic performance; and they can therefore be taken as evidence that by the second and third centuries A.D. only detached scenes were recited by actors, to the accompaniment of music and complemented by solo singers and chorus. It is further surmised that these recitals took place usually at private festivals and public funerals. Certainly the way that the painter in the Cyrenean painting has placed the three actors on pedestals would indicate that recital was the norm for such a performance. This may have been the mode of performance envisaged by Seneca when he wrote his tragedies.

## Statuettes and Masks

An ivory statuette from the second century A.D. features (*a*) a mask with a pronounced *onkos* or cone-shaped extension of the mask above the forehead, (*b*) a full-length, decorated costume, and (*c*) what appear to be particularly exaggerated *cothurnoi*, elevated boots designed to increase an actor's stature. (See Pickard-Cambridge, *Dramatic Festivals*, fig. 63.) Although believed at one time to represent a tragic actor from fifth-century Athens, the statuette clearly represents a Roman stage-figure. The exaggerated expression of the tragic mask is repeated in a great many Roman marble masks found in various parts of the Empire and frequently found illustrated in books on the theatre (for example, Bieber, figs. 536–541). It is tempting to link such expressions with the appearance of the actors who are reputed by Lucian ("The Dance") and Philostratus (*Life of Apollonius* V.9) to have so frightened the audience in Hispalis in Spain that it fled from the theatre. Numerous terracotta masks of the Atellan farce, which by the time of the Empire had replaced comedy, have also been found, as well as some figurines of mimes. But whether of marble or terracotta, we must remember that these masks are renderings in a different medium for a different purpose of masks originally made from linen, cork, or wood, and designed to fit over an actor's head.

When all is said and done, pictorial monuments purporting to illustrate the Roman theatre can provide testimony of a general and secondary nature only. Their relationship to actual performance is questionable, and with the exception of the miniatures on the manuscripts of Terence, there is no direct connection between the monuments and the text of any extant play. Nevertheless, it would be foolish to ignore what they *can* tell us. However informed by non-theatrical traditions and conventions, they do represent what someone thought looked like a stage presentation or a theatrical mask and were presumably so understood by contemporary viewers. Such evidence can at least partially inform us of the fundamental iconography of the theatre if not of its specific detail.

## ARCHAEOLOGICAL REMAINS OF THEATRES

The last recorded performance of a new Roman play was in 31 B.C. The earliest known permanent Roman theatre anywhere is the odeon at Pompeii, which dates from 75 B.C. The earliest theatre at Rome, the theatre of Pompey, was erected in 55 B.C. And the best known, that of Marcellus, was not built until 11 B.C. While there is every likelihood that tragedy and comedy continued to be performed in these theatres, we have no record of any extant play being performed at any of them, and it seems probable from the available evidence that the literary drama was gradually replaced by the more farcical and extemporaneous mime, and especially by pantomine, a variant in which a more serious theme was presented in dumb-show by a masked actor accompanied by a chorus and musicians. For this reason, there is no single Roman theatre that approaches in importance or significance the theatre of Dionysus at Athens. Nevertheless, some hundreds of Roman theatres of various types remain, scattered throughout Europe, North Africa, and the Near East, in various states of preservation, and their excavation and study have added to our picture of the Roman theatre and its role in Roman culture.

Even a brief consideration of the variety of structures devoted to theatrical performance of one kind or another is helpful in determining both the Roman attitude towards the theatre and the variety of influences that went into defining that attitude. Broadly speaking, Roman theatres can be classified as (1) odeons, small theatres intended for musical performances; (2) amphitheatres; (3) Roman theatres proper, designed and built along the lines described by Vitruvius; (4) classical Greek or Hellenistic theatres rebuilt by the Romans according to their own lights and for their own purposes; and (5) Graeco-Roman theatres, built on a hillside and characterized by the extended semi-circular auditorium of the late Greek theatre, but also featuring the elaborate *frons scaenae* of the Roman theatre. (Bieber provides an excellent summary of the archaeological evidence in Chapters 13 and 14.)

So far as odeons are concerned, two of these small theatres, which could seat approximately 1,000 spectators, are of special interest. The one at Pompeii was erected about 75 B.C. and is consequently the oldest purely Roman theatre that has been preserved. The auditorium and the orchestra are semi-circular; there are vaulted entrances, a curtain slot, and a protective parapet separating the lower seating area reserved for dignitaries from the rest of the audience; and the entire structure was intended to be covered with a roof. All of these features typify the Roman theatre. The second odeon that merits some attention is that of Herodes Atticus, erected in A.D. 16l at the southwest corner of the Acropolis. Again we find the semi-circular orchestra, a high spacious stage, and an elaborate *frons scaenae*. As odeons go, this one is large, seating some 5,000 people. It is still in use.

The oldest extant example of an amphitheatre, designed to accommodate chariot-racing, gladiatorial combats, and animal baitings as well as various kinds of spectacular entertainment of a less bloody nature, is also to be found at Pompeii. Erected at the same time as the odeon, this amphitheatre held a modest 12,000 spectators. Others were far larger. The most famous—or infamous—of the amphitheatres, the Colosseum at Rome, seated 50,000, had a circumference of nearly a kilometer, and was more than forty meters high. Built about A.D. 75, the Colosseum derives its name from a colossal sculpture of Nero, erected by the Emperor at one side of the structure. The statue has vanished, but the name—place of the Colossus—remains, as does an impressive part of the outer structure itself. The north side of the outer wall is standing, together with much of the inner wall and the skeleton structure between the inner wall and the arena. The interior has been gutted. Nine fragments of a plan of Rome in marble from the reign of the Emperor Alexander Severus (A.D. 222–235) represent parts of the amphitheatre. (See Henri Jordan, *Forma Urbis Romae*, 1874.)

Throughout the ancient Greek world were a variety of theatres, built into hillsides, which the Romans adopted for their own purposes. The large theatre at Pompeii is an example. Originally erected after the Greek manner between 200 and 150 B.C., it was remodelled during the reign of Augustus. The original two *paraskenia* were removed and the open *paradoi* vaulted; a deep, low stage backed by an elaborately decorated *frons scaenae* was built; the orchestra became semi-circular. Orchestra, stage, and auditorium became an architectural unity.

A different effect resulted from the Romanization of the Hellenistic theatres of Asia Minor. The construction of the high back wall in these theatres prevented the cutting of deep niches for *reqia* or statues of the emperors which are found in the adaptations of southern Italy; consequently, the decoration of the *frons scaenae* is very shallow. Perhaps of more importance, the stage remained at the elevated Hellenistic level. An example is the theatre at Ephesus in Turkey, which was constantly being remodelled throughout the first century A.D.

Even the theatre of Dionysus was not spared Roman improvement. A new stage was constructed about A.D. 60, evidently featuring a large marble *frons scaenae*, and the orchestra was also paved with marble. Later the stage was extended into the orchestra so far that it closed off the *paradoi*. The marble parapet that walled off the auditorium from the orchestra could have served as protection against animals and as a means of transforming the orchestra to allow for water spectacles.

The rebuilt theatres discussed above are sometimes referred to as "Graeco-Roman" theatres, but it is probably preferable to reserve the designation for those theatres, confined principally to southeastern Asia Minor, where the traditional hillside auditorium arranged in an extended semi-circle is joined with the Roman *frons scaenae*. The front wall of the podium is broken by small doors, evidently designed to allow the entry of animals into the orchestra. Such theatres were intended to accommodate the bloodier entertainments usually associated with amphitheatres.

It might be argued that the amphitheatre is a more purely Roman invention than the theatres modelled on the theatres of Pompey and Marcellus, but Rome has traditionally been credited with developing a form of theatre architecture that, while reminiscent of the Greek, reflected a new attitude towards dramatic entertainment and a new self-contained architectural unit. These new theatres are found mainly in Europe, Italy, and North Africa. The best preserved—and therefore the most commonly illustrated—are at Orange in France and at Aspendos in Turkey. Both have high and impressive façades, and both have provision for a canopy and stage roof. Above all, both exhibit a complete fusion of auditorium and stage house, and both adhere remarkably closely to Vitruvius' specifications—an attribute that has endeared them all the more to scholars eager to underscore the reliability of the architect. (We might recall that it was the combination of Aspendos and Vitruvius that so misled Donaldson in his study of the Greek theatre.)

In the final analysis, however, theatre historians are most interested in the theatres erected in the city of Rome itself in the first century B.C. Unfortunately, neither the theatre of Pompey (55 B.C.), the theatre of Balbus (13 B.C.), nor the theatre of Marcellus (11 B.C.) has very successfully weathered the ravages of time and man. Indeed, there are no physical remains at all of the theatre of Balbus. Fragments of the Marble Plan, however, indicate the locations of all three theatres, and in the case of the theatre of Pompey provide a plan of the theatre. The archaeological remains of Pompey's theatre are difficult to analyze. Although its general plan is discernible in the pattern of buildings built over its ruins, and traces of arches and vaults can be seen in the basements of the area, very little of the original structure is visible, and it is difficult to connect the parts that remain in a coherent fashion. We are a bit more fortunate so far as the theatre of Marcellus is concerned. About one-third of the outer curvilinear wall is still standing.

The picture of the Roman theatre that archaeology presents to us is characterized by a variety of structure, by the ability of the Romans to adapt many kinds of theatres for their own purposes, and by an aesthetic based in architectural unity and decorative detail. And in spite of the fact that the literary drama of the Republic was not performed in such theatres, it can be and has been assumed that the temporary theatres erected for the production of plays by Plautus and Terence must have included some of the general features typical of the permanent theatres. Said Bieber in 1939: "We may conclude . . . that this practical, unified form [of the theatre of Pompey] was tried out at Rome in the many wooden theatres which were continually being torn down, before the best form was finally executed in stone" (p. 345). The accuracy of this assumption is, of course, subject to the same scepticism accorded the similar assumption concerning the Greek theatre, and Bieber omits the remark in the 1961 revision of *The History of the Greek and Roman Theater*.

But particular details of the architecture of the theatre of Pompey—and of other later theatres as well—pose a question concerning the nature and purpose of these permanent structures. It has long been a tenet of theatre historians that the Roman theatre became increasingly a secular and commercial enterprise. Although the theatre was almost always associated with official religious festivals, or *ludi*, a commonly held belief has it that the practical Romans were not an especially religious people and that there was more form than substance in the association of theatre and religion. This attitude has been crucial in the interpretation of a seeming peculiarity of the theatre that Pompey built: It included a temple and four smaller shrines within its structure. According to various ancient authorities—Gellius, Pliny, Suetonius, and Tertullian—Pompey constructed a temple of Venus at the top of the central part of the auditorium or *cavea*, so the rows of seats doubled as curved steps before the temple, and he dedicated the entire structure as a shrine rather than as a theatre. The Christian Tertullian in his *De Spectaculis* (10.5) began the traditional scepticism concerning Pompey's motives by declaring that the dedication of the edifice as a shrine was a ruse on the builder's part to avoid censure for having built a permanent theatre. It has also been commonly held that Pompey's theatre was unique, an architectural experiment which was not repeated, and that even the pretense of religious significance disappeared from the physical theatre after 55 B.C. But the work of archaeologists over the past seventy-five years has provided information that can be used to challenge the generalization that theatres and shrines were completely separated during the Empire. John Arthur Hanson in *Roman Theater-Temples* (1959) cites over twenty examples of such structures that, he maintains, confirm that the theatre of Pompey was not *sui generis* but part of a consistent architectural tradition:

What is common to all is a location on the central axis of the theatre overlooking the orchestra with the front facing the stage building, with provision for a statue of the divinity. Most have a colonnaded façade and many are approachable by special steps or entrances through the back wall of the *cavea*. [p. 77]

The significance of this view is three-fold. First, since this particular structure has no precedent in Greek practice, it further serves to differentiate the Roman theatre from the Greek. Second, it provides a more cogent reason for Christian antipathy to the Roman theatre than simply a distrust of mimetic entertainment, however frivolous or barbaric; it was pagan religion and not just the theatre that drew the ire of the Church Fathers. And finally, although it seems clear that the theatre was the dominant element of the combination, we must ask ourselves if an element of religious belief did not continue to inform the theatrical experience of audiences, even in the declining years of the Roman Empire.

## WRITTEN SOURCES

Most of the reservations concerning written sources for the Greek theatre are equally applicable to the written sources for the Roman theatre. The writers often lived long after the events they describe; they usually refer to theatrical affairs only incidentally; and their purposes, perspectives, and prejudices must be taken into account when evaluating their work. Some of the names are familiar from our considerations of the Greek theatre: Plutarch, Vitruvius, and Pollux among the ''major'' sources; Gellius, Athenaeus, Diogenes Laertius, and Photius among the compendiasts. But Roman literature, history, and scholarship provide a large amount of fresh material to be sorted and evaluated; and a new wrinkle is added in the determinedly Christian point of view taken by later writers.

### Horace

There are no literary remains dealing with or mentioning the theatre prior to the first century B.C., and we therefore have no eye-witness accounts of any theatrical production during the Golden Age of Roman drama. The last years of the Republic, however, saw incidental references to the theatre by the didactic poet Lucretius (94–55 B.C.), by the poet and critic Horace (65–8 B.C.), and, most importantly, by the prolific man-about-letters Cicero (106–43 B.C.). In *The Nature of the Universe*, Lucretius on two occasions mentions awnings over the theatre. Horace's *Ars Poetica* is devoted mainly to problems of literary composition and advice to the prospective writer. He stresses *decorum,* off-stage violence, traditional and consistent characterization, a five-act structure, and the necessity of mingling profit and pleasure. Like Aristotle, Horace was to exercise a considerable influence in the Renaissance, but his work tells us very little about the contemporary or earlier theatre. He offers a very brief "history" of drama, in which he credits Thespis with inventing tragedy and having it performed on wagons by men who smeared their faces with wine-lees, and notes that Aeschylus added the mask, the robe, the plank stage, and the buskin. Old Comedy, he writes, declined when its vice and violence were restrained by law. He also comments that native Roman poets tried all styles of drama, including Roman drama with Roman subjects. What is interesting, of course, is not the authenticity of Horace's history, but the fact that it probably represents an accepted tradition. So far as the origins of specifically Roman drama are concerned, Horace in *Epistles* (II.1.139–163) describes the development of the Fescennine verses from rustic festivals, their decline when it became necessary to restrain their abusive nature by law, and their replacement by the Greek dramatic form after the Punic wars. The similar fates of Old Comedy and the Fescennine verses suggest a formulaic rather than a historical account. Of some interest too in this same epistle is what Horace evidently intended as a description of a typical theatrical performance (11.177–213), in which spectacle has replaced drama.

### Cicero

But our fullest picture of the Roman theatrical world is provided by Cicero, who was clearly familiar with both Greek and Latin dramatic texts and with the contemporary world of theatre and performance. F. Warren Wright, in *Cicero and the Theater* (1931), collected all of Cicero's references to theatre and drama and found that, besides naming many plays and quoting from many of them, Cicero mentions twenty-one playwrights by name, together with over twenty actors and actresses. "No other Roman Writer," concludes Wright, "has given us such a picture of the theatre, and the vividness of the picture is by no means due solely to the volume of Cicero's extant works. It is in part due to his own taste" (p. 79). Of particular interest is Cicero's discussion of oratory and its relationship to acting in *De Oratorio*. This work, together with the *Institutio Oratoria* by the rhetorician Quintilian (ca. A.D. 38–100), has proved useful in arriving at an estimate of Roman acting. Also, Cicero is the main source for our knowledge of Roscius, whose name has become synonymous with "actor." In fact, Cicero once argued on behalf of the actor in court, and his oration *Pro Q. Roscio Comoedo Oratio* has been duly preserved. A passage in the speech (IV.20) provides a brief comparison between the plaintiff, one Gaius Fannius Chaerea, and the pimp Ballio, a character in Plautus' *Pseudolus,* whom Roscius is held to have impersonated on the stage. This is the only extant role known to have been acted by Roscius. Incidental theatrical references and bare factual detail are not often in themselves very helpful, but taken together, with various other bits and pieces of information, they can provide the basis for cautious inference and speculation. For instance, using Cicero, the text of *Pseudolus*, and various literary, historical, and archaeological information, Charles Garton has attempted to determine the nature of Roscius' performance (*Personal Aspects of the Roman Theatre*, pp. 169–188).

## Pliny the Elder

A later work, *Natural History* by Pliny the Elder (A.D. 23–79) covering 20,000 matters deemed by its author worthy of preserving, is to a large extent a formless and inaccurate hodge-podge of information gleaned from a couple of thousand other books. But Pliny is the only writer to have left us descriptions of the temporary theatres that the Romans were in the habit of erecting and tearing down before Pompey built his theatre in 55 B.C. Pliny refers to two such structures: one built by the aedile M. Aemilius Scaurus in 58 B.C. and one erected by C. Curio in 50 B.C. (XXXVI.24). The first is described as having three stories—of marble, glass, and gilded wood—and accommodating 80,000 spectators. The second is described as consisting of two wooden theatres, back to back, that could be swiveled about on pivots to face one another and thereby form an amphitheatre. Most scholars have remained sceptical about Pliny's testimony.

## Written Evidence concerning Mime and Pantomime

By the first century of the Christian era, mime and pantomime had replaced the literary drama. There are unflattering references to mime actors and actresses and their performances in Juvenal's *Satires* (A.D. 110–130) and in Martial's epigrams (ca. A.D. 64–98). But neither writer tells us much about the ways in which they acted. The novelist Apuleius (fl. ca. A.D. 150) in *The Metamorphoses*, or *The Golden Ass* (X.29–34), includes a description of a pantomime on the subject of the Judgment of Paris, ostensibly performed in the amphitheatre at Corinth. Although he was writing fiction, Apuleius had no reason to distort the essential nature of a kind of performance with which he was doubtless familiar.

A more analytical if enthusiastic account of pantomime is provided by Lucian of Samosata (fl. ca. A.D. 170). In the dialogue commonly translated as "The Dance," Lucian offers a conventional defense of the art, pointing to the gods, heroes, and nations that have practised it, and to the poets and philosophers who have sanctioned it. Much of this is most likely not to be taken entirely seriously, but the description of the pantomime itself and its comparison with other theatrical forms, especially tragedy, provides a useful picture of second-century theatre.

The unsavory nature of the acting profession implied in Procopius' *Historia Arcana*, or *Secret History* (ca. A.D. 550), is secondary to the author's vicious attack on the Emperor Justinian and the Empress Theodora, a one-time actress. Moreover, Procopius' palpable exaggeration and obvious scandal-mongering make the *Secret History* less a work of scholarship than a personal diatribe. That the mime and its performers may have deserved a more charitable estimation is borne out by an extant oration by Procopius' pupil, Choricius of Gaza. In his *Apologia Mimorum*—defense of mimes—Choricius notes that the performers deserve the fame and the riches they acquire through their art; that most of them lead perfectly respectable lives; that not all mimes lack dignity; and that the depiction of adultery and foolishness in some performances ought not to be taken out of context, but recognized as an accurate reflection of human behaviour. Choricius' oration is an important document, and his reasonable and logical exposition stands in sharp contrast to the mindless condemnations of the mime and its performers penned by many of his contemporaries.

### Historians

A good deal of information concerning the theatre, both specific and incidental, can also be gleaned from ancient historians, although the modern reader might well be reminded that in the ancient view the writing of history did not necessarily include an automatic genuflection before fact. Moreover, certain morally based assumptions underlie much of the best Roman history. The most important was the assumption of the continuing decline of Roman virtue: Specifically, the Empire was looked upon as a decadent descendant of the republic. Even so loyal an Augustan as Livy (59 B.C.–A.D 17) shared the assumption. When in Book VII of his *History* he related the origins of Roman drama, he justified doing so in order "that it might be seen how sober were the beginnings of an art that has nowadays reached a point where opulent kingdoms could hardly support its mad extravagance" (ii.13). Tacitus (ca. A.D. 55–115) developed the assumption into a theme: not only does the Republic serve in his work as a standard against which to measure the corrupt and stagnant Empire, but in the *Germania* (A.D. 98) he draws a further contrast between the immorality and corruption of the hyper-civilized Empire and the unsophisticated vigor of the Germanic tribes which the less perceptive among his contemporaries considered barbaric. With the advent of Christianity, the idea was broadened to include the distinction between Christian (good) and pagan (bad). Under these circumstances, any association of theatre with Rome, with the Empire, or with paganism was bound to bring it into disrepute. And since the only theatre that historians and commentators knew was indeed Roman, imperial, and pagan, we ought not to wonder at their condemnation of it. When such historians are cited as evidence for theatre history, therefore, we must be careful to consider their testimony in the light of their biases.

It is to historians that we must look when attempting to determine the early history of the theatre in Rome; but of course they were writing long after the fact, they seldom divulge their sources, and there is every likelihood that speculation and theory supplemented fact and tradition. Livy is especially valuable, describing in his seventh book (ii.4–13) how the flute music and dance imported from Etruria in 364 B.C. were imitated and assimilated by young Romans who added jests and rude verses; and how the native professional actors became known as *histriones* after the Etruscan word for "player," and how they performed a kind of musical medley "to melodies which were now rather written out to go with the flute, and with appropriate gesticulation." The historian then notes that some years later Livius Andronicus abandoned this *satura* and began to compose plays with plots, which he himself acted, until the loss of his voice necessitated his acting the role through gesture while a boy sang the lyrics to the accompaniment of a flute. From this time on, writes Livy, actors spoke only dialogue. But once again, the young men revived an entertainment consisting of improvised jests, which became known as *exodia*, and, usually combined with Atellan farces, were performed as after-plays. The amateur—and therefore respectable—nature of these performances is reflected in Livy's comment that the performers were allowed to serve in the army, a privilege denied professional actors. Although we must remember that Livy had no direct knowledge of the process he was describing, he does tend to reproduce tradition relatively faithfully, without undue rationalization, and his account has therefore at least the validity of received opinion.

Livy's slightly younger contemporary, the historian Valerius Maximus (fl. A.D. 25), in general confirms Livy's account of the origins of the Roman theatre in his *Facta et Dicta Memorabilia* (II.iv.4). He deviates only in crediting the Roman youth with the earliest songs and dances, to which the Etruscan import was added. It is not clear, however, whether Valerius and Livy had access to the same information, or whether Valerius was simply paraphrasing Livy. Tacitus too refers to Etruscan origins and to the disreputable nature of professional acting. In the *Annals* (XIV.21), he records the arguments of those who supported the institution in A.D. 60 of a five-yearly stage competition on the Greek model. It had been urged that such public entertainment had long been a Roman custom, that various kinds of performance had been imported from Etruria and Asia, that in the 200 years since Lucius Mummius had first given such a show at his triumph (146 B.C.) no upper-class Roman had ever demeaned himself by professional acting, and that a permanent theatre was more economical than a series of temporary ones.

Several other passages in Livy refer to matters theatrical (XXXIV.54; XLI.27; XL.51), but prompting the most discussion has been the one in which he cites a Senatorial decree of 174 B.C. that seats should not be allowed at theatrical productions (*Epitome* XLVIII). Valerius Maximus attests to the same (II.iv.2). Moreover, a hundred years later Tacitus has opponents of the theatre claim that in the early days not only were theatres temporary structures, but that no seats were provided for the spectators. Partially on the basis of Tacitus' report, some modern scholars have interpreted Livy's testimony as evidence that there were no seats in Roman theatres before Mummius' triumph in 146 B.C. It seems more likely, however, that the decree by the Senate was in effect from 174 to 146 at most, and that seating of some sort was provided for the audiences of Plautus and Terence.

Such then is the evidence from historians concerning the early Roman theatre. What is perhaps most striking is that we learn precious little about the theatre contemporaneous with the historians. It is true that Livy and Tacitus were concerned principally with affairs of state and normally touched on the theatre only incidentally. And the same might be said of their successors, citations from whose writings we find sprinkled throughout studies of the Roman theatre. The interest of most historians, certainly from the time of Velleius Paterculus (ca. 19 B.C.–ca. A.D. 32), was chiefly in biography, and by the time of Suetonius (ca. A.D. 69–ca. 140) chiefly in the biographies of emperors. And as the activities of the emperors became more bizarre and outrageous, so did the descriptions of their lives, culminating in the later parts of the so-called *Augustan History*, probably written at the end of the fourth century.

Suetonius' *Lives of the Caesars* presents a wealth of varied information concerning the first twelve Caesars, Julius to Domitian, although the author is not averse to including a spicing of gossip. Of considerably more interest to theatre historians is Suetonius' *De viris illustribus* (A.D. 106–113), which includes biographies of Horace and Terence. (See *Suetonius*, tr. J. C. Rolfe). The *Life of Terence* has come down to us prefixed to Donatus' commentary on the playwright (fourth century A.D.), which itself survives only in a sixth-century compilation of copies found in two Terence manuscripts. Although it constitutes our main source of information concerning Terence, the *Life* is filled with contradictions, and it is likely that Suetonius fleshed out any gaps in his narrative with stock themes and anecdotes. He also derived biographical material from Terence's own writings.

The *Scriptores Historiae Augustae*, or *Augustan History*, is still very often cited under the names—most likely fictitious—of its supposed authors: Aelius Spartianus, Julius Capitolinus, Aelius Lampridius, Vulcatius Gallicanus, Trebellius Pollio, and Flavius Vopiscus. In truth, these biographies of the emperors from Hadrian to Diocletian (A.D. 117–284) are now considered to be the work of one man who, for whatever reason, chose to hide behind his list of bogus historians. The first half of the *Augustan History*, from Hadrian to Heliogabalus, seems to have some basis in fact; but the later lives are principally fiction. The kind of information we can glean from these sources is illustrated by the revelation that in stage performances of acts of adultery Heliogabalus ordered that what was usually simulated should actually be done. Whether such reports reflect more on the theatre or the emperor, they do give some indication of the atmosphere surrounding public performances.

### Scholarship

Roman scholarship really began at the end of the second century B.C. with the work of L. Aelius Stilo (fl. 100 B.C.), the teacher of both Cicero and the greatest of Roman scholars, Marcus Terentius Varro (116–27 B.C.), himself a pupil of Aristarchus at Alexandria. Of Stilo's work, which included the establishment of a canon of twenty-five plays of Plautus and an edition of the playwright Ennius, only fragments remain. Varro's continued interest in Plautus is reflected in the *fabulae Varronianae*, which remained the basis of the Plautine canon. Information derived from his *Antiquitates Rerum Humanarum et Divinarum* has been preserved only in the compilations and citations of later authors—Gellius' *Noctes Atticae*, Macrobius' *Saturnalia* (ca. A.D. 400), and St. Augustine's *The City of God* (A.D. 413–26). Another scholarly source is Dionysius of Halicarnassus (fl. 30–8 B.C.), whose *Roman Antiquities* survives mainly in the form of tenth-century excerpts. The value of the work lies in its preservation of accounts by previous historians, but it also includes a long description of a *pompa*, or sacred procession that normally preceded a theatrical presentation (VII.72). This description may include details from Dionysius' own experience as well as from his acknowledged source, one Fabius Pictor. One further writer from this early period also provides a valuable source for the literary history of the early Empire: that is, Marcus Annaeus Seneca (ca. 55 B.C.-ca. A.D. 40), the father of the dramatist, whose surviving books of *Controversiae* and *Suasoriae* reflect a long and active intellectual life.

The most erudite of the Augustan scholars, Verrius Flaccus, had his lost *De Significatu Verborum*, the first Latin lexicon, epitomized in the late second century by Sextus Pompeius Festus, who in turn was epitomized by Paul the Deacon in the late eighth century. And the various compendia of Gellius, Athenaeus, and Diogenes Laertius (discussed in Chapter 2) appeared in the second and third centuries A.D. But it was the fourth century which witnessed a significant revival of Roman scholarship. In the early part of the century appeared Nonius Marcellus' *De Compendiosa Doctrina*, a dictionary that incorporates excerpts from a wide range of authors, including Varro and Ennius. The most famous and influential grammarian of the century, Aelius Donatus, produced his important commentary on Terence (and incidentally preserved for us Suetonius' *Life*) which, as we have noted, survives in a sixth-century compilation. Donatus also wrote treatises on comedy and tragedy. Later in the fourth century Servius compiled his grammar, based on Donatus and intended for school use. Finally appeared the *Ars Grammatica* of Diomedes, who relied on earlier grammarians in his discussion of Republican authors. He is possibly most famous for his dubious remark that Roscius was the first Roman actor to wear a mask, and that he did so to conceal a squint. A far earlier date for the introduction of the mask is attested by Cicero, Festus, and Donatus. The following century saw Macrobius' *Saturnalia* and Martianus Capella's *De Nuptis Philologiae et Mercurii*, a compilation of half-digested learning borrowed from many places—both of which provide material for the historian's mill, although much of it proves to be chaff.

### Christian Writers

There is one group of writers, whose comments on the Roman theatre have drawn a great deal of attention, but who because of their very specific orientation must be interpreted with some care. These are writers deliberately espousing the viewpoint of Christianity, which by the end of the fourth century had been made the official religion of the Roman Empire. Christian writers, besides harboring the basically conservative viewpoint of many Roman writers who decried the decline of Roman virtue, had their own reasons for disliking theatrical performances. In the first place, the theatre was associated with pagan festivals (a point stressed by Hanson in *Roman Theater Temples*); and in the second place, mimes ridiculed Christian rites (although in fairness we should note that in this respect Christianity was not an exclusive target). Charges of licentiousness and immorality were common among Christians and non-Christians alike. The idea that Christian antipathy to the theatre was based on a doctrinal aversion to mimetic performance is no longer taken seriously. In many ways the Christian writers were merely echoing and extending the point of view expressed or implied in Livy and Tacitus and Suetonius. Perhaps a single example will serve to illustrate the point. In *De Gubernatione Dei*, Salvianus (ca. 400–ca. 480) echoes Tacitus in contrasting the vice and decadence of Roman civilization with the virtue and vigor of the barbarians; and then he goes on to point to the latter's victory as God's judgment on Rome and as an incentive to Christians to purify their lives and strengthen their faith. And, of course, the Church itself became the subject of a continuing history, which supplements that of the secular historians. Eusebius of Caesarea (260–340) covers the period from the foundations of Christianity to 324. His work was continued by Gelasius (d. 395) and by Theodoret (ca. 393–ca. 466), who brought the narrative down to 428.

The Christian writings concerning theatrical performance most often cited are those of Tertullian, Arnobius, Lactantius, Salvianus, Gregory of Nyssa, Jerome, Chrysostum, and Augustine—men whose active careers spanned the period ca. 180–430. In addition, the various councils of the early Christian Church tried to deal with an institution that they considered an affront to their faith and morals, but that was clearly popular among laymen. Translations of the writings of the Church Fathers are available in several series, including *The Fathers of the Church: A New Translation*. Proceedings of the Church Councils are available in Latin in *Sacrorum Conciliorum Nova et Amplissima Collectio*, edited by J. D. Mensi (1769–92).

By far the most important early Christian document dealing with the stage is Tertullian's *De Spectaculis* (ca. A.D. 200), which has come down to us in a single ninth-century manuscript (Paris, Lat. 1622). The author argues (1) that since spectacles are idolatrous in their origin, it is impossible for a Christian to participate in them without being guilty of idolatry and without injury to his faith, and (2) that attendance at such amusements excites violent passions and therefore undermines moral discipline. "If the literary accomplishments of the stage delight you," he admonishes, "we have sufficient literature of our own, enough verses and maxims, also enough songs and melodies; and ours are not fables, but truths, not artful devices, but plain realities" (29.4). For Tertullian does find some features of the theatre worthy; nevertheless, he explicitly warns that they are "droppings of honey from a poisoned cake" (27.5). What is of more significance for theatre history is that in the process of demonstrating his case Tertullian provides a history and a description of theatrical spectacle (5–13)—including performances in the circus, theatre, stadium, and amphitheatre—unparalleled in extant ancient literature. "Without it [*De Spectaculis*]," notes a recent translator, "our literary sources on the subject would amount only to a number of passages found here and there in the works of ancient authors, leaving us with lamentable blanks in our knowledge about the various kinds of spectacles in antiquity" (Rudolph Arbesmann, *The Fathers of the Church*, XL, 39).

## CONCLUSION

The available evidence for the Roman theatre leaves us with an oddly disjointed picture, but one thing at least seems clear: The picture is out of focus primarily because not only did the Romans themselves not distinguish the theatre from other forms of public entertainment, but they treated it at best as something peripheral to their primary concerns and at worst as something antithetical to their very Romanness. Even where evidence is available it is often inconclusive and of secondary importance. In this category we can include much of the pictorial evidence, inscriptions, and passing literary allusions. The extant plays are, of course, of fundamental importance, but their small number is frustrating. The theatres that have survived are also clearly important sources of information, but it remains impossible to connect them with the performance of any extant play. Among the written sources, the following seem of primary importance: (1) Livy's account of the origins of the Roman theatre, (2) Cicero's many references to matters theatrical, (3) Lucian's dialogue on the dance, (4) Choricius' defense of mimes; and (5) Tertullian's *De Spectaculis*. To these we can possibly add Pollux and Vitruvius. And that is all.

## REFERENCES

Apuleius. *The Golden Ass*. Tr. Robert Graves. Harmondsworth, 1950.

Athenaeus. *Deipnosophistae*. Tr. C. B. Gulick. 7 Vols. Cambridge, Mass., and London, 1927–41.

[*Augustan History*]. *Lives of the Later Caesars*. Tr. Anthony Birley. Harmondsworth, 1976.

Augustine (Saint). *The City of God*. Tr. Demetrius B. Zema, Gerald G. Walsh, Grace Monahan, and Daniel J. Honan. *The Fathers of the Church: A New Translation*, vols. 8, 14, 24. New York, 1950–54.

Beare, W. *The Roman Stage*. 3d ed. London, 1964.

Bieber, Margarete. *The History of the Greek and Roman Theater*. Princeton, 1939; rev. 1961.

Bonario, Mario. *Romani Mimi*. Rome, 1965.

Choricius of Gaza. *Apologia Mimorum*. In *Choricii Gazaei: Opera*. Ed. Richard Foerster. Stuttgart, 1972 [1929].

Cicero. *Works*. Tr. H. Caplan et al. 26 Vols. Cambridge, Mass., and London, 1913–61.

*Corpus Inscriptionum Latinarum.* 16 Vols. Berlin, 1862–1975.

Dessau, Hermann. *Inscriptiones Latinae Selectae.* 3 Vols. in 5. Berlin, 1892–1916.

Diogenes Laertius. *Lives and Opinions of the Eminent Philosophers.* Tr. R. D. Hicks. 2 Vols. Cambridge, Mass., and London, 1925.

Dionysius of Halicarnassus. *Roman Antiquities.* Tr. E. Cary. 7 Vols. Cambridge, Mass., and London, 1937.

Donatus, Aelius. *Commentum Terenti.* Ed. Paul Wessner. 3 Vols. Stuttgart, 1966 [1902–5].

Duckworth, George E. *The Nature of Roman Comedy: A Study in Popular Entertainment.* Princeton, 1952.

Eusebius of Caesarea. *Ecclesiastical History.* Tr. H. J. Lawlor and J.E.L. Oulton. New York and Toronto, 1927–28.

*Fathers of the Church, The: A New Translation.* 65 Vols. New York or Washington, 1947–72.

Flickinger, Roy C. *The Greek Theater and Its Drama.* 4th ed. Chicago, 1936.

Garton, Charles. *Personal Aspects of the Roman Theatre.* Toronto, 1972.

Gellius, Aulus. *Noctes Atticae.* Tr. J. C. Rolfe. 3 Vols. Cambridge, Mass., and London, 1927–28.

Hanson, John Arthur. *Roman Theater-Temples.* Princeton, 1959.

Horace. *Satires, Epistles, Ars Poetica.* Tr. H. Rushton Fairclough. Cambridge, Mass., and London, 1926.

Jocelyn, H. D., ed. *The Tragedies of Ennius.* Cambridge, 1969.

Johnston, Mary. *Exits and Entrances in Roman Comedy.* Geneva, New York, 1933.

Jones, Leslie Webber, and C. R. Morey. *The Miniatures of the Manuscripts of Terence prior to the Thirteenth Century.* 2 Vols. Princeton, 1931.

Jordan, Henri. *Forma Urbis Romae.* Berlin, 1874.

Juvenal. *The Sixteen Satires.* Tr. Peter Green. Harmondsworth, 1967.

Livy. *History.* Tr. B. O. Foster, et al. 14 Vols. Cambridge, Mass., and London, 1919–59.

Lucian. "The Dance." In *Lucian,* vol. V. Tr. A. M. Harmon. Cambridge, Mass., and London, 1936.

Lucretius. *The Nature of the Universe.* Tr. R. E. Latham. Harmondsworth, 1951.

Macrobius. *The Saturnalia.* Tr. Percival Davies. New York and London, 1969.

*Martial Epigrams.* Tr. Walter C. A. Ker. 2 Vols. Cambridge, Mass., and London, 1920.

Mensi, J. D., ed. *Sacrorum Conciliorum Nova et Amplissima Collectio.* 31 Vols. Florence, 1769–92.

Mooney, J. J., ed. and tr. *Hosidius Geta's Tragedy "Medea."* Birmingham, 1919.

Mountford, J. F. *The Scholia Bembina.* Liverpool, 1934.

Nicoll, Allardyce. *Masks, Mimes, and Miracles.* London and New York, 1931.

Philostratus. *Life of Apollonius.* Tr. C. P. Jones. Ed. G. W. Bowersock. Harmondsworth, 1970.

Pickard-Cambridge, A. W. *The Dramatic Festivals of Athens.* Rev. John Gould and D. M. Lewis. Oxford, 1968.

Photius. *Bibliothèque.* Tr. (French) R. Henri. 4 Vols. Paris, 1959–65.

Platnauer, M., ed. *Fifty Years (and Twelve) of Classical Scholarship.* Oxford, 1968.

Platner, Samuel Ball, and Thomas Ashby. *A Topographical Dictionary of Ancient Rome.* Oxford, 1929.

Pliny the Elder. *Natural History*. Tr. H. Rachman, W.H.S. Jones, and D. E. Eicholz. 10 Vols. Cambridge, Mass., and London, 1938–63.

Pollux. *Onomasticon*. Ed. Immanuel Bekker. Berlin, 1846.

Poulsen, Frederik. *Etruscan Tomb Paintings: Their Subjects and Significance*. Tr. Ingeborg Andersen. Oxford, 1922.

Procopius. *Secret History*. Tr. Richard Atwater. Ann Arbor, 1961.

Quintilian. *Institutio Oratoria*. Tr. H. E. Butler. 4 Vols. Cambridge, Mass., and London, 1921–22.

Reynolds, L. D., and N. G. Wilson. *Scribes and Scholars: A Guide to the Transmission of Greek and Latin Literature*. 2d ed. Oxford, 1974.

Ribbeck, Otto, ed. *Comicorum Romanorum Fragmenta*. 3rd ed. Leipzig, 1898.

———. *Tragicorum Latinorum Fragmenta*. 3d ed. Leipzig, 1897.

Seneca, Marcus Annaeus. *The Suasoriae of Seneca the Elder*. Ed. and tr. W. A. Edward. Cambridge, 1928.

Suetonius. *Lives of the Caesars*. Tr. Robert Graves. Harmondsworth, 1957.

———. *Suetonious*. Tr. J. C. Rolfe, 2 vols. Cambridge, Mass., and London, 1914.

Tacitus, Cornelius. *Agricola, Germania*. Tr. H. Mattingly. Harmondsworth, 1948.

———. *The Annals of Imperial Rome*. Tr. Michael Grant. Harmondsworth, 1956.

Tertullian. *De Spectaculis*. In *Disciplinary, Moral and Ascetical Works*. Tr. Rudolph Arbesman, Emily Joseph Daly, and Edwin A. Qain. *The Fathers of the Church: A New Translation*, vol. 40. New York, 1959.

Trendall, A. D. *Catalogue of Phlyax Vases*. 2nd ed. *Bulletin of the Institute of Classical Studies*, Supplement No. 19. London, 1967.

Valerius Maximus. *Facta et Dicta Memorabilia Libri Novem*. Ed. C. Kempf. Hildesheim, 1976 [1854].

Vitruvius. *The Ten Books of Architecture*. Tr. Morris Hicky Morgan. New York, 1960 [1914].

Warmington, E. H., tr. *Remains of Old Latin*. 4 Vols. Cambridge, Mass., and London, 1935–36.

Webster, T.B.L. *Hellenistic Poetry and Art*. New York, 1964.

———. *Monuments Illustrating New Comedy*. *Bulletin of the Institute of Classical Studies*, Supplement No. 11. London, 1961.

———. *Monuments Illustrating Old and Middle Comedy*. *Bulletin of the Institute of Classical Studies*, Supplement No. 9. London, 1960.

———. *Monuments Illustrating Tragedy and Satyr Play*. *Bulletin of the Institute of Classical Studies*, Supplement No. 14. London. 1962.

Wright, F. Warren. *Cicero and the Theater*. Smith College Classical Studies No. 11. Northampton, Mass., 1931.

# 4

# THE MEDIEVAL THEATRE

## SCHOLARSHIP

The writing of medieval theatre history has undergone changes over the past century similar to those reflected in the writing of the history of the classical theatres. There has been a gradual shift in emphasis from an exclusive attention to dramatic texts—usually religious—to a more serious consideration of the elements of performance, and an accompanying redefinition of theatre to include various non-verbal forms such as royal entries, city pageants, tournaments, and courtly dance-games. The result has been a revaluation of the quality and significance of the medieval theatre, which, when judged on the basis of the text alone and according to strictly literary standards, seems vastly inferior to the theatre of the Greeks or the Elizabethans. "The dialogue has not the richness of texture," writes a recent apologist, "that would make a constant re-reading of the words rewarding" (Rosemary Woolf, *The English Mystery Plays,* p. 100). What *has* proved rewarding is the consideration of this theatre and its extant texts in the light of the theatrical conditions that gave them their initial artistic life.

This approach, which in recent years has brought the study of the medieval theatre close to the centre of theatrical research, did not always enjoy the status of self-evident truth it is now generally accorded. The preference of eighteenth- and early nineteenth-century historians for dramatic literature was reinforced, if not determined, by the nature of the evidence available to them. It consisted mostly of dramatic texts and ecclesiastical written records. It was to take many years of painstaking investigation of exceedingly fragmentary evidence even to begin the reconstruction of the ephemeral, occasional, textless entertainments that made up a large part of the medieval theatre. And such investigation was unlikely to be undertaken so long as the criterion for attention was literary merit, so long as the medieval drama was seen as an aberration in dramatic history, so long as historians could find no discernible pattern within it, and so long as there seemed to be no relationship between the drama of the Middle Ages and the classical drama which preceded it and the Renaissance drama which succeeded it. In short, the medieval theatre was not worth explaining, and it could explain nothing; it was therefore ignored.

It is true that a few antiquarians were responsible for collecting and publishing records and information concerning theatrical productions at specific places. In 1816, G.A.J. Hécart published the principal documents from Valenciennes in *Recherches historiques bibliographiques, critiques et littéraires sur le théâtre à Valenciennes*; and in 1825 Thomas Sharp produced *A Dissertation on the Pageants or Dramatic Mysteries Anciently Performed at Coventry*. Such work has often proved of inestimable value to later historians, particularly in those instances where the original documents have since been lost or destroyed. But in general, antiquarian interest was in the facts of the past, rather than in their interpretation or in historical process or explanation. What was needed, then, in order to draw the attention of historians to the medieval theatre, was a theory of historical process that would enable them to interpret and explain the factual evidence being haphazardly collected by antiquarians, a theory that would in itself prompt new fact-finding inquiries and help to determine which facts were relevant and which not, a theory that could bring about a shift in perspective from value-oriented literary appreciation to historical explanation. The theory that served this purpose was the product of historical empiricism and the concept of an evolutionary process from the simple to the complex. The monumental scholarly works that resulted remain indispensible compendia of facts— no matter what revisions have been made in the theory which prompted their collection and shaped their interpretation.

Among the earliest of the new scholars was L. Petit de Julleville, who, between 1880 and 1886, published five data-filled volumes devoted to the medieval theatre of France. A new attitude is immediately apparent. Petit de Julleville begins the first volume of *Les Mystères* (1880) by pointing out that the generally accepted beginning of French drama, Charles VI's granting of letters of patent to the Confrérie de la Passion in 1402, is in fact totally in error, that the fifteenth century was actually the culmination of an evolutionary process that had its beginnings in the liturgy of the Catholic Church. And he rehearses the process now so familiar from innumerable repetitions in popular histories and handbooks: The Latin liturgical drama was slowly transformed, via accretion and elaboration, into a vernacular and secularized drama, performed by the laity in the streets and public squares. And in the recently discovered twelfth-century *Jeu d'Adam* he found a concrete example of an intermediary point in this process.

Of at least equal importance, however, was Petit de Julleville's recognition that the medieval theatre differed from the classical theatre in its emphasis on spectacle, its immense and varied action unlimited in time or space, in its fusion of the marvelous with a detailed realism. As a consequence, he included a consideration of the *mise en scène*, which had been almost completely ignored in the eighteenth century. And in the second volume of *Les Mystères* he provides a chronological list of performances given between 1290 and 1603, quoting from original production records and documents where possible. His emancipation from text-centered history is attested by a similar list of *Mystères Mimes*, "mystères sans paroles," performed between 1313 and 1564. His work on the conditions of performance continued in *Les Comédiens en France au moyen âge* (1885), in which he discusses the various groups and constituencies that provided actors for the medieval stage in France, for, as he asks in a question all too often forgotten, "What can be said of a theatre without actors?" (p. 11). He had few illusions about the literary merits of the drama he discussed: "Our farces, our *moralités* are not literary works" (*La Comédie et les moeurs*, p. 6).

E. K. Chambers, in *The Mediaeval Stage* (1903), went even further than had Petit de Julleville in his deliberate neglect of the literary side of medieval drama. He claims to be concerned with the collection of social and economic facts, with "as many facts with as precise references as possible" (I, vii). That he was largely successful in his aims underscores the point that Chambers viewed the medieval theatre simply as a pre-condition for what was of real value to follow; he was eager "to state and explain the pre-existing conditions which . . . made the great Shakespearean stage possible" (I, v-vi). Although he argues that modern drama evolved from the liturgy, the farce of the mimes, and the classical revivals of Humanism, he clearly assumes that the medieval drama itself evolved along the lines laid out earlier by Petit de Julleville. The liturgy itself was the seed from which theatre developed, and "from such beginnings, grew up the great popular religious drama of the miracle-plays, with its offshoots in the moralities and the dramatic pageants." The process of change Chambers labelled *secularization*, and his assumption of its inevitability governs the arrangement and discussion of the material which fills his two impressive volumes. He does for the English medieval theatre what Petit de Julleville had done for the French.

Similar theoretical assumptions underlie the work of the great French theatre historian, Gustave Cohen, whose long and distinguished career is most fittingly represented by *Histoire de la mise en scène dans le théâtre religieux français du moyen-âge*, first published in 1906 and revised in 1926, and by *Le Théâtre en France au moyen-âge* (1928–31). Cohen believed that literature and theatre evolved in much the same way as had biological species, according to laws that ensured that the same cause always had the same effect. We noted when discussing the origins of the theatre that it was Cohen who articulated the analogy between theatrical development in the Middle Ages and theatrical development in ancient Greece. Like Petit de Julleville, Cohen recognized the spectacular nature of the medieval religious drama and devoted an entire book to the elu-

cidation of its *mise en scèene*. The realistic detail of the presentation, also noted
by Petit de Julleville, he attributed to the need of child-like medieval man to
be able to see and feel characters whom religious tradition had presented as
incomplete sketches. And his need was the basis of the medieval dramatic in-
stinct, which expressed itself, according to Cohen, not only in the amplification
and ornamentation of the text, but in the elaborated *mise en scène*, in the development of scene decoration, stage machinery, and costume.

Cohen, however, was not satisfied simply to reconstruct the theatrical conditions for each period of theatrical history; he also insisted on studying and
explaining the evolution of these conditions: It is necessary, he argued, to demonstrate that the *mise en scène* is the expression of the culture where it developed. Finally, Cohen cited with approval the comparative method championed
by the French literary critic Ferdinand Brunetière, who in 1889 had expounded
his theory of the ''evolution'' of literary genres. But the theatre historian goes
further in his comparative method, filling in and clarifying his description of
the French *mise en scène* by reference to contemporary theatrical practice in
Spain, Italy, Germany, England, and the Low Countries. ''The historian,'' he
writes, ''however modest he may be, ought not to isolate himself in his subject;
he must elucidate it as well from without'' (*Histoire de la mise en scène*, p.
13).

Cohen's contribution to theatre history is great. He systematically surveyed
archival documents, memoirs, city records; he examined and analyzed in detail
texts and textual rubrics—in original manuscripts when they were available. He
utilized the comparative method judiciously, and he used the evolutionary theory creatively, in order to make some sense out of a wealth of disparate material. Above all, he constantly sought to explain the medieval theatre as a human, social, and artistic institution. Cohen was, of course, sometimes wrong
in detail, and the theory of evolutionary development that he both assumed and
espoused has come under attack. But however much later historians have revised the history of the French medieval stage, they have always found it pru-
dent to begin by consulting Cohen.

The last of the new pioneers in the writing of medieval theatre history is the
American Karl Young, whose *Drama of the Medieval Church* appeared in 1933.
Here are collected and discussed hundreds of Latin liturgical plays, previously
available only in widely scattered and sometimes badly prepared editions and
in manuscript. Young's purpose was primarily literary, and he consequently ex-
cludes consideration both of the music, which in some instances is included in
the manuscripts, and of the *mise en scène*. We might wonder, therefore, at the
influence of the work on historians of the medieval theatre. The answer lies in
Young's assumption of the evolutionary theory which the very arrangement of
his work tends to canonize. ''Within a single chapter,'' he explains, ''the several versions of the same play are arranged in what might be called the *logical*
order of development, from the simplest to the most complex and elaborate.
Presumably this is, in general, also the *historical* order. . . .'' (I, viii-ix). Young

readily admits that it is impossible to demonstrate the validity of this idea and notes that the simplest forms sometimes appear in the latest manuscripts and vice versa. He therefore describes his method as "primarily descriptive, rather than historical." Nevertheless, his obvious enthusiasm for his subject is predicated on a historical sequence.

Historical empiricism and evolutionary theory combined then to provide the hypotheses upon which Petit de Julleville, Chambers, Cohen, and Young arranged and ordered their factual data. Unfortunately, these hypotheses tended to harden into dogma as they were reproduced in textbooks, taught in schools and universities, and uncritically accepted even by scholars. As is often the case in such circumstances, where theory has served to provide fresh perspectives on a neglected field and to stimulate investigation, dogma could only serve as an article of faith in a system of orthodoxy.

A case in point is that of Hardin Craig, who in 1955 published *English Religious Drama*, destined to be the last hurrah of the evolutionary orthodoxy. In spite of a keen critical eye and a solid factual foundation, Craig seems always to miss the point of studies such as those of Chambers and Young, both of whom he acknowledges. Like them, he adheres to the evolutionary theory of dramatic development, which saw the drama moving from Latin to the vernacular, from the religious to the secular, from church to street, from clergy to laity, from the simple to the complex. But unlike Chambers—and certainly unlike Cohen—his bias is predominantly literary, and the theatrical element is simply dismissed: "To be sure, the machinery of theatres, stages, and actors somewhat as we know them came into existence as it was needed . . ." (p. 1). Left, then, with the texts of plays and only the most rudimentary notion of dramaturgy and staging conventions (based mainly on Aristotle and Roman comedy), Craig not surprisingly finds little to admire in the English drama of the Middle Ages. It lacked dramatic technique, dramatic purpose, artistic self-consciousness, and theory: "The technique of the mystery and miracle plays and of the main current of English popular drama consisted merely in telling a story on a stage by means of dialogue, impersonation, and action" (p. 9). Merely.

Craig resisted any challenge to the orthodox explanation of dramatic development, but in spite of his considerable reputation he was unable finally to counter a reassessment of the medieval theatre based on (*a*) a consideration of new evidence gleaned from government and municipal records, (*b*) a fresh look at the assumptions underlying the evolutionary "secularization" theory, (*c*) a view of theatre expanded to include various kinds of non-literary performance, and (*d*) a new realization that the surviving dramatic texts are worthy of serious study. While much of this revisionist work was done in English and was concerned mainly with the medieval theatre of England, the tendencies it reflects are generally true of Continental scholarship as well.

It is now conceded that the prime document in the revisionist revaluation was Harold C. Gardiner's *Mysteries' End* (1946). Gardiner challenged the idea that the religious drama of medieval England had flourished, undergone secularization, and finally declined and died, through a process of natural growth and decay. He argued instead that the plays remained religious to the end, that there was no legislation of the Catholic Church in opposition to the religious stage as such, but only to its "extraneous abuses," that the medieval drama of England was deliberately suppressed by the Protestant monarchs, Henry VIII, Edward VI, and Elizabeth I. The real villain "was Reformation distaste for the religious culture of the past . . ., a distaste, moreover, which was stimulated and kept alive by the wishes of the government" (p. xiii). Father Gardiner's carefully documented argument threatens nevertheless to become the self-evident truth of a new orthodoxy; and we should try therefore to understand his methods and assumptions.

*Mysteries' End* is a good example of the process by which history is often written. Theories do not normally arise from collected facts. Rather, a new interpretation of the facts, a new theory, is forced upon the historian by a change in perspective often brought about by and dependent on larger matters of faith and vision. In Gardiner's case, we find a priest's clear preference for medieval Catholic culture over the values of the Reformation, together with a strong desire to see the medieval theatre as worthy of the Catholic culture that produced it. The result was that Gardiner did indeed find evidence of the deliberate suppression of the religious drama, and so altered once and for all the theory of its decline. But he also forced a reassessment of the drama itself, and it became for him good drama. The same tests that elicited Craig's condescension prompted Gardiner's admiration. What had changed was the value system from which they were viewed.

The significance of Gardiner's study went to a large extent unnoticed for almost a decade. In the meantime, the successful performances of English cycle plays in 1951 contributed to the growing feeling that the medieval theatre was one of substance and significance. Then, in 1955, appeared F. M. Salter's *Medieval Drama in Chester* which, through a careful reassessment of the Chester records, confirmed Gardiner's challenge of the "secularization" theory of the decline of the religious drama, while at the same time it emphasized the complexity and the quality of the drama itself. Finally, Richard Southern, in *The Medieval Theatre in the Round* (1957; rev. 1975), demonstrated the undoubted abilities of the author of the early fifteenth-century morality *The Castle of Perseverance*.

The revisionist history of the medieval theatre—in England at least—received its most comprehensive treatment in Volume I of Glynne Wickham's *Early English Stages*, which appeared in 1959. Originally intending to write a single volume devoted to pageantry and its connection with the growth of the stage, Wickham was prompted by a chance reading of Salter's book to produce a multi-volumed work that attempts "to trace the history of English stagecraft from its beginnings to the advent of the proscenium-arched scenic theatre that became public property shortly after the Restoration of the Monarchy in 1660" (I, vii). From the first, then, Wickham realized that he was in a battle with earlier scholars, with the exceptions of Gardiner, Salter, and Southern. He breaks specifically with the evolutionary school in postulating two distinct religious dramas "of single Christian origin but of independent motivation: the drama of the Real Presence within the liturgy and the imitative drama of Christ's Humanity in the world outside" (I, 314). Rather than being a direct development of the liturgical drama, Wickham argues that the vernacular drama was the creation of thirteenth-century friars, priests, and clerks, related to the earlier drama by techniques and subject-matter but with a different purpose.

Wickham's insistence on the theatrical context for any consideration of the medieval drama, on interpreting texts and stage directions in the light of the practices and methods of the tournament and the street pageant, confused some reviewers, including Hardin Craig, who could not make connections between text-centered "drama" and textless ceremony, occasional and ephemeral. Such a connection becomes possible only when the religious drama is considered in terms of what it has in common with performances of all kinds—spectacle. "It becomes both possible and reasonable," writes Wickham, "to consider the stagecraft of Tournaments, Royal Entries, the Miracle Cycles and the Elizabethan Public Theatre as so many different manifestations of a single homogeneous tradition of stage spectacle, acting and production" (I, 113). Moreover, this emphasis on the visual aspect of the medieval theatre also drew attention to the language of icon and emblem, of visual symbol and allegory: "We must anticipate a whole language of signs and learn to read it" (I, 85). Both a cause and a consequence of this perspective is the affirmation of the sophistication and worth of the early drama, and the richness of the civilization that produced it. And no longer is it necessary to be a priest of the Roman Catholic Church to recognize this worth and this richness.

Many of the points made above concerning historical method and Darwinian assumption are made in a highly sophisticated form in O. B. Hardison's *Christian Rite and Christian Drama in the Middle Ages* (1965), the opening chapter of which constitutes a comprehensive theoretical refutation of the earlier orthodoxy. Hardison is, nonetheless, basically a literary scholar, interested in literary rather than theatrical structures. Indeed, some of the most often cited studies published since 1960, while acknowledging the intrinsic merits of the medieval drama, have been essentially literary studies: e.g., V. A. Kolve's *The Play Called Corpus Christi* (1966), Rosemary Woolf's *The English Mystery Plays* (1972), and Eleanor Prosser's *Drama and Religion in the English Mystery Plays* (1961). Even these studies, however, reflect the growing recognition that the medieval drama, if it is to be profitably discussed at all, must be approached as texts designed for the stage and not for the study.

Medieval theatrical conditions and conventions continue to be explored by scholars such as Elie Konigson (*L'Espace théâtral médiéval*, 1975), Alan H. Nelson (*The Medieval English Stage*, 1974), and Fletcher Collins (*The Production of Medieval Church Music-Drama*, 1972). The careful examination of public and ecclesiastical records of all sorts, as well as of texts and rubrics, pioneered by Cohen and Chambers and given new life by the revisionists, has now become commonplace. But perhaps the most significant new emphasis has been on the use of contemporaneous pictorial material to illuminate dramaturgy and stage practices. Earlier historians were either ignorant or sceptical of its value. Cohen, for example, used miniatures found in manuscripts, painting, and sculpture with extreme caution, and only when his other sources proved inadequate. But now, study after study has appeared in which evidence derived from stained glass, mural paintings, sculpture, and manuscript illuminations has played a major part.

## DRAMATIC TEXTS

Unlike the extant dramatic texts from Greece and Rome, which are severely limited in number and which in each case date from a relatively concentrated period of time and were originally performed at a single location, medieval texts number in the hundreds, were composed and performed at various places all over Western Europe, and appeared at various times over a 600-year period from the middle of the tenth to the middle of the sixteenth century. (See Appendix for a detailed discussion.) They were, moreover, composed in all the major vernacular languages of Europe—English, French, German, Italian, Spanish—as well as in Latin, the *lingua franca* of the Middle Ages. Indeed, so vast is the bulk of material that there is currently no satisfactory bibliography or catalogue of the extant texts. The following reference works are either available or in progress:

1. C. J. Stratman's *Bibliography of Medieval Drama* (1954; rev. 1972) is intended primarily for students of the English drama, and the editor therefore includes for England a reasonably complete listing of the extant manuscripts together with their locations. The Latin liturgical drama is similarly well served. But for the vernacular theatre of the rest of Europe we must make do with the cataloguing of printed editions of plays. The entries for Germany, Italy, and Spain are particularly sparse.

2. A more comprehensive project is under way at the University of Leeds in England. *The Leeds Descriptive Catalogue of Medieval Drama*, the first volume of which was expected to appear in 1980–81, is intended to provide essential information on the dramatic texts of medieval Europe; the terminal date is 1500. The emphasis will be on subject matter, and the contents of the plays are to be described as fully as possible, but other information will also be included: bibliographical information, indications of staging information to be found in a manuscript or book, the names associated with the play (e.g. author, reviser, scribe, performer). (See note by Peter Meredith in *Research Opportunities in Renaissance Drama*, 1978.)

3. Two volumes on the theatre are promised in the new *Grundriss der Romanischen Literaturen des Mittelalters* by Hans R. Jauss and others, an encyclopedic work designed to cover all the medieval literatures of the Romance languages. The first volume will list all extant texts in a Romance language (French, Provençal, Italian, Spanish, Portuguese), along with information about manuscripts and editions; the second volume will consist of historical surveys of the various dramas.

Also unlike Greek dramatic texts, which, as we have seen, are totally synthetic, medieval dramatic texts appear in various kinds of manuscript, and by the late fifteenth century in printed editions as well. Some few seem to be directors' or prompters' copies; even fewer represent individual actors' copies. Some manuscripts are fairly luxurious, clearly prepared as reading copies and perhaps intended for presentation to a noble personage. Medieval plays were commonly produced annually, or at least on a semi-regular basis, and there are indications in some of the manuscripts of changes introduced for a specific occasion. A few manuscripts appear to have been prepared for use at a particular time and place, and they were subsequently preserved in that state. We find manuscripts that are illustrated or accompanied by pictorial miniatures, and manuscripts that include notes and even stage-plans. And finally, there are manuscripts of plays that in all likelihood were not performed at all. Their variety, complexity, and number make medieval dramatic texts particularly bewildering and difficult to interpret as evidence for theatre history. We can, nonetheless, categorize these texts, at least in a rough way, according to the amount and worth of the information they are able to provide the theatre historian.

In the first place, while play texts may be considered prime evidence for their own staging, they constitute such evidence only if we can reasonably assure ourselves that they were indeed performed. Therefore, the least useful category of dramatic texts is that comprising plays for which there is no evidence, textual or otherwise, of their ever having been performed. In some instances it may be possible to demonstrate that they could not be performed, or that they were indeed not performed. We assume, however, that most of the plays that have come down to us were performed. This assumption is based on either internal textual evidence or on extra-textual testimony or inference. Still, however, the fact of performance itself does not tell us where or when or under what circumstances; nor can we be sure that the text we read is precisely the text that was enacted.

The bare text of a play is rendered more valuable if it is accompanied by rubrics providing stage directions and details of performance. On occasion, however, rubrics can be confusing, and even when they are not confusing they can be too vague for use. They always need careful interpretation. And under even the best of circumstances, unless the performance can be documented as to time and place from some other source, stage-directions tend to provide a general rather than a specific picture. A case in point is *Le Mystère d'Adam*, whose rubrics promise so much but have been so variously interpreted. And little wonder. We are informed that Paradise is to be set up in a *loco eminenciari*, in a high or elevated place; that the actors are to make their actions appropriate to the subject matter; that devils at one point are to run *per plateas*, about the place, making appropriate gestures; that Cain and Abel go *ad locus remotum et quasi secretum*, to a remote and secret place. The problem is that, while the stage directions are sufficient guides for a modern producer to stage the play effectively, using modern resources and techniques, they do not explain precisely what was available for their realization in the twelfth century, especially at the first performance. It has proved impossible to reconstruct that stage. Nagler's rueful comment after surveying the difficulties in interpreting the stage directions seems apt: "Even abundant rubrics will produce only vague notions" (*Medieval Religious Stage*, p. 3).

Similarly, those texts illustrated with miniatures usually promise more than can with any confidence be inferred. Aside from the usual hesitation about deriving details concerning one art from another art, we cannot be sure that the illustrator was attempting to reflect stage practice or even to provide a scene from the play's scenario. It is virtually a certainty, for instance, that the pictures illuminating the texts of *Les Miracles de Notre Dame* and *Le Passion D'Arras* were not executed with either the theatre or the plays' specific texts in mind.

The few texts that can be demonstrated to have been used at a particular time and at a particular place are especially valuable, and it is in the treatment of such texts that the literary scholar and the theatre historian most obviously part company. On the basis of editorial and philological principles—worked out in the nineteenth century for classical authors and in the early twentieth century for modern authors—literary and textual scholars compare and collate the variant copies of what is considered to be a single literary work, in order to reconstruct a single authoritative text. Perhaps the key word here is "authoritative." It is assumed that a single conception governs the "true" text and that it is the scholar's responsibility to determine that conception and to establish a text that conforms to it. This assumption underlay the attempt to reconstruct an original *Tirol Passion* on the basis of five distinct manuscripts. We are operating under a similar assumption when we refer to Greban's *Passion* as though the essential "play" exists independently of the various manuscripts that provide the acting versions of it. And the same tendency underlies our predilection for categorizing liturgical plays on the basis of their subject matter, and then considering the various treatments simply as local variants. But theatre historians are interested—or at least ought to be interested—in the local variants, in the texts performed at a specific place and time. Where such a text exists, the origin or origins of that text are of secondary consideration: It has become what we might call a "document of production," as valuable in its own way as a prompt-book, a director's notes, a stage-plan, or an eye-witness account. Thus the importance, for instance, of the manuscripts preserved in the municipal library at Troye, containing the text of the play performed there in 1490. Literary scholarship has determined that it consists of the beginning of *Le Vieux Testament* and parts of Greban's *Passion*. But such knowledge provides no help in interpreting this particular text as a production document. Given the variable nature of the texts available to us, and the incomplete bibliographical information concerning them, we ought not to be surprised to find scholars somewhat at odds over their treatment and interpretation.

Playing the "game of rubrics," according to A. M. Nagler, "is entertaining for the researcher, though it may sometimes be harmful to his scholarly health'' (*The Medieval Religious Stage*, p. 1). Nagler is dubious about the value of play texts as evidence for their own staging, and his scepticism appears to have prompted him to consider the study of manuscripts and original printed texts as something outside the theatre historian's purview: ''The theatre historian is not concerned with the restoration of the text; ceding this difficult task to qualified philologists, he employs the best available text and, above all, its explicit or implicit stage directions'' (p. xi). The problem with this seemingly sensible procedure—that is, to rely on an expert where we are ourselves not expert—is, as we have seen, that the aims of the theatre historian and the philologist are not identical. And Nagler was challenged on the point in a review of *The Medieval Religious Stage* in the *Educational Theatre Journal*: ''To my mind,'' writes Alan H. Nelson,

an edition, however scholarly, must not be regarded as a substitute for nor (worse yet!) an improvement upon the source, but rather as a key which will make easier the task of reinspecting the original. There is no substitute for facsimiles, microfilms, or a willingness to travel: the philologist's eye may easily miss or dismiss a detail which is crucial to the theatre historian [XXIX (1977), 575].

The textual editor is interested in the single ''authoritative'' text that underlies the various versions; the theatre historian is far more concerned with the variations. It is common for historians and theatre critics to consider the text as a score for speech and action, a score that can be realized only in performance. It therefore matters whether the score was altered to accommodate different instruments: That is what the history of theatre is about.

## PRODUCTION DOCUMENTS

Dramatic texts can sometimes qualify as documents of production. Other such evidence includes prompt-books, stage plans, contracts, and municipal or guild records and accounts that refer to specific and identifiable performances. We are fortunate in possessing a number of these documents, mostly from the fifteenth and sixteenth centuries, and mostly from France and Germany. We can hope that, as the systematic collection and publication of records continues, the number of production documents will grow. The following account provides, as examples, introductions to the best known and most commonly cited materials, including the only known instance of an eye-witness account, and a consideration of five specific performances from the Continent for which the documentation is especially rich. It concludes with a brief discussion which stands on the periphery of the category.

### Prompt-Books

There are three prompt-books or director's copies—called variously *abregiés*, *livres de conduite du régisseur*, or *Dirigierolle*—that have attracted attention. The first consists of director's notes by one Baldemar von Peterweil, prepared for a mid-fourteenth-century production of a lost Passion play at Frankfurt, Germany. It is printed by R. Froning in *Das Drama des Mittelalters* (pp. 340–374). Peterweil's notes provide brief stage directions, the order of the appearance of the actors, and the first lines of speeches and songs. Our second example, from the city of Mons in present-day Belgium, is much more elaborate and will be discussed in conjunction with other documents concerning a performance in that city in 1501. A third prompt copy for the Alsfeld Passion play, discovered in 1891, has been little discussed. The only reference to it in English is by Nagler, who cites a German article of 1904 and notes that it does us little good in any event (*The Medieval Religious Stage*, p. 34).

### Stage Plans

Six stage plans of varying complexity and detail have survived in conjunction with dramatic texts or other performance documents. The earliest and simplest are the schematic drawings of circles and stations in the manuscript of the Cornish *Ordinalia*. Another is that included in the manuscript containing the *Macro Plays*, which illustrates a circular playing area for *The Castle of Perseverance*. A castle stands in the middle of the circle, and there are scaffolds, ascribed to Deus, Flesh, Mundus, Belial, and Covetous, indicated at five points outside the circumference. Rubrics suggest that the playing area was to be encircled with a ditch filled with water if possible, otherwise that it be "strongly barred all about," and that no one was to sit on the central Castle of Perseverance "for letting of sight." Instructions are given too that "not over many stytelerys be within the place." Scholarly opinion is divided as to the specific interpretation of the drawing. In the most elaborate discussion of the problem, Richard Southern argues in *The Medieval Theatre in the Round* that the playing area was surrounded by a moat, and the scaffolds erected inside the moat. The audience took up its place, then, between the scaffolds, and in the central area as well—with, of course, the exception of the prohibited Castle itself. Southern's theory of this theatre-in-the round has been widely accepted, although scholars such as Glynne Wickham and A. M. Nagler continue to question it on the grounds of the impropriety of an unruly audience's presence in the *platea*, and the logistical difficulties of digging a ditch and disposing of the earth.

The stage plans from the Continent suggest a different method of staging. On the last page of the manuscript of the Alsfeld Passion play (1501) is a rudimentary sketch indicating the position of several mansions—eleven to be precise—arranged with "Ortus" at the top, "Thronus" at the bottom, four "castra" on the left, and five more mansions in a row on the right. (See Nagler, *The Medieval Religious Stage*, p. 33, for a reproduction of the plan.) A plan found in the manuscript of the Tirol Passion play performed in 1514 at Bozen (modern Bolzano), the work of one Vigil Raber, is the only such document that illustrates the performance of a Passion play in a church. (The Church unfortunately no longer exists and we are consequently dependent upon descriptions of it.) The plan, reproduced by Nagler (p. 48), presents a central rectangle—a temple?—within a larger rectangle, the whole surrounded by several mansions. On one side is a large door from which a kind of runway leads to the playing area. Theories of the size and location of this stage within the church are conjectural and inconclusive.

A third plan, found in the mid-nineteenth century in the Fürstlich Fürstenbergische Hofbibliothek at Donaueschingen, has generated a good deal of confusion. The drawing was found on a loose sheet, enclosed with the manuscript of the Donaueschingen Passion play (1845), and it was long regarded as the stage plan for the performance of that play—even though the written characters are of sixteenth-century origin. The mismatch of plan and text has finally persuaded Nagler at least that the plan was not intended for the Donaueschingen Passion play; and he offers substantial arguments that it was intended instead for the Villingen Passion, also found in the Donaueschingen library, but dating as we have seen from about 1585. His discussion of the controversy (pp. 36–47) illustrates the way in which an *idée fixe* can continue to keep hardworking and intelligent men at an unprofitable task, in this instance trying to reconcile the plan with the text of the Donaueschingen Passion play. The sketch itself provides for a number of mansions on either side of a series of three arches, with a cluster of mansions and a cross at the top. (Nagler reproduces the plan on p. 41.)

Closely associated as evidence with these stage-plans are illustrations of the stage-settings for a performance at Valenciennes in 1547 and a performance at Cologne in 1581. The Valenciennes document is discussed below. The illustration from Cologne depicts the stage-plan for a production of the Latin play *Laurentius*. It shows typically medieval "houses" and emblems on a platform set upon barrels (five of which are visible) and features entrances in the form of curtained arches at the rear and sides of the platform. (The illustration is reproduced in Jean Jacquot, ed., *Le Lieu théâtral*, Plate I. See also the discussion by Carl Niessen, pp. 191–214.) (A final plan, for a performance at Lucerne in 1583, will be discussed in the context of all the evidence for that production.)

### Archival Documents

Other documents that have a direct bearing on particular performances are contracts between the organizers of performances and those charged with preparing or executing certain elements of those performances. We have, for example, an agreement signed on April 20, 1453, between the Barcelona City Council and one Johan Calon, for the construction of new pageants. We also have a contract of 1528 between twelve citizens of Pithiviers and a priest, Jean Hamelin, who was charged with directing the *Mystère de Saint Jacques*. We have a carpenter's contract from Aix-en-Provence dated 1444. And for a play of Sainte-Christophe, performed in 1540, there is preserved among the notarized acts of the City of Paris contracts with carpenters (no. 1513) and musicians (no. 1514). Such documents, taken together with the records and accounts of guilds and municipalities, can provide considerable information concerning the organizational, economic, and social underpinning of a medieval theatrical performance.

Not all such records and accounts can rightly be regarded as production documents, in that the information they provide is generally rather than specifically applicable. Those to be discussed here are clearly associated with specific performances. We have an "order of processing"—*ordung des vmbgangs*—from Freiburg, and there are a few similar documents relating to a performance at Zerbst in 1511–12. Orders of Procession are also to be found in Spain from 1424. In England, at York, we find an entry in the Memorandum Book by the town clerk, Roger Burton, consisting of the *Ordo paginarum ludi Corporis Christi*, a schedule of the crafts and their plays, dated 1415. A further entry from 1417 informs us of the locations of the twelve stations where the individual pageants were to be performed. Records from Norwich (1565) and York (1433) offer suggestive detail concerning the construction of pageants for a play of the Fall and a Doomsday play respectively. In France, there are accounts in the Bibliothèque D'Angers that attest to some of the trials, tribulations, and troubles experienced by the town in mounting a production in 1486. (See Petit de Julleville, *Les Mystères*, II, 50–51.)

A particularly important document also survives from the town of Seurre in Burgundy. Now in the Bibliothèque Nationale (fr. 24332), it contains a *mystère*, a farce, and a morality, all by the same playwright, André de la Vigne— eloquent testimony to the varied bill of fare an audience could expect in 1496. But the real treat lies in an accompanying *procès-verbal* or official report, prepared by the author himself. Thanks to this document—printed in Petit de Julleville, *Les Mystères*, II, 68–71—we know where, when, by whom, and for whom *Le Mystère de Saint Martin* was written and performed. And we are given details of the performance itself, particularly concerning the use of music and musical instruments. But such reports are, unfortunately, rare, even for the wellresearched French theatre, and we must normally content ourselves with far less, or at least with information less directly applicable to specific performances.

### An Eyewitness Account

There survives an eyewitness account of two medieval performances in two churches in Florence, Italy, left to us by the Russian Bishop Abraham of Souzdal. The performances in question were witnessed by the good bishop on March 25 and May 14, 1439. The first was an Annunciation play at the Church of the Santissima Annunziata; the second was a play of the Ascension at the Church of Santa Maria del Carmine. This document, described by Nagler as "a source without parallel in the history of the medieval theatre" (*The Medieval Religious Stage*, p. 25), previously available in English only in an abridged version in Joseph Spencer Kennard's *The Italian Theatre* (pp. 51–53), was printed in 1957 in *Educational Theatre Journal* (IX, 208–213) in a translation by Orville K. Larson. The detail and completeness of the descriptions are remarkable, although in the absence of texts, Nagler's opinion that the performances could be reconstructed with little difficulty seems a bit sanguine.

## Five Performances

Five performances from the Continent are particularly well documented and regularly cited and discussed by theatre historians: (1) Mons (1501), (2) Romans (1509), (3) Bourges (1536), (4) Valenciennes (1547), and (5) Lucerne (1583). Clearly, all of them are late, and extrapolation in time or space on the basis of evidence associated with these productions must be undertaken with care. On the other hand, the conservative nature of medieval society in general and of the religious theatre in particular would suggest that at best the principles of staging involved—if we are able to determine them—probably do not differ from those of earlier and less copiously documented performances.

Records from the city of Mons in present-day Belgium indicate that a Passion play was performed there on a fairly regular basis throughout the fifteenth century, but the nature of the play and details concerning its performance were for many years unknown. In 1913 Gustave Cohen found a reference to a manuscript containing information about a 1501 performance at Mons in Léopold Devillers' *Analectes montois* (1869) and began to search for this otherwise unknown document. He finally discovered in the manuscript collection of the Mons town library not one but two *livres de conduite* that, he reports, "regulate with an astonishing detail, the comings and goings of each actor, the entrances onto the scene, the orchestral interludes, and above all the complicated operation of the stage machinery." Like the Frankfurt *Dirigierolle*, the Mons *Abregiet* indicates the order of entrance of the characters (but including the actor's name) and the first lines of each speaker. From these Cohen was able to determine that the text used was based on Greban's *Passion*, with additions from that of Jean Michel. As it happens, in the archives at Mons there does exist the *livre des dépenses*, the account book, for the same performance of 1501 for which Cohen found the director's prompt-book. Cohen subsequently published all the documents in *Le Livre de conduite du régisseur et le compte des dépenses pour le Mystère de la Passion joué à Mons en 1501* (1925).

The performance at Romans in 1509 of *Le Mystère des Trois Doms* was for many years known solely on the basis of a manuscript discovered at Romans by Paul-Emile Giraud and published by him in 1848 in a limited edition of only twenty copies as *Le Composition, mise en scène et représentation du mystère des Trois Doms*. The manuscript, bearing the title *Conclusion et despence faicte pour le jeu et mistere des troy doms de Romans de l'an 1509*, contains a list of the actors involved (there were ninety-six roles), an account of the presentation, a detailed accounting of expenses, and the carpenters' contract. We learn of the materials used by the carpenters, the colours used by the scene-painters, the kind and number of musical instruments used, the price of admission, and the management of the playing area. A brief eye-witness account by one of the actors, one Louis Perrier, a judge in Romans, adds to our information by telling us the size of the acting area. Perrier's "Notice" was discovered by Giraud as well and was published in 1887 along with his even more important discovery of the *text* of *Les Trois Doms*. Again, however, the edition was severely limited: only 200 copies were printed. To complete the unusually precise documentation for this production, we can add a map of Romans completed about 1612, which clearly shows the courtyard of the Franciscan monastery where the play was performed. (The relevant detail from the map is reproduced in Nagler's *Medieval Religious Stage*, p. 21.)

The performance at Bourges in 1535 of *Le Mystère des Actes des Apôtres* by les frères Greban can be reconstructed on the basis of the following evidence:

a. Two manuscript versions of the text, one in Paris, the other at Bourges, and five editions of the play, all dating from the first half of the sixteenth century. Unfortunately, we cannot be absolutely sure of the exact text enacted at Bourges. Raymond Lebègue in *Le Mystère des Actes des Apôtres* (1929) maintained that the 1538 edition represents the text played in 1536, but Nagler argues that this edition has sections removed which might have offended Protestant readers, and that the manuscripts are not prompt copies. In his opinion, "we can come fairly close to the text as it was performed, but absolute authenticity . . . cannot be expected here" (*The Medieval Religious Stage*, p. 24).

b. An account, presumably by Jacques Thiboust, a local merchant, of the procession of the actors in their costumes on April 30, published in 1836 as *La relation de l'ordre de la triomphants et magnifique monstre du Mystère des Actes des Apôtres faite à Bourges*. Thiboust offers detailed descriptions of the costumes for the 700 or so participants, as well as of the pageant wagons that began and ended the procession.

c. A manuscript in the Bourges library contains a list of persons appearing in the play, and an *Extrait des feintes*—a not very precise source of information concerning mansions and stage effects. (The manuscript was printed by A. de Girardot in 1854.)

d. Jean Chaumeau's *Histoire de Berry*, published in 1566, provides the information that the performances at Bourges took place in the "fosse des arenes" or sandpit. Chaumeau also refers to the remains of an amphitheatre in the Roman sense. (A German chronicler who witnessed the preparations for the play also applies the term "amphitheatre" to the location of the performance.) Chaumeau's description concludes: "le dict Amphithéâtre estoit à deux etaiges surpassans la sommité des degrez" (quoted by Nagler, *Medieval Religious Stage*, p. 23). Finally, a map of Bourges from 1597 includes the celebrated sandpit. Even though most of this evidence dates from a period nearly sixty years after the fact, it is mutually confirming, and there seems no reason to doubt that the performance did indeed take place in an old Roman amphitheatre.

One of the two best known and most frequently cited performances of a medieval play is that at Valenciennes in 1547. It is the subject of a book-length study by Elie Konigson, and the frontispiece of one of the two manuscripts preserved in the Bibliothèque Nationale (Collection J. de Rothchild I.7.3), ostensibly showing the stage used for the production, graces every text and handbook that deals with the medieval theatre. Indeed, it is this frontispiece with the miniatures illustrating both manuscripts that have done the most to immortalize Valenciennes. Unlike the miniatures adorning the *Arras Passion* or *Les Miracles de Notre Dame*, those illustrating the Valenciennes manuscripts have some claim to consideration as production documents. Although executed thirty years after the original production, they are the work of the designer of that production, Hubert Cailleau, assisted by Jacques des Moëles, "conducteur de pluiseurs secrets." We have in addition a relatively large number of other documents relating to the 1547 performance: (*a*) the actors' contract, (*b*) an account of receipts and costs, and (*c*) the names and roles of most of the participants. Moreover, an early chronicler of Valenciennes, Henri d'Outreman, was the son of one of the participants in the performance, described as "superintendent et jueur de aulcunes parchons et avecq che conducteur des secrets, lesquels il estoit oportun en enfer." The younger Outreman has left us an account of the 1547 production in his *Histoire de la ville et comté de Valenciennes* (1639). (The documents are printed in Petit de Julleville's *Mystères*, II, 144–156, and in Konigson's *Represéntation d'un mystère de la Passion à Valenciennes en 1547.*)

The last—and latest—of the well documented performances from the Continent is that at Lucerne, Switzerland, in 1583. The materials for reconstructing this performance are so complete and detailed that the otherwise cautious Nagler was moved to announce that "an authentic replica of the 1583 production could be staged on the Weinmarkt tomorrow, as a tourist attraction" (*The Medieval Religious Stage*, p. 29). The evidence that prompts this confidence consists of the following, all preserved in the Burgerbibliothek of Lucerne:

a. The text of the play for the first half of the first day. The remainder of the play has been reconstructed on the basis of seven other incomplete manuscripts dating from 1545 to 1616. There seems to be rare agreement, nonetheless, that the resulting text—however synthetically arrived at—is indeed the text performed in 1583.

b. The memoranda of Renward Cysat (1545–1614), associated with the performances of the Passion play at Lucerne as an actor as early as 1571, and the director of the 1583 production. (See M. Blakemore Evans, *The Passion Play of Lucerne.*)

c. Two stage plans—for the first and the second days of the performance respectively—sketched by Cysat (reproduced by Nagler, pp. 30–31), both executed in exceptional detail. Moreover, the place of performance, the Weinmarkt of Lucerne, remains much as it appeared in the sixteenth century. Text, place, stage plans, director's notes—the theatre historian could scarcely hope for more.

## Some Questionable Documents of Production

It is clear that some documents or accounts that purport to pertain to a particular production, or to performances at a specific place within a limited time span, can be included among documents of production only in circumstances in which their connection with the performance is clear and where the connection itself attests to the probable accuracy of the evidence. The histories of Chaumeau and Outreman are examples, as are Cailleau's miniatures. Other documents, including some pictorial monuments, are more doubtfully characterized as production documents, and the evidence they present must be verified from independent sources. Nevertheless, such evidence has occasionally been accorded the weight of a production document. In particular, the following have been so treated: (*a*) two seventeenth-century English accounts that have served as the basis for our conception of a typical English pageant wagon (*b*) another seventeenth-century document and a mid-fifteenth-century miniature which together provide the evidence for the presence of the Ordinary or pageant-master on stage during the actual performance of a play (*c*) a series of carvings in the choir-stalls at St. Stephen's Cathedral in Vienna, which are sometimes cited as evidence for the setting of the Viennese Passion play, performed between 1505 and 1512 and (*d*) an eye-witness account of a performance of the English morality play, *The Cradle of Security*.

Sir William Dugdale, in *Antiquities of Warwickshire* (1656), refers to the staging of plays at Coventry, and on the basis of reports "by some old people, who in their younger years were eyewitnesses of these *Pageants* so acted," he records that the producers of the cycle "had Theaters for the several Scenes, very large and high, placed upon wheels." An earlier account of pageant wagons used at Chester, in David Rogers' *Breviary* (1609–23), has been even more influential. It has been generally accepted as the principal source for the reconstruction of an English pageant wagon. The breviarye exists in five manuscripts, which agree on the following points: (*a*) that a pageant was a high scaffold with two rooms, a higher and a lower; (*b*) that the lower room was a tiring-room for the actors; and (*c*) that the upper room, "being all open at the top," was where the actors played. On the other hand, the manuscripts differ on the number of wheels on which the pageant was set: Two copies indicate six wheels and three copies indicate four. Nevertheless, Thomas Sharp, in *A Dissertation on the Pageants or Dramatic Mysteries Anciently Performed at Coventry* (1825), based his pictorial representation of an English pageant wagon on Rogers' and Dugdale's descriptions, and his relatively modest, four-wheeled car has constituted the popular conception of a pageant wagon ever since.

Rogers' reliability has been challenged on various practical grounds concerning the necessary size, structure, and maneuverability of the wagon as determined by the demands of the Chester plays. But a comparison with available guild accounts tends to support Rogers, at least insofar as it does not demonstrate that he was wrong. The point, however, is this. Regardless of the accuracy or inaccuracy of Dugdale's and Rogers' accounts, their authority does not derive from the date and nature of the documents themselves, as it would for true documents of production. Neither are eye-witness accounts, and their testimony is too far removed from the events and performances they purport to describe for them to be treated as independent sources.

The evidence for the presence of a director-prompter among the actors of a play consists of a fifteenth-century miniature by Jean Fouquet depicting the martyrdom of Saint Apollonia, and an anecdote preserved in Richard Carew's *Survey of Cornwell* (1602). Fouquet's miniature has usually been taken as representing a theatrical production of a play on the subject of Saint Apollonia, and a figure carrying a book and staff on the "stage" has been regarded as depicting the *régisseur*. On the face of it, the theatricality of the painting is inescapable, although the lack of any text of the play with which to compare it makes it impossible to reconstruct a performance in any detail. On the other hand, it has been pointed out that the miniature was painted between 1452 and 1460 as part of a collection of miniatures for the *Book of Hours* of Etienne Chevalier, preserved in the Musée Condé de Chantilly, and that it is the only one of the scenes executed by Fouquet that is placed in a theatrical context. The question of why only this picture is theatrical is but one of the many problems that arise when scholars undertake the analysis of this unique and much-reproduced painting. And among the more perplexing difficulties is what to make of the *régisseur*-figure. The only other evidence to suggest his role is provided by Carew, whose account is very late and whom all historians of the theatre caution must be treated with a degree of scepticism. But the unlikeliness of the arrangement has not prevented a constant reference to the miniature—which is admittedly impressive even if problematic—and a consequent dignifying of Carew's *Survey*.

One further instance of a work of art as a possible production document needs mentioning. Among the true documents of production we have the account-books of the Brotherhood of the Body of the Lord, which was responsible for the production of the Passion play at Vienna between 1505 and 1512. The accounts are particularly helpful regarding costumes and properties, but little else. However, one of the two men in charge of the Brotherhood, Wilhelm Rollinger (the other was Matheus Heuberger), was a woodcarver when he was not directing the Corpus Christi procession and theatricals, and he participated in the carving of forty-six biblical scenes on the choir-stalls of St. Stephen's Cathedral between 1476 and 1486–87. The facts that the carved scenes of Christ's Passion coincide with scenes from the play (so far as it has been possible to determine it from the accounts) and that one of the carvers was also a director of the play has led to speculation that carvings and stage presentations were of a piece. Nagler is more cautious, pointing out that in actuality the carvings can tell us less about the costumes than do the accounts. And he sounds the theoretical note of skepticism we have heard before: "At the New Market, Rollinger was the Regierer; in his workshop he was a pictorial artist" (*The Medieval Religious Stage*, p. 102). Unfortunately, the student who wishes to look at the carvings must now be contented with photographs (reproduced in Paul Stix, *Die Wiener Passion*): The choir stalls were destroyed by fire in April 1945.

Finally, we have in Ralph Willis' *Mount Tabor* (1639) an account of the author's witnessing as a young boy in the city of Gloucester a performance of *The Cradle of Security*. Willis notes that he stood between his seated father's legs, and it is therefore clear that he was of relatively tender years at the time. In 1639 Willis was seventy-five years of age; therefore, the date of the performance was about 1570. What is noteworthy about the description is the obviously *non*-abstract nature of the characters as perceived by a small boy. "This sight took such impression on me," writes Willis, "that, when I came towards mans estate, it was as fresh in my memory as if I had seen it newly acted." We cannot make ourselves contemporary with performances of long ago—even Willis could not return to his childhood—but his recorded memory is precious testimony to the common experience that can humanize the historian's reconstruction of the past. (Willis' account is printed in F. P. Wilson, *The English Drama 1485–1585,* pp. 76–77.)

## PLACES OF PERFORMANCE

Medieval plays were performed in a variety of places, indoors annd out. Few of the locations were intended to be used exclusively as theatres, and even fewer have survived intact to be examined in their original state. Moreover, the "stage" and "settings" were equally variable and more often than not temporary as well. We simply do not have the physical remains of medieval theatres. But the places of performance of many plays can be determined, in some instances very specifically; and time and humankind have had a maximum of 1000 years to destroy city squares and churches, as opposed to the two and one-half millenia between ourselves and fifth-century Athens. It is possible, therefore, for theatre historians to come to at least as accurate a knowledge of medieval "theatres" as they have of classical theatres.

We can derive information of a general nature by surveying the towns and cities where plays are known to have been performed. We can examine streets and town squares, buildings and courtyards that we know to have survived the centuries, in order to construct a generalized picture of the physical environment of the medieval world. We can examine still extant guild-halls, banqueting-halls, church interiors, and monasteries in order to gain some idea of the possibilities of an indoor performance. And, of course, in some specific instances we are fortunate enough to be able to pinpoint the precise location of a particular performance, while in others we are able to determine that a given location was used as an acting place. When knowledge of and the continued existence of a location coincide, we may count ourselves doubly fortunate. But while accounts may tell us the place and ancient maps sometimes portray or indicate it, and while a few plans may suggest how the place was used as a theatre, the actual physical evidence for specific medieval theatrical structures is very limited.

Many of the churches, which figure so prominently in the history of medieval theatrical presentation, have either been destroyed or so altered that it is impossible to reconstruct their interiors in exact detail. St. Martial at Limoges was destroyed in the eighteenth century, Beauvais Cathedral Choir in 1225, and the cathedral at Rouen in 1200. In fact, of the churches known to have been the settings for performances of liturgical plays, only two, at Padua and at Cividale in Italy, remain architecturally intact. Also, the two churches in Florence where Bishop Abraham of Souzdal witnessed performances in 1439 still exist. But even a general knowledge of Romanesque church architecture is important for an understanding of medieval staging practice. For as O. B. Hardison both puts the question and answers it:

Should the nave, chancel, presbyterium, and altar of the church be considered a stage, and its windows, statues, images, and ornaments a ''setting''? As long as there is clear recognition that these elements are hallowed, that they are the sacred phase of parallel elements turned to secular use on the profane stage, it is possible to answer yes. [*Christian Rite and Christian Drama*, p. 79]

The ambience of a theatrical experience originally conditioned by an all-encompassing religious context was not likely to have been completely abandoned simply because the church building itself ceased to be the normal locale for the performance of religious plays. The principles of dramaturgy, the patterns of symbolism, the habits of conceptualization, and the techniques of emblematic representation, devised and perfected within the church building—these continued to inform the theatre during the Middle Ages and into the Renaissance as well.

The remains of Roman amphitheatres were also utilized for the performance of medieval plays, as we have seen in the case of Bourges. True archaeological data can therefore be of some use in these instances, provided it is possible to determine the state of preservation at a relatively specific date between the thirteenth and sixteenth centuries. Similar techniques and reservations are applicable in Cornwall, where earthen rounds evidently served as substitutes for ancient amphitheatres. The only surviving example is the Piran Round near Perranporth, although there is some doubt as to its use as a theatre in the medieval period. William Borlase provides the earliest description of the round in his *Natural History of Cornwall* (1758). In an earlier book, *Observations on the Antiquities Historical and Monumental of Cornwall* (1754), the same author describes a similar round near the church of St. Just-in-Penwith. Borlase's descriptions would suggest that these rounds were of a good size, nearly forty meters in diameter and with banks two to three meters high; six or seven tiers of seats were available for spectators.

All in all, we are able to get a very good idea of the kinds of locations and settings commonly employed for the performance of the medieval drama. But since staging arrangements normally depended upon temporary structures, a knowledge of a location can do more to indicate what was possible or impossible than to suggest a positive visual definition of the playing area. So far as open-air theatre is concerned, William Tydeman, in *The Theatre in the Middle Ages* (1978), deduces five general principles of staging (pp. 141ff.): (1) that, whenever possible, a preexisting location was used, preferably enclosed or at least well-defined; (2) that the shape of the playing area was circular, square, or rectilinear, with the audience accommodated on at least two sides, and more often all around; (3) that the playing area was normally large; (4) that the use of mansions, under whatever names, constituted the fundamental staging principle; and (5) that the most common arrangement of mansions is that found at Lucerne in 1583.

Other scholars have attempted to be more specific, and in the process usually more schematic. In *Histoire de la mise en scène,* Cohen, basing his argument principally on Cailleau's miniatures, developed the most widely accepted idea of the *décor simultané,* and envisaged mansions in a line. The shape of the line might vary, but the principle remained constant. Certainly the concept is superior to the bizzare notion, promulgated in the eighteenth century by les frères Parfaict, that the stage emblems are arranged *vertically.* More recently, in *Le Cercle magique* (1973), Henri Rey-Flaud, basing his contention on Fouquet's miniature of Saint Apollonia, has argued for a theatre-in-the-round as the usual method for performing late medieval plays, at least on the Continent. And in *L'Espace théâtral médiéval* (1975), Elie Konigson postulates that the governing architectural line in the presentation of the liturgical drama was an east-west axis with hell or Galilee in the west, castle, town, or palace in the centre, and heaven, temple, or manger in the east. He goes on to theorize that the same principle informed performances outside the church as well. The town square was considered the centre of the east-west axis and the mansions arranged accordingly. Where the playing area was circular, this same axis determined the arrangement of the sets. Such theories concerning staging practices are clearly dependent upon more than the physical remains of known playing areas, but they do help us to envisage the possible uses to which those areas could be put.

## WRITTEN RECORDS

Given the close relationship between the Christian religion and the bulk of the medieval drama, the Church's attitude towards the theatre from the fall of Rome to the end of the sixteenth century is obviously of some importance. Theatre historians, therefore, have dutifully combed through the proceedings of Councils and Synods and the writings of a multitude of theologians and religious scholars in an effort to determine that attitude and to trace any changes it may have undergone. Moreover, the drama sponsored and supervised by religious authorities themselves has prompted historians to examine monastic and cathedral records and accounts with an equal zeal, in an attempt to gather information about the performance and the dissemination of the religious drama.

As we saw when dealing with the Roman theatre, the records of the early Church Councils and the writings of the Church Fathers indicate in general a strong antipathy to the theatrical performances of the late Empire. The evidence

is more difficult to interpret for the period between the cessation of Roman theatricals in the fifth century A.D. and the beginnings of the liturgical drama in
the tenth century. It is not clear, for example, that Churchmen always knew
what they were writing about. Isidore of Seville (ca. 560–636) is his *Etymologiae* seemingly provides a storehouse of knowledge and lore on a multitude
of subjects, including the theatre. But there is little indication that any of his.
etymologically—often fancifully—derived definitions of such terms as *theatro,
scena,* and *orchestra* are based on anything more than his reading—and misunderstanding—of earlier commentators like Tertullian. But while it might be argued that Isidore's ignorance is based on the non-existence of things theatrical
during the so-called Dark Ages, we must be cautious of leaping to this conclusion as well. There are continuous references during the period from about 550
to 950 to *mimi, scurrae,* and *histriones.* The canons established by the Concil-
ium Trullanum of 692, one of the most important of the early Church Councils,
leave little doubt that mimes were flourishing, and they imply by their number
and vehemence that prohibitions were having disconcertingly little effect. (See
Mensi, *Sacrorum Conciliorum,* XI, 943–975.) And the sometimes close association of the clergy itself with the theatre is attested by Photius, Patriarch of
Constantinople, who in the ninth century pronounced a three-year pen-
ance on any priest who attended theatrical spectacles. Moreover, Allardyce
Nicoll in *Masks, Mimes, and Miracles* (p. 145) points out that while Isidore
describes the stage and theatre architecture in the past tense, he uses the present
tense in his references to *mimes* and *histriones,* thereby indicating a first-hand
acquaintance with these ubiquitous performers.

It seems, too, that in order to interpret this continuing Christian commentary
accurately, we should recognize not only that Churchmen distinguished between the "regular" Roman theatre and that represented by the *mimes* and *histriones* and *joculatores,* but that they made a similar distinction between popular, often sacriligious and scurrilous, entertainment and the Christian drama
performed as an act of worship or instruction to the faithful. In no other way
is it possible to reconcile over 500 years of Christian theatre with the never-
ending hostility expressed by many members of the clergy towards theatrical
performers. In a passage from an early fourteenth-century *Penitential* (printed
in Chambers, *Mediaeval Stage,* II, 262–63), we find the author, Thomas de
Cabham, Bishop of Salisbury, distinguishing three types of *histriones* according to the kind of entertainment they provide. All three are equally damned.
But Cabham does note that *joculatores* sing of the deeds of heroes and saints,
and bring comfort to men. It was the disreputable performances and reputations
of these secular entertainers that seem to have bothered Church authorities, and
they consequently offer repeated warnings, not against dramatic performances
*per se,* but against patterning those performances after the indecent manner of
the *mimes.* This seems to be the gist of St. Ailred's accusation in *Speculum
Caritatis* (1142–43) that English clerics were using unseemly theatrical gestures, and of a letter of March 12, 1445, from the Faculty of Theology at the

University of Paris to the bishops of France, complaining of the behavior of priests and monks during the Feast of Fools, a ribald New Year's celebration held by the lower clergy in cathedrals and collegiate schools. (See Chambers, *Mediaeval Stage*, I, 294.)

The popular conception of the Church as the implacable enemy of the theatre is in fact erroneous. As Gardiner pointed out in 1946 in *Mysteries' End*, it is necessary to specify which "Church" is being referred to whenever generalizations concerning the relationship between religious authorities and the theatre are attempted. Passion plays and mystery cycles may have come under attack by Christian clerics in the sixteenth century, but these were after all *Catholic* dramas being condemned by *Protestant* clergy. And even before the Reformation proper, the ostensibly universal Catholic Church was not united in its attitude towards the theatre. Anti-establishment movements like that of the Lollards in the fourteenth century attacked the theatre and in a sense forced Church authorities into defending it. A collection of Lollard tracts in the British Library (Add. MS. 24202) includes *A Tretise of Miraclis Pleyinge* which, in condemning the practice, provides a summary of the Church's counter-arguments in favour of the theatre as well. (*A Tretise of Miraclis Pleyinqe* is printed in *Selections from English Wycliffite Writings*, ed. Anne Hudson, pp. 97–104.) Indeed, the picture of the Church as the villain of theatre history derives—for English speakers at least—from a work by a man who made no distinctions of purpose or context in attributing a constant anti-theatre viewpoint to Christianity in general. The Puritan William Prynne in 1633 published his *Histriomastix*, a massive collection of anti-theatrical Christian sentiment that has served too well as a starting point for considerations of Church-theatre relations. Prynne was, after all, only interested in negative commentary. Historians cannot afford such partisan luxury.

Archival material from cathedrals, churches, and monasteries is also relevant to the drama: It is in breviaries, ordinalia, tropers, and the like where we are most likely to find liturgical play texts and descriptions of ceremonies. To these we can add occasional account books, capitular statutes, and sacristans' manuals. Sometimes a document of supreme significance, such as the *Concordia Regularis*, comes to light. At other times theatre historians have found that some preliminary work has already been done. A seventeenth-century manuscript in the archives of the Church of Nuestra Señora de Pilar in Zaragoza in Spain, for instance, contains all the ceremonials of several Spanish cathedrals. While it seems likely that much of this archival material—especially in Spain—is still awaiting systematic investigation, there is no guarantee that its sacred depository has ensured or will ensure its survival. We have noted on several occasions the destruction in this century of evidence that had otherwise weathered the chaos of centuries. One more example may be cited here. In 1872 Ernesto Monaci published in *Rivista di Filologia Romanza* (I, 257–260) some partially edited inventories of theatrical furnishings possessed by the Confraternity of St. Dominic in Perugia, Italy. It is fortunate that he did so, for the inventories themselves were destroyed near the end of World War II in an anti-Fascist uprising.

Long among the chief depositories of material useful to the theatre historian have been the municipal libraries, archives, and town halls of the centres where medieval plays were performed, and the records and accounts of the various organizations (guilds, *confréries*, and so on) charged with arranging performances. In England, one of the earliest investigators of such records was the antiquarian Thomas Sharp, who made full use of ancient books and documents belonging to the Corporation of Coventry, together with the remaining account books of the trading companies and guilds. Sharp published a great deal of this "hitherto unexplored" source material in 1825 in his *Dissertation*—again a very fortuitous circumstance, for the collection of Coventry manuscripts that he used was destroyed in a fire at the Birmingham Free Reference Library in 1879. Of the original documents consulted by Sharp, only the Coventry *Leet Book* still survives (Coventry Corporation MS. A.3). A few years later R. Davies published *Extracts from the Municipal Records of the City of York* (1843). And in 1903 E. K. Chambers presented what was for many years the standard survey of such records for England in Appendix W of *The Mediaeval Stage*.

On the Continent, a beginning was made in Spain with M. Carboneres' *Relación y explicatión histórico de la solemne procesión del Corpus* (1873). Carboneres prints expense accounts from the first decade of the fifteenth century, which provide some insight into the Corpus Christi procession of Valencia. In France, the process of collecting and publishing such records, begun by G.A.J. Hécart in 1816, was undertaken on a systematic basis by Petit de Julleville in the 1880s. He speculated how much more information lay buried in as yet unexplored archives, and he expressed the hopeful expectation that in time new information would be added to the historian's storehouse (*Mystères*, II, 1–2). His hope was at least partially fulfilled in the patient researches of Gustave Cohen.

Nevertheless, many years passed without the publication of new collections of archival documents. In 1961, writing of the English medieval stage, Arnold Williams noted that, outside the texts, everything we know about the plays comes from the town and guild records of York, Chester, Coventry, Beverley, and Norwich (*The Drama of Medieval England*, p. 91). But scholars were busily at work even as Williams wrote. In 1965 appeared Giles E. Dawson's *Records of Plays and Players in Kent 1450–1642*, and in 1974 Stanley J. Kahrl's *Records of Plays and Players in Lincolnshire 1300–1585*.

By far the most ambitious project in this regard, however, is being undertaken at the University of Toronto, where the first volumes of *Records of Early English Drama* were published in 1978. The stated aim of the project "is to locate, transcribe, and publish systematically all surviving external evidence of dramatic, ceremonial, and minstrel activity in Great Britain before 1642" (Newsletter, 1976: 1, p. 1). The estimated fifty volumes—the first three of which, containing the York and Chester records, have already appeared—will clearly be devoted to more than the handful of places mentioned by Williams. In fact, work on at least twenty additional cities and counties is in progress at one stage or another, and editors continue to be recruited for yet-unexplored areas. The records involved are shared among six jurisdictions: (1) crown, (2) county, (3) town, (4) parish, (5) ecclesiastical and monastic, and (6) private, including that of academic and guild organizations. And the records themselves are classified into four types: (1) Legal Documents (deeds, contracts, leases, statutes, wills, etc.), (2) Administrative or Ministerial Proceedings (accounts, books of procedure, inventories, minutes, registers, etc.), (3) Judicial Proceedings (court rolls, minutes, pleas, sessions, etc.), (4) Miscellaneous Records (broadsheets, diaries, letters, chronicles, etc.). The historian who systematically consults, collects, and categorizes in such a way is unlikely to overlook much. The way and the extent to which this information will affect the writing of theatre history is yet to be seen.

The difficulties associated with the interpretation of theatrical references in medieval documents can be illustrated by a controversy that flared briefly in the mid–1940s concerning the question of "theatres" in the twelfth century. In an article in *Speculum* in 1945, R. S. Loomis cited nine passages from seven authors, dating between 1126 and 1236, "which disclose familiarity with the word *theatrum* and its derivatives and with something called *ludi scenici*" (XX, 95). Gustave Cohen, in a commentary appended to the article, cautiously noted the possibility that these references are evidence of classical scholarship rather than of familiarity with contemporary theatres, but opined that "it seems sound and conservative" to infer that the state of theatrical affairs in the thirteenth century was already much as it was in the fifteenth: that is, there may not have existed any permanent theatre, "but there were some play-houses in the form of a circus, often in the ruins of a Roman amphitheatre" (p. 98). The Loomis-Cohen thesis was challenged the following year by Dino Bigongiari in *Romantic Review*. Bigongiari pointed to two faulty premises on which the argument was based: (1) that the persistence of specific words implies a survival of the things referred to and (2) that literary texts faithfully reflect contemporary conditions. He went on to chastise Loomis and Cohen for failing "to distinguish between what is obviously rhetorical, moralizing or encyclopedic antiquarianism and what is genuinely representative of contemporary conditions" (XXXVII, 201). His conclusion is, or ought to be, a commonplace, but given the predilection of scholars to "make something" of the evidence they find, it is worth repeating. "It seems . . .," wrote Bigongiari, "as though the utilization of a text from a medieval author becomes valid for historical purposes only after the history of the passage and the value of its terms are known" (pp. 223–224).

## THE EXTRA-LITERARY DIMENSION

When we turn to the more formal accounts of historians and chroniclers, we find our attention shifted from the streets to the courts of Europe, from townspeople and the clergy to the aristocracy and the nobility. Occasionally, it is true, the performances referred to are religious in nature. The chronicle of Miguel Lucas de Iranzo, Constable of Castile (printed in *Memorial histórico espa-ñol*, VIII, 75–76), contains evidence of religious entertainments of some sort being performed in the houses of the nobility in 1461–62. But more often chroniclers and historians virtually ignore the religious drama that provides the bulk of the dramatic literature from the period; and they thereby offer indirect testimony concerning its socio-economic context. Trade and religious guilds, city governments, and bourgeois merchants—these were responsible for the Passion plays, the mysteries, the cycles, the early moralities. And professional and semi-professional actors were similarly responsible for the farces and moral interludes of the late fifteenth and the sixteenth centuries. Historians had other interests: the lives and activities of court and nobility, affairs of state, national and international relations. When we turn to their narratives for information concerning the theatre, therefore, we find that the performances described are for the most part of a different order from what we have hitherto been examining—and we are led into a world of mumming, disguising, and masking; of processions, tournaments, and entries; of banquets, weddings, and coronations. The task of the theatre historian becomes one of integrating these disparate data, together with those derived from the examination of the religious and secular drama, into a coherent picture of the kinds of performance in the Middle Ages that qualify as theatrical.

Information about royal entries, civic pageantry, tournaments, mummings, disguisings, dances, and masques is derived from many different sources: chroniclers and historians, royal statutes and accounts, civic records, official descriptions, occasional letters—a miscellaneous array of records both public and private, published and unpublished. Too rarely, however, at least until relatively recently, have theatre historians concerned themselves with this material. Chambers devoted almost one-half of *The Mediaeval Stage* to the folk-drama, but all but ignored the public ceremonials and aristocratic private pastimes and entertainments that flourished simultaneously with the religious theatre that was his main concern. And most later studies, including the volumes of *Les Fêtes de la Renaissance*, published by the Centre National de la Recherche Scientifique (1956–75), are more concerned with Renaissance than with medieval pageantry. Between 1918 and 1926, Robert Withington published his *English Pageantry*, still the most useful survey of the subject. But his conclusions concerning the possible relationship between pageantry and the more literary miracle-plays are disconcertingly modest: "It is true that these performances [of miracle-plays] would be pageants, were they not something more, but they must be considered dramatic productions—given, if you will, under pageantic conditions" (II, 297). With this we may compare Wickham's assertion, over a quarter of a century later, in *Early English Stages*, that such "pageantic" forms as tournaments "supply the theatre historian with information that concerns not only medieval dramatic spectacle and auditoriums but also a secular dramatic form, however rudimentary, which deserves consideration alongside the literary Miracle Plays of the period" (I, 50). What theatre historians are now trying to do is to discover the principles underlying all medieval performance, be it religious or secular, verbal or non-verbal, and on the basis of constant comparison and cross-reference, to reconstruct a coherent and satisfying picture of the medieval theatre, distorted as little as possible by modern preference and preconception. An important dimension of the performance of *The Castle of Perseverance* is lost, for example, if we do not recognize, as a medieval audience undoubtedly would, that the assault on the castle is based on the *pas d'armes*, a form of tournament in which a restricted passage is defended by one or more champions against all comers.

The word "tournament" incorporates a range of quasi-military pastimes: mock-battles between groups of men; the *joust*, which was called a *tilt* if the combat was between mounted men armed with lances, or *barriers* if fought on foot with swords; and the *pas d'armes*, the most elaborate and spectacular of medieval tournaments, and the one most nearly approaching the status of artistic entertainment.

Tournaments were closely associated with ideals of chivalry, of social and military conduct, and their proper form is documented from several sources. A full account of early tournaments, for instance, is provided in *L'Histoire de Guillaume le Maréchal* (ca. 1220 ; ed., Paul Meyer, 1891–1901) and by Jacques Bretex in *Les Tournois de Chauvenci* (1285; printed 1895). In England the *Statuta Armorum* (British Museum MS. Rawlinson 277; printed 1810) regulated tournaments. In France, René d'Anjou, father-in-law of Henry VI, was the author of a textbook on the conduct of tournaments, *Le Livre des tournois* (Bibliothèque Nationale, MS. fr. 2692; a printed edition was published in 1946). A late description of tournament procedures is provided by A. Favyn in *A Theatre of Honour and Knighthood* (1623). Other information is available in collections in the Bibliothèque National (fr. 1436, 21809), the British Museum (Cotton Titus C.l; Harleian 293; Lansdowne 285), and the College of Arms in London (1st M. 6, 16). (Some of the important documents are included as Appendices in F. H. Cripps-Day, *The History of the Tournament*.)

Of particular interest are the descriptions of *pas d'armes* that are specific as to time, place, and participants. Among the most thoroughly documented are the following:

1. The *Pas de la Bergière* (1449), organized by René d'Anjou at Tarascon in Provence and described by Loys de Beauvau, Seneschal d'Anjou. The description has been printed by T. Comte de Quatrebarbes in *Oeuvres Complètes du Roi René* (1845).

2. The *Pas d'Armes de la Sauvaige Dame* (1469), performed at Ghent and described by Olivier de la Marche. The manuscripts, in the Bibliothèque de Valenciennes, have been edited by B. Prost in *Traités du Duel Judiciaire* (1872).

3. A *pas d'armes* at the English court in 1524 is fully described in Edward Hall's *Union of the Noble and Illustrious Chonicle Families*, (1548). There also exists in the College of Arms a pen drawing of the emblematic castle constructed for the occasion (MS. M.6. 57b).

Based on these descriptions and others, Glynne Wickham offers a synoptic description of the conventional formula adhered to by the *pas d'armes* in the fifteenth century:

A lady or ladies commission a favoured knight or knights to serve them. This fact is elaborated into a mimed heroic drama. The knight invents a reason to explain his presence in the lists on behalf of the lady. This usually takes the form of an allegory built round the knight and the lady who, together with their servants, assume the dress appropriate to the character in the allegory whom each represents and set it in action against a suitable setting. [*Early English Stages*, I, 25]

Wordless they may have been, but there is no doubt that these *pas d'armes* were mimetic performances.

Records and descriptions of various kinds of civic pageantry, usually processional and usually involving noble personages, are also valuable in coming to an estimation of the extent of theatrical activity in the Middle Ages. Wickham provides a selected list of such street pageants in London, Paris, and Saragosa between 1207 and 1445, the descriptions of which indicate a growing use of scenic and stage properties and devices (*Early English Stages*, I, Appendix E). Documentary evidence concerning Spanish festivals and entries is collected in J. Alenda y Mira's *Relaciones de solemnidades* (1903); and texts and documents from France in *Les Entrées royales françaises de 1328 à 1515* by B. Guénée and F. Lehoux (1968). A complete list of English pageants is provided by Withington in the first volume of *English Pageantry*. These pageants concerned celebrated events of national or international significance: a royal wedding, a military victory, the visit of a king or a foreign dignitary, a coronation. And such events were not only cause for celebration, they were cause for the celebrations to be recorded for posterity.

The sources of information for such events, besides the usual official and archival material, are often chroniclers and historians. One of our chief authorities for English history of the fourteenth century is Thomas Walsingham (d. 1422?), who describes in his *Historia Anglicana* the pageant and the emblematic castle constructed for the coronation of Richard II in 1377 (quoted and translated by Wickham in *Early English Stages*, I, 54–55). Other sources include the thirteenth-century chroniclers Matthew Westminster and Matthew Paris, whose histories were published and used by John Stow in the sixteenth century. Stow (1525?–1605) was an indefatigable chronicler and antiquary: his *Survey of London* (1598) is particularly useful in its detailing of city customs. Edward Hall's *Union of the Two Noble and Illustrate Families of Lancaster and York* (1548) provides a considerable amount of information on court pageantry, especially for the period after 1529, when Hall became an eye-witness to the events he describes. For French history between 1325 and 1444 we are indebted to Jean Froissart (ca. 1337–ca. 1410), possibly the most famous of medieval chroniclers, and his successor, Enguerrand de Monstrelet (d. 1453). Froissart,

for example, describes the entry of Isabella of Bavaria into Paris in August 1389;
and Monstrelet does the same for Henry VI's French coronation in 1431.

Some other, not so obvious, sources include poems by Richard Maydiston
on Richard II's entry into London in 1392 (Bodleian MS. E. Museo, 94; printed
and translated by Wickham, I, 64–70), and by John Lydgate on Henry VI's
entry into London in 1432 (printed in *Minor Poems*, II, 643–44).

Medieval pageantry and mimetic entertainment were, of course, not confined
to the lists and the streets. Courtly entertainments—variously referred to as disguisings, mummings, *entrements*, or *maschere*—appear to have been a constant
feature of aristocratic life throughout Europe. Our sources of information are
basically the same as they were for civic pageantry: historians and chroniclers,
and in some instances accounts and records of the preparations and the performance, including official or semi-official histories by the attendant-heralds.
Froissart's eye for surface detail makes his *Chronicle* particularly useful. He
records, for example, that at a banquet given by Edward III in 1364 "the young
Lord de Couci danced and sang splendidly when his turn came" (quoted by
Tydeman, *Theatre in the Middle Ages*, p. 76)—an early indication of the tendency of the nobility to participate themselves in their entertainments. Froissart
is responsible too for our information concerning the notorious entertainment in
1393 at the wedding of Charles VI of France, at which four young men burned
to death when their wax-laden costumes caught fire. And he records another
spectacle in 1389, which included among its stage properties a pavilion, a ship,
and a castle representing Troy. He describes a celebration of 1378, in honour
of the Emperor Charles IV's visit to his nephew Charles V of France, depicting
Geoffrey of Boulogne's conquest of Jerusalem. The entertainment was devised
by Phillippe de Mézières, the author of a Latin religious play and *L'Histoire de
Griseldis*. Another description of this *entrement* is contained in the manuscript
*Chronique de Charles V* in the Bibliothèque Nationale (fr. 2813), a great illustrated volume dating between 1375 and 1379. (The manuscript has been edited
by R. Delachenal in *Les Grandes Chroniques de France* II, 234–244.)

In England, John Stow's *Survey of London* contains a description of a mumming before Richard II at Christmas 1377; and Hall's *Chronicle* records that,
in 1512, "on the daie of the Epiphanie at night, the Kyng with a xi. other were
disguised, after the manner of Italie, called a maske, a thyng not seen afore in
Englande . . ." (p. 526). Although the use of a text is occasionally implied in
some of the accounts of such celebrations, we actually possess what seem to
be the texts of mummings or disguises from the early years of the fifteenth century. Between 1427 and 1435, John Lydgate wrote a series of seven poems,
labelled by their author variously as "A Mumming," "A Ballad for a Mumming," "A Disguising," "A Ballad in wyse of Mummers Disguised." Evidently, the "performance" normally consisted of the entrance of a "Herald"
with a "letter" containing a poem, and the reading of the poem to the audience
as disguised mummers mimed the action specified in the verse. Because these
texts have come down to us, we are perhaps inclined in retrospect to credit

Lydgate with a breakthrough in dramaturgy that may not have been apparent to his contemporaries. Without detracting from his ingenuity, it is wise to remember the context within which he fashioned his little entertainments. As Wickham reminds us,

The nucleus which Lydgate seized upon was the mumming. Borrowing allegories from romance and scriptural sources, he gave this folk-custom, involving disguise of the person, a literary frame. From the Miracle Plays and Street Pageants he borrowed the idea of speaking actors, if he did not have them closer to hand among the minstrels already. From the Tournament he borrowed the Herald to present his characters and to explain their significance. [*Early English Stages*, I, 207]

The study of this non-literary theatre, then, can cast considerable light on productions such as Lydgate's "mummings." But more important, it provides theatre historians with a more broadly based conception of the expectations of a medieval audience. It focusses attention on the spectacular dimension of performance that that audience obviously approved. It indicates the reciprocating relationship between religious and secular pageantry, between the allegorical characters of the moralities and those of the street theatre. But above all, the study of tournaments and entries and *entremets* aids in fashioning a key to the symbolic and allegorical significance of the visual iconography of colour and costume and scenic device that was as much a part of dramatic presentation as it was of heraldry. What is essential for an appreciation of the non-literary theatre can enrich immeasurably our appreciation of the literary drama. Indeed, it might be argued that it is the visual aspect of the medieval theatre, not the texts, that rewards repeated study.

## FOLK-DRAMA

One further non-literary theatrical form remains to be considered: the drama of the folk. Histories and chronicles from late Roman and early medieval times provide us with information regarding pagan and Celtic dramatic rituals and attendant folk-drama and dance. Tacitus in the *Germania* (XXIV) notes that the only public show among the German tribes was a form of sword-dance. From the Venerable Bede's *History of the English Church and People* (ca. 731) we learn of the pagan beliefs and customs that continued even after the conversion of England to Christianity. In the late twelfth century Giraldus Cambrensis (Gerald of Wales) comments in *Gemma Ecclesiastica* and *Itinerarium Cambriae* on the performances in Wales of processional dance-songs; and it is recorded a hundred years later in *The Chronicle of Lanercost* that even priests occasionally joined the wanton dancing. Finally, a late account, Olaus Magnus' *Historia de Gentibus septentrionalibus* (1555), describes how the Goths and Swedes still continued the sword-dancing noted by Tacitus, but confined the performance to Shrovetide, "the time of masking." (Chambers collects and discusses this material in *The Mediaeval Stage*.) These accounts, together with clerical denun-ciations of such pagan activities as those described, texts of mummers' plays collected and written down in the eighteenth and nineteenth centuries, and var-ious survivals of May-day festivals, folk-ceremonies, and processional song-dances throughout Europe, constitute our main source of information about the medieval folk-theatre.

The interpretation of the material we have is still heavily indebted to anthro-pological theory, particularly that expounded by the Cambridge anthropologists during the early years of this century. Indeed, William Tydeman in *The Theatre in the Middle Ages* (pp. 1–21) not only quotes both Murray and Gaster but offers, in a mind-boggling juxtaposition reminiscent of the earlier origin-seek-ers, references to pre-historic art, the activities of Australian aborigines, ancient Aztec ceremonials, the Horn Dance from Staffordshire, and a Basque carnival contest. And however influenced by game theory and ideas of mimetic perfor-mance, Tydeman understands the various performances as expressions of a uni-versal vegetation-myth, linked to seasonal rhythms and designed to guarantee fertility and new life. A similar point of view is expressed by Glynne Wick-ham, who in addition suggests an explanation for the incorporation of pagan ritual into Christian worship. He finds the common source of all ancient reli-gious customs in the climate, in the seasons, in food and survival—in energy:

Loss of energy terminating in death, and the renewal of energy culminating in procrea-tion, provided the constants and the polarities linking the old religious beliefs of suc-cessive generations and cults with those of the Christian fathers who themselves preached life eternal beyond the grave in the person of the risen Christ. [*The Medieval Theatre*, p. 126]

Whether or not we are prepared to accept this interpretation of the folk-drama, or this explanation for the linking of pagan and Christian religious practices and beliefs, the fact remains that the evidence attests to the survival of older beliefs and rituals and ceremonies into the Middle Ages, and as Tydeman argues, "any account of medieval stage conditions must acknowledge the presence of . . . traditional ceremonies, stemming from primitive pagan rites, and never quite assimilated or extinguished by Church or State" (p. 21).

## ART AND THEATRE

We have had occasion to refer to several examples of art as possible evi-dence for theatre history. Those miniatures executed as manuscript illumina-tions have been of particular interest to theatre historians, although only Cail-leau's illustrations for the 1547 performance at Valenciennes have qualified as production documents. Fouquet's miniature depicting the martyrdom of Saint Apollonia and Rollinger's choir-stall carvings have similarly been noted. We may add to these illustrations of a procession of biblical tableaux at Louvain in

1594, and a painted panel by Daniel van Alsloot, now in the Victoria and Albert Museum in London, commemorating the entry of Archduchess Isabella into Brussels in 1615, featuring pageant-cars. (The pictures are reproduced in Edward van Even's *L'Omgang de Louvain* and Leo van Puyvelde's *L'Ommegang de 1615 à Bruxelles* respectively.) There also exist three engravings in *De Amphitheatro liber*, editions of which appeared in 1584, 1598, and 1604, that ostensibly represent the amphitheatre of Doué in le Maine-et-Loire. At one time held to portray a true ancient theatre, the engravings are now dismissed by Elie Konigson as merely vague approximations of a real place (*L'Espace théâtral médiéval*, p. 194).

While these illustrations are the most commonly cited pictorial evidence concerning the medieval theatre, other, less obvious and less well-known—even obscure—works of art are reproduced somewhat eclectically by Allardyce Nicoll in *Masks, Mimes, and Miracles* in support of his contention that the popular entertainment represented by the mime continued in an unbroken tradition through the Dark Ages. Among them are the following:

a. a set of miniatures in some manuscripts of sermons or "dramatic homilies" by Jacobus of Coccinobaphus (fig. 146) that, Nicoll observes, "certainly seem theatrically inspired" and provide a "realistic depiction of stage scenes" (p. 211);

b. a set of miniatures in a fourteenth-century manucript, *Li Romans d'Alixandre*, in the Bodleian Library, depicting performing animals, fools, and puppets (figs. 115–119, 121);

c. a miniature from a lost codex from Landsberg, Germany (fig. 20), again depicting puppets;

d. an illustrated Terence manuscript in the Bibliothèque de l'Arsenal in Paris (fig. 102), which Nicoll believes to be "a delineation, probably realistic, of the *ioculatores* of ·the medieval period" (p. 157);

e. a collection of masks—whose connection with the theatre is uncertain—preserved in the Tiroler Landesmuseum Ferdinandeum in Innsbruck (fig. 130);

f. reliefs, also in Innsbruck (figs. 110–130), that depict the medieval fool;

g. a series of eleventh-century frescoes in the Cathedral of Saint Sophia in Kiev (fig. 107), which again attest to the continuing presence of the ubiquitous mimes.

These are interesting illustrations, and they may even be evidence of what Nicoll claims they are, but it is difficult to escape the impression that they are the result of a determination to prove a point rather than of a systematic survey and analysis of European art and artifacts.

In point of fact, the systematic study of the relationship between medieval art and theatre began with a historian of art rather than of the theatre. One of the earliest and most influential of art historians who concerned themselves with the relationship was Emile Mâle who, during the first half of the twentieth century, contributed a voluminous scholarly commentary on the religious art of medieval France, culminating in the many editions of four large volumes: *L'Art* *religieux du XII<sup>e</sup> siècle en France, L'Art religieux de la fin du moyen âge en France, L'Art religieux du XIII<sup>e</sup> siècle en France*, and *L'Art religieux après le Concile de Trente.* The gist of Mâle's thesis is that the liturgical drama and the mystery plays had a profound influence on the visual arts, which he saw incorporating in the late Middle Ages realistic and dramatic details derived from theatrical presentation. Among the examples he cites as proof of his argument he includes Fouquet's miniature and Cailleau's manuscript illuminations; but more often he refers to bas-reliefs, stained glass windows, wall-paintings, and altar-pieces. These, Mâle suggests, tell us what people saw when they went to the theatre. And in some instances, works of art, like the mysteries, show simultaneous action.

Mâle tended to see the main value of the medieval drama in the service to artists and attributed what little merit it did possess to the *tableaux vivants*, which he considered the essential element of the medieval theatre. In this respect he was in agreement with the ideas of theatrical scholarship being pioneered at the same time by Gustave Cohen. Cohen, nevertheless, was in this, as in other things, cautious: he preferred texts and archival documents, and consulted pictorial art and sculpture only as a last resort. The contentious issue of the direction of influence—even Mâle eventually admitted the possibility that it went both ways—Cohen neatly sidestepped without invalidating pictorial art as evidence for theatre history by suggesting that both art and theatre had a common provenance and a common purpose. Moreover, Cohen argued, the source and purpose were the same regardless of the medium—scene, stone, wood, or glass. Implicit was the assumption of the sameness of the iconographic content.

Later theatre historians proceeded on the grounds laid out by Mâle and Cohen, very often ignoring the latter's note of caution. M. D. Anderson, in *Drama and Imagery in English Medieval Churches* (1963), while acknowledging the difficulties inherent in limited evidence, in determining the source of a distinctive feature common to both drama and art, and in the lack of reliable information concerning the practices of medieval craftsmen, argues that the probability that medieval art was inspired by the drama is so great that the work of medieval artists constitutes a record of what they had seen on the stage. Such a direct interaction makes for direct evidence, and Anderson does not hesitate to suggest that contemporary art on a theme which is known to have been dramatized can provide evidence of what even a lost play was like.

Rosemary Woolf finds the possible relationship between art and theatre similarly illuminating, although, like Cohen, she postulates a parallel development in arts practised by men in close contact with one another and working within the same iconographic tradition. And she further conceptualizes the relationship between art and theatre as a process that might at times have been the actual historical sequence: ". . . if one postulates the following series, religious painting, tableau of the same subject, mime, play, it is unclear at what point one would want to cry halt and draw the line between a difference in degree and a difference in kind" (*The English Mystery Plays*, p. 97). On the basis of this postulation, Woolf suggests that the development of the dramatic cycle form was influenced by iconographic cycles on church walls or in manuscripts—a theory elaborated by Alan H. Nelson in *The Medieval English Stage* (1974): "If we seek the sources of the generic integrity of the episodic cycles, we perhaps should look to pictorial traditions rather than to liturgical plays, liturgical texts, or theological doctrines" (p. 10). It is perhaps worth noting that both Woolf and Nelson alter Mâle's theory of influence so that, at the least, art and theatre act upon one another. Indeed, in the example cited, the direction of the influence is from art to theatre.

One of the most consistent applications of the idea that art and theatre, as expressions of the same iconographic tradition, can illuminate one another is Fletcher Collins' *The Production of Medieval Church Music-Drama* (1972). Collins surveys medieval Christian art for information concerning characterization, movement and gesture, costume, makeup, properties, and furnishings. He points out that there exists remarkable agreement between the playwrights and the artists as to what constitutes a major episode from the biblical narrative, and that consequently art works from the same period as the plays constitute reliable sources of information with respect to scenic requirements as well. Collins acknowledges that there is little hope of establishing a direct relationship between extant art and drama and therefore resorts to the idea of medieval homogeneity to support a necessarily second-best methodology. "For the most part," he writes,

we must be content with those representations wherever made, that bring into focus some facet of the theatrical image. Medieval single-mindedness in visual expression encourages us to correlate almost any artist's image, in whatever medium, with that of playwrights and audiences of the same period. [p. xi]

The generalized nature of Collins' study is underscored by the fact that, rather than citing and describing particular art objects, he refers his readers to the *Index of Christian Art*, a collection of approximately 125,000 photographs that constitutes, in its entirety, the evidence to support the claims he makes. (The *Index* is located at Princeton University, with photographic copies available at several other centres in the United States and Europe. See H. Woodruff, *The Index of Christian Art*, 1942.) We are a long way from the miniatures of Cailleau and Fouquet.

Since, as we have seen, it is next to impossible to identify a particular visual monument as a true production document, such insight into staging practice as the visual arts afford is dependent in general on several assumptions: (1) that pictorial art borrowed iconographic motifs from the religious theatre, or that both derived these motifs from a common source; (2) that the artistic medium plays a limited role in determining the conventions of the art; (3) that the religious content of the several contemporaneous arts was presented in an iconographically similar manner; (4) that individual artistic predilection and local variation represent insignificant aberrations from a generalized norm; and (5) that a general idea of pictorial iconography can provide a general idea of theatrical representation, which can in turn be refined by reference to the dramatic text and to selected examples from the pictorial arts.

Some of these assumptions have been challenged, in particular the notion that the direction of influence was from theatre to art rather than the other way round. There have been serious doubts raised as to whether visual art more than very rarely was modelled on stage settings; indeed, the counter-argument is more frequently made—that the theatre can at least in some instances be seen as an extension of the visual arts. We have seen that Woolf, for instance, postulates an art-to-drama sequence. And the theory of the development of the vernacular cycle plays from the *tableaux vivants*, argued by several historians, is one of the better known specific examples. But whether or not we are justified on the basis of these hypotheses in extrapolating a new generalization concerning the relationship between art and theatre is another matter. Clifford Davidson, in *Drama and Art: An Introduction to the Use of Evidence from the Visual Arts for the Study of Early Drama* (1977), is convinced that the theatre borrowed from art: "The conservative nature of drama is proof of its derivative character; it is rarely innovative with regard to either iconography or ways of visualizing scenes" (p. 13). Despite Davidson's confidence, his assertion is impossible to either prove or disprove.

The assumptions that the medium had an insignificant effect on iconography, and that the local or individual variations in artistic expression are of little importance, have been similarly questioned. Elie Konigson, although he admits the common "réalité figurative" of art and theatre, warns that the "réalité concrète" of the visible sign or icon is expressed by different techniques on canvas, in stone, or on the stage (*L'Espace théâtral médiéval*, p. 233). And it has also come to be recognized that there is much profit to be derived from the careful analysis of specific and local visual evidence, indeed that the temptation to hypothesize a general medieval visual tradition can lead to distortion of the meaning and significance of the evidence. "Our methodology," writes Davidson in an article in *Comparative Drama*, "will avoid merely the tracing of iconographic ideas apart from their hermeneutic context, for it is true that iconographic configurations may have different meanings in different periods and different settings" (XIII [1979–80], 301).

Whatever the precise nature of the relationship between medieval art and medieval theatre, it is clear that consideration of it has directed the attention of theatre historians to a vast array of materials that at first glance might seem tangential to the theatre, but that, on further consideration, can be seen as constituent parts of a large picture wherein the theatre arts too have their place. Iconographic motifs in religious art—stained glass, sculpture and carving, wall-paintings—have their counterparts in the heraldic emblems of the tapestries and paintings reflecting the pageantry, feasting, and social life of the Middle Ages. And both have their parallels in the liturgical and vernacular theatre, in tournaments, pageants, and entries, and in the *tableaux vivants* appropriate to all medieval theatre. If the drama is to be understood as something seen as well as something heard, the visual arts executed in non-ephemeral media must be the key to reconstructing the ephemeral theatrical spectacle and to coming to some appreciation of the full emotional range and complexity of the medieval theatre.

## CONCLUSION

It is tempting to add to this heading, "in which nothing is concluded." Procedures for the finding, categorizing, and evaluating of evidence for the medieval theatre are still being developed. It is also not clear whether we are dealing with a single theatre distinguished by a finite number of variations or whether those variations themselves constitute separate theatres that must be analyzed and evaluated on an individual basis. Moreover, any breakdown into constituent parts can be made in various ways: (1) on the basis of geography or language, (2) on the basis of purpose or auspices or place of performance, (3) on the basis of historical chronology, or (4) on the basis of several of these factors. For what we call the medieval theatre is both vast and heterogeneous; and more than one observer has recoiled from what is seen as an untamed jungle. At one time, not so long ago, as we have seen, the difficulties of access to this rich theatrical world seemed more formidable than any reward that might derive from exploring it. "Small wonder then," wrote Glynne Wickham in 1959, "that few have ventured into the archives of our medieval dramatic heritage when quicker profits can patently be made by ignoring it" (*Early English Stages* I, xxiii). Happily we have since discovered that hard-won riches too have their value, and the study of the medieval theatre now rivals in intensity that of the classical or Elizabethan theatres.

## REFERENCES

Alenda y Mira, J. *Relaciones de solemnidades y fiestas públicas de España*. Madrid, 1903.

Anderson, M. D. *Drama and Imagery in English Medieval Churches*. Cambridge, 1963.

Axton, Richard. *European Drama of the Early Middle Ages*. London, 1974.

Bigongiari, Dino. "Were There Theatres in the Twelfth and Thirteenth Centuries?" *Romantic Review* XXXVII (1946), 201–224.

Bills, Bing D. "The 'Suppression Theory' and the English Corpus Christi Play: A Re-Examination." *Theatre Journal* XXXII (1980), 157–168.

Borlase, William. *Natural History of Cornwall*. Oxford, 1758.

———. *Observations on the Antiquities Historical and Monumental of Cornwall*. Oxford, 1754.

Bretex, Jacques. *Les Tournois de Chauvenci*. Ed. P.I.J. Delmotte. 2 Vols. Valenciennes, 1835.

Brody, Alan. *The English Mummers and Their Plays: Traces of Ancient History*. Philadelphia, 1969.

Carbonares, Manuel. *Relación y explicatión histórico de la solemne procesión del Corpus, que annualmente celebra la cuidad de Valencia*. Valencia, 1873.

Carew, Richard. *The Survey of Cornwall*. Ed. F.E. Halliday. London, 1953 [1602].

Cargill, Oscar. *Drama and Liturgy*. New York, 1930.

Chambers, E. K. *The English Folk-Play*. Oxford, 1933.

———. *The Mediaeval Stage*. 2 Vols. Oxford, 1903.

Cohen, Gustave. *L' Histoire de la mise en scène dans le théâtre religieux français du moyen-âge*. 2nd ed. Paris, 1926.

———. *Le Livre de conduite du régisseur et le compte des dépenses pour la mystère de la Passion joué à Mons en 1501*. Strasbourg and Paris, 1925.

———. *Le Théâtre en France au moyen-âge*. 2 Vols. Paris, 1928.

Collins, Fletcher. *The Production of Medieval Church Music-Drama*. Charlottesville, 1972.

Collins, Patrick J. *The N-Town Plays and Medieval Pictorial Cycles*. Kalamazoo, 1979.

Craig, Hardin. *English Religious Drama of the Middle Ages*. Oxford, 1955.

Cripps-Day, Francis Henry. *The History of the Tournament in England and in France*. London, 1918.

Davidson, Clifford. *Drama and Art: An Introduction to the Use of Evidence from the Visual Arts for the Study of Early Drama*. Kalamazoo, 1977.

———. "On the Uses of Iconographic Study: The Example of the *Sponsus* from St. Martial of Limoges." *Comparative Drama* XIII (1979–80), 300–319.

Davies, R., ed. *Extracts from the Municipal Records of the City of York*. Dursley, 1976 [1843].

Dawson, Giles E. *Records of Plays and Players in Kent 1450–1642*. Malone Society Collections VII. Oxford, 1965.

Delachenal, R., ed. *Les Grandes Chroniques de France, Chroniques des regnes de Jean II et Charles V*. 4 Vols. Paris, 1910–20.

Dietrich, Julia C. "Folk Drama Scholarship: The State of the Art." *Research Opportunities in Renaissance Drama* XIX (1976), 15–32.

Dugdale, William. *Antiquities of Warwickshire*. London, 1656.

Evans, M. Blakemore. *The Passion Play of Lucerne*. New York, 1943.

Even, Edward van. *L'Omgang de Louvain*. Brussels and Louvain, 1863.

Favyn, A. *A Theatre of Honour and Knighthood*. London, 1623.

Frank, Grace. *The Medieval French Drama*. Oxford, 1954.

Froissart, Jean. *The Chronicle of Froissart*. Tr. Lord Berners 1523–25. Ed. W. P. Ker. 6 Vols. London, 1902.

Froning, R., ed. *Das Drama des Mittelalters*. 3 Vols. Stuttgart, 1891–92.

Gardiner, Harold C. *Mysteries' End: An Investigation of the Last Days of the Medieval Religious Stage*. New Haven, 1946.

Gibson, Gail McMurray. "Long Melford Church, Suffolk: Some Suggestions for the Study of Visual Artifacts and Medieval Drama." *Research Opportunities in Renaissance Drama* XXI (1978), 103–115.

Girardot, Auguste-Théodore de, ed. *Mystère des Actes des Apôtres représenté à Bourges en avril, 1536*. Paris, 1854.

Giraud, Paul-Emile, *Le composition, mise en scène et représentation du mystère des Trois Doms joué à Romans*. Lyon, 1848.

———, and Ulysse Chevalier, eds. *Les Mystère des Trois Doms, joué à Romans en 1509*. Lyon, 1887.

Guénée, Bernard, and Françoise Lehoux. *Les Entrées royales françaises de 1328 à 1515*. Paris, 1968.

Hall, Edward. *Union of the Two Noble and Illustrate Families of Lancaster and York*. Ed. H. Ellis. London, 1809 [1548].

Hardison, O. B. *Christian Rite and Christian Drama in the Middle Ages*. Baltimore, 1965.

Hécart, G.A.J. *Recherches historiques, bibliographiques, critiques et littéraires sur le théâtre à Valenciennes*. Paris, 1816.

Holinshed, Raphael. *Chronicles of England, Scotland, and Ireland*. 6 Vols. New York, 1965 [1807-08].

Hudson, Anne, ed. *Selections from English Wycliffite Writings*. Cambridge, 1978.

Hunningher, Benjamin. *The Origin of the Theatre*. New York, 1961.

Iranzo, Miguel Lucas de. *Crónica del Condestable Miguel Lucas de Iranzo*. In *Memorial histórico español*, vol. VIII. Madrid, 1855.

Isidore of Seville. *Etymologiae*. Ed. W. M. Lindsay. 2 Vols. Oxford, 1911.

Jacquot, Jean, ed. *Le Lieu théâtral à la Renaissance*. Paris, 1964.

Jauss, Hans R., E. Koehler, et al. *Grundriss der Romanischen Literaturen des Mittelalters*. Heidelberg, 1972-

Kahrl, Stanley J. *Records of Plays and Players in Lincolnshire 1300–1585*. Malone Society Collections VIII. Oxford, 1974.

———. *Traditions of Medieval English Drama*. London, 1974.

Kennard, Joseph Spencer. *The Italian Theatre from Its Beginning to the Close of the Seventeenth Century*. 2 Vols. New York, 1964 [1932].

Kolve, V. A. *The Play Called Corpus Christi*. Stanford, 1966.

Konigson, Elie. *L'Espace théâtral médiéval*. Paris, 1975.

———. *La Représentation d'un Mystère de la Passion à Valenciennes en 1547*. Paris, 1969.

Lancashire, Ian. "REED Research Guide." *Records of Early English Drama: Newsletter* (1976: 1), pp. 10–23.

Larson, Orville K. "Bishop Abraham of Seuzdal's Description of Sacre Rappresentazioni," *Educational Theatre Journal* IX (1957), 208–213.

Lebègue, Raymond. *Le Mystère des Actes des Apôtres, contribution à l'étude de l'humanisme et du protestantisme français au XVIᵉ siècle*. Paris, 1929.

Loomis, Laura Hibbard. "Secular Dramatics in the Royal Palace, Paris, 1378, 1389, and Chaucer's 'Tregetoures.' " *Speculum* XXXIII (1958), 242–255.

Loomis, R. S. "Were There Theatres in the Twelfth and Thirteenth Centuries?" *Speculum* XX (1945), 92–98.

Lydgate, John. *Minor Poems*. Ed. N. H. MacCracken. 2 Vols. London, 1934.

Mâle, Emile. *L'Art religieux de la fin du moyen âge en France*. 3rd ed. Paris, 1925.

———. *L'Art religieux du XIIᵉ au XVIIIᵉ siècle*. Paris, 1961.

———. *The Gothic Image: Religious Art in France of the Thirteenth Century*. Tr. Dora Nussey. New York, 1972.

———. *Religious Art in France: The Twelfth Century*. Ed. Harry Bober. Tr. Marthiel Mathews. Princeton, 1978.

Marshall, John. "The Chester Pageant Carriage—How Right Was Rogers?" *Medieval English Theatre* I (1979), 49–55.

Mensi, J. D., ed. *Sacrorum Conciliorum Nova et Amplissima Collectio*. 3 Vols. Florence, 1769–92.

Meredith, Peter. "The Leeds Descriptive Catalogue of Medieval Drama." *Research Opportunities in Renaissance Drama* XXI (1978), 91–93.

Meyer, Paul, ed. *L'Histoire de Guillaume le Maréchal, Compte de Striguil et de Pembroke, Regent d'Angleterre de 1216 à 1219, poème français.* 3 Vols. Paris, 1891–1901.

Michael, Wolfgang F. "The Staging of the Bozen Passion Play." *The Germanic Review*, XXV (1950), 178–195.

Mill, Anna J. *Medieval Plays in Scotland.* Edinburgh and London, 1924.

Monaci, Ernesto. "Appunti per la storia del teatro italiano: Uffizi drammatici dei disciplinati dell' Umbria," *Revista di Filologia Romanza*, I (1872), 257–260.

Nagler, A. M. *The Medieval Religious Stage.* New Haven and London, 1976.

Nelson, Alan H. "Early Pictorial Analogues of Medieval Theatre-in-the-Round." *Research Opportunities in Renaissance Drama*, XII (1969), 93–106.

———. *The Medieval English Stage.* Chicago and London, 1974.

———. Review of A. M. Nagler, *The Medieval Religious Stage* in *Educational Theatre Journal*, XXIX (1977), 574–575.

Nicoll, Allardyce. *Masks, Mimes, and Miracles.* London and New York, 1931.

Niessen, Carl. "La Scène du 'Laurentius' à Cologne." In *Le Lieu théâtral à la Renaissance,* ed. Jean Jacquot (Paris, 1964).

Pacht, Otto. *The Rise of Pictorial Narrative in Twelfth Century England.* Oxford, 1962.

Penn, Dorothy. *The Staging of the 'Miracles de Nostre Dame par personnages' of the Ms. Cangé.* New York, 1933.

Petit de Julleville, L. *La Comédie et les moeurs.* Paris, 1886.

———. *Les Comédiens en France au moyen âge.* Paris, 1885.

———. *Les Mystères.* 2 Vols. Paris, 1880.

———. *Répertoire du théâtre comique en France au moyen-âge.* Paris, 1886.

Prosser, Eleanor. *Drama and Religion in the English Mystery Plays.* Stanford, 1961.

Prost, Bernard, ed. *Traités du Duel iudiciare, relations de pas d'armes et tournois.* Paris, 1872.

Puyvelde, Leo van. *L'Ommegang de 1615 à Bruxelles.* Brussels, 1960.

René d'Anjou. *Oeuvres complètes.* Ed. Theodore Compte de Quatrebarbes. 4 Vols. Angers, 1845.

———. *Le Livre des tournois du Roi Rene.* Paris, 1946.

Rey-Flaud, Henri. *Le Cercle magique: Essai sur le théâtre en rond à la fin du moyen âge.* Paris, 1973.

*Records of Early English Drama.* Ex. Ed. Alexandra F. Johnston. Toronto, 1978-

*Records of Early English Drama: Newsletter.* Toronto, 1976-

Runnalls, Graham A. "Medieval French Drama: A Review of Recent Scholarship." *Research Opportunities in Renaissance Drama*, XXI (1978), 83–90; XXII (1979), 111–136.

Salter, F. M. *Medieval Drama in Chester.* Toronto, 1955.

Sharp, Thomas. *A Dissertation on the Pageants or Dramatic Mysteries Anciently Performed at Coventry.* Foreword A. C. Cawley. Totowa, New Jersey, 1973 [1825].

Sheingorn, Pamela. "On Using Medieval Art in the Study of Medieval Drama: An Introduction to Methodology." *Research Opportunities in Renaissance Drama*, XXII (1979), 101–109.

Shergold, W. D. *A History of the Spanish Stage from Medieval Times until the End of the Seventeenth Century.* Oxford, 1967.

Southern, Richard. *The Medieval Theatre in the Round*. Rev. ed. London, 1975 [1957].
————. *The Staging of Plays before Shakespeare*. London, 1973.
*Statuta Armorum*. In *Statutes of the Realm* (London, 1969), I, 230–321 [1810].
Sticca, Sandro. *The Latin Passion Play: Its Origin and Development*. Albany, 1970.
Stix, Paul, ed. *Die Wiener Passion*. Vienna, 1950.
Stow, John. *Annales, or, A General Chronicle of England*. Continuation by Edmond Howes. London, 1615, 1631.
————. *A Survey of London*. Ed. C. L. Kingsford. 3 Vols. Oxford, 1908–27 [1598].
Stratman, Carl J. *Bibliography of Medieval Drama*. 2d ed. 2 Vols. New York, 1972.
Stuart, Donald C. *Stage Decoration in France in the Middle Ages*. New York, 1910.
Tydeman, William. *The Theatre in the Middle Ages: Western European Stage Conditions c. 800–1576*. Cambridge, 1978.
Wickham, Glynne. *Early English Stages 1300–1660*. 3 Vols. in 4. London, 1959–81.
————. *The Medieval Theatre*. London, 1974.
————. *Shakespeare's Dramatic Heritage*. London, 1969.
Williams, Arnold. *The Drama of Medieval England*. East Lansing, 1961.
Wilson, F. P. *The English Drama 1485–1585*. Ed. G. K. Hunter. Oxford, 1969.
Withington, Robert. *English Pageantry: An Historical Outline*. 2 Vols. New York, 1963 [1918–26].
Woodruff, H. *The Index of Christian Art at Princeton University. A Handbook*. Princeton, 1942.
Woolf, Rosemary. *The English Mystery Plays*. London, 1972.
Young, Karl. *The Drama of the Medieval Church*. 2 Vols. Oxford, 1933.

# Appendix

## A REVIEW OF
## MEDIEVAL DRAMATIC TEXTS

### LATIN PLAYS IN THE CLASSICAL TRADITION

It is usually assumed that the few secular plays in Latin that we possess, dating from the tenth and twelfth centuries, are essentially literary exercises, neither intended for nor undergoing performance, and serving at best as evidence for a continuing Roman literary tradition rather than a theatrical one. This evaluation seems almost certainly valid in the case of the tenth-century nun Hroswitha who, during her years in the nunnery of Gandersheim in Germany, produced six plays modelled on Terence but based on legends of holy and chaste women. Although the earliest and most complete manuscript containing the plays—now in the Bayerische Staatsbibliothek in Munich—dates from the tenth or eleventh century, Hroswitha's dramas appear to have remained unknown until their publication in 1501.

The provenance and nature of the medieval Latin *commedia*, written in the twelfth century at Blois, Orléans, Vendome, and Tours, and later in England and Italy, are another matter. Some scholars consider them merely versified tales but others, including Benjamin Hunningher in *Origin of the Theater*, argue for the existence of a secular theatrical tradition in the twelfth century, and that some at least of these compositions were actually performed. Several of the manuscripts in fact do contain speakers' names and some stage-directions in apparently later glosses. This is true of two pieces by Vitalis of Blois—*Geta* and *Aulularia* (an adaptation of the pseudo-Plautine *Querolus*)—and of the anonymous *Babio*. Most scholars, however, continue to hold that these texts were written as school texts and that the added stage-directions reflect adaptations for recitation or unpretentious classroom performance.

### LITURGICAL DRAMA

The drama produced between the tenth and the sixteenth centuries under the aegis of the medieval Church flourished throughout Europe, and the manuscripts containing the plays that are to be found in various church and monastic libraries are sufficiently similar to suggest that liturgical and literary influences passed freely throughout Christendom. There are enough individual differences, however, to allow the historian to trace developments geographically as well as chronologically, and to note individual variations to meet local requirements. Many of the extant texts are relatively late compositions: Fully one-half of the 500–600 plays in Karl Young's *Drama of the Medieval Church* are from the fifteenth and sixteenth centuries. Approximately one-third of the plays were discovered in breviaries; another one-fifth in *ordinalia*, which indicate the order and content of various church ceremonies (also known as *liber consuetudina, directoria, agenda, consueta*); and most of the rest in tropers, *libri responsales*, and similar books of chant.

The liturgical drama ranges in length and complexity from the simple question-and-answer of the *Quem Quaeritis* trope to the elaborate Christmas and Easter plays of the thirteenth century and even later. It is extremely difficult to determine any particular pattern of development in this drama, certainly on a continent-wide basis; for even a cursory examination indicates that the process was different in Italy and Spain than in the rest of Europe. The destruction of the monasteries in England in the sixteenth century undoubtedly resulted in the loss of much relevant material in that country. It is even difficult to categorize the plays except in terms of their subject-matter: When we do, we find that the liturgical drama consists principally of variations on sixteen basic "plays." But, of course, this begs the question of whether each variation is not in effect a different play.

In general, the manuscripts are something of a disappointment so far as theatre historians are concerned. They give no indication of being directors' copies or rehearsal scores, and it is theorized, quite reasonably, that the extant manuscripts were prepared by scribes from the choir director's working copy for inclusion in a permanent service book, which was then deposited in the monastic or church library. Some of the manuscripts do contain musical annotation, a valuable source of information for anyone wishing to reconstruct a performance. Unfortunately, although Edmond de Coussemaker provided the music in his *Drames liturgiques du moyen âge* in 1860, he was unable to transcribe the medieval notation into modern notation, and historians were unable to make use of the information. Young provided no musical notation at all. Since 1933, however, musicologists have successfully translated the musical notation, and editions of liturgical plays that include the music have been published. (See especially the several editions by W. L. Smoldon and Noah Greenberg, and Fletcher Collins' *Medieval Church Music-Dramas*.) And finally, in 1980 appeared Smoldon's *Music of the Medieval Church Dramas*, the most comprehensive treatment to date of this long neglected dimension of the liturgical drama. Smoldon seems to have envisaged his work as a companion to Young's *Drama of the Medieval Church*, for which he expresses great admiration. He insists that since we are in fact dealing with opera, the texts of such pieces must include the available music. He discusses the dramas and their music chronologically, and in an appendix (pp. 419–430) lists the surviving manuscripts that have retained their musical settings. (Photographs of the manuscripts, once belonging to Smoldon, are now in the library of the University of London.)

### France

The richest collections of liturgical drama are in France, associated with various cathedrals and churches, monasteries, and convents. The cathedrals include those at Beauvais, Laon, Rouen, Nevers, and Paris; the main churches are at Amiens, Bayeaux, Fleury,

Limoges, Rouen, and Tours. Monasteries and convents include St Martial of Limoges, Fleury, Compiègne, Mont-St-Michel, Fécamp, St-Ouen, Origny-Ste-Benoîte, Notre-Dame de Troyes, Ste-Croix de Poitiers. At least half a dozen manuscripts, some dating from the tenth and eleventh centuries, come from the Benedictine monastery of St. Martial at Limoges (Bibliothèque Nationale MSS. lat. 1118, 1119, 1139, 1240, 784, 887). Several more come from Rouen (B.N. MSS. lat. 904, 1213; and Bibliothèque de la Ville de Rouen, MSS. 252, 384, 222). The most significant of the early collections, however, is the so-called *Fleury Play-Book*, presumably written in the monastery of St-Benoit-sur-loire at Fleury and now preserved in the city library at Orléans (MSS. 201). It is a composite manuscript, dating from the twelfth or thirteenth century, and undoubtedly representing the mature repertory of the monastery. It includes musical notation and, in at least one instance—*The Conversion of St. Paul*—rubrics containing information about staging.

In rare cases we know the name of the playwright responsible for a liturgical play. A wandering scholar of the twelfth century, Hilarius, sometime pupil of Abelard, is one such playwright. He is the author of three plays, a *Raising of Lazarus*, an *Iconia Sancti Nicolai*, and a *Daniel*, which are preserved in a manuscript in the Bibiliothèque Nationale (MSS. lat. 11331). Each play is preceded by a statement indicating the number of *dramatis personae* needed, and the text also indicates that at the end of *Lazarus* and of *Daniel* either the *Te Deum* or the *Magnificat* was to be sung, depending upon the point in the service where they were to be performed.

About the same time as Hilarius produced his *Daniel*, or shortly thereafter, the students at the Cathedral School of Beauvais wrote their own version of the play. The manuscript was used by Coussemaker in 1860, but it disappeared during the latter part of the nineteenth century and was not rediscovered—by E. K. Chambers—until the turn of the century. It now resides in the British Museum (MS. Egerton 2615). The Beauvais *Daniel* is generally considered to be the finest specimen of twelfth-century drama extant. Thanks at least in part to its being both performed and recorded in this century, it is also very likely the best known.

The persistence of this Latin religious drama is attested by Phillippe de Mézières' *Representatio Figurata in Festo Praesentationis Beatae Virginis Mariae in Templo*, performed at Avignon, probably in 1372. The manuscript, now housed in the Bibliothèque Nationale (MSS. lat. 173330), is particularly significant in that it contains, besides the text of the play, correspondence and commentary by Mézières, together with detailed directions for the play's staging. Albert B. Weiner provided a translation of crucial sections in *Philippe de Mézières' Description of the "Festum Praesentationis"* (1958); and Robert S. Haller has translated the entire play (1971).

## Germany

The earliest manuscripts in a German-speaking area of Europe containing liturgical plays were produced at the Benedictine monastery of St. Gall in Switzerland, where they are preserved in the Stiftsbibliothek. But once again the later manuscripts are more interesting from the point of view of the information concerning performance that they contain. The two most significant are the Tegernsee *Antichristus* (twelfth century) and the Carmina Burana manuscript from Benediktbeuren (thirteenth century). The former exists in two manuscripts in the Staatsbibliothek in Munich (1at. 19291, 19411); the extensive rubrics indicate that mansions were placed at three points of the compass, but are otherwise remarkably silent on the details, or the place, of staging. The manuscript from the Benedictine Monastery of Benedicktbeuren in Bavaria, also in the Staatsbibliothek in Munich (1at. 4660, Carmina Burana), dates from about 1230, although the plays it contains—a Christmas play and two Passion plays—may date from an earlier time. The stage directions are relatively extensive and the *mise en scène* clearly very complex.

## Italy

When Young's *Drama of the Medieval Church* appeared in 1933, the principal liturgical dramatic documents from Italy were three manuscripts from the Cathedral of Friuli, dating from the fourteenth century. Of these, supposedly on deposit in the Reale Museo Archeologico (MSS. CI, CII, and T.VII), Young was able to find only the first two, and was therefore forced to reprint the third from Coussemaker's edition of 1860. T.VII still awaits its E. K. Chambers.

Shortly after Young published his work, there was discovered at the Monastery of Monte Cassino a nearly complete Passion play in Latin, which was subsequently published in 1936 by D. M. Inguanez. This remarkable play dates from approximately 1150 and is thus a century older than any other known Passion play. It has been possible to establish a close relationship between this text and a fourteenth-century fragment from Sulmona Cathedral, found in the Archivio capitolare di S. Panfilo. The Sulmona fragment provides the lines for the actor playing the fourth soldier, *Officium Quarti Militis*. (Inguanez' text is reprinted in Sandro Sticca, *The Latin Passion Play*, pp. 66–78. Sticca also compares the Montescassino and Sulmona Passions, pp. 84–113.)

## Spain

The liturgical drama of Spain was for many years neglected. In fact, of the hundreds of plays collected and published by Young, only four are from Spain, all from the same manuscript associated with the Cathedral at Ripoll and now held in the museum at Vich. Admittedly, the situation in Spain poses difficulties for the researcher: Many of the possible manuscript repositories, especially in ecclesiastical libraries and archives, have not been catalogued; and the manuscripts that have been found are located in collections and libraries, both public and ecclesiastical, in France and England as well as in Spain. There is the further problem that much of the Spanish peninsula had been cut off from cultural and religious developments in the rest of Europe by the Moorish occupation; and it was therefore assumed—correctly it appears—that the liturgical drama was confined mainly to Catalonia, that area of northeast Spain bordering France. Richard B. Donovan, however, in *The Liturgical Drama in Medieval Spain* (1958), besides noting evidence of liturgical dramatic activity in the northern centres of Silos, Compostella, and Zaragoza, points out that by the fourteenth century at least liturgical plays were being performed in the Cathedral in the Castilian city of Toledo.

The earliest Spanish liturgical drama is to be found in two late eleventh-century manuscripts from the Benedictine Monastery of Silos, near Burgos. Both manuscripts are now located in the British Museum (Add. MSS. 30848, 30850). In the Cathedral library at Compostella, there was discovered in 1932 a twelfth-century Easter play although Donovan reports that he could not find the manuscript in 1954. However, a fifteenth-century manuscript in the same library contains the same play, and what is of more importance, provides directions for staging it. (Donovan prints the manuscript on pp. 53–54.) A 1497 breviary also includes the play, with two additional sequences and some detail concerning the dress of the participants. Elsewhere, Santiago contributes a *Visitatio Sepulchri*, and the city of Huesca two *Quem Quaeritis* tropes.

The evidence for liturgical drama at Toledo consists of an eighteenth-century manuscript in the library of the Academia de la Historia in Madrid (2–7–4 MS. 75) by Felipe Fernandez Vallejo. In one chapter of this work the author provides the text and description of a ceremony performed on Christmas Eve at Toledo in the eighteenth century, and further notes that he took it from an earlier manuscript by Juan Chaves de Arcayos, prebendary at the Toledo Cathedral 1598–1643. In another chapter there is a second description of another ceremony performed on Christmas Eve—the prophecy of the Sibyl. Another eighteenth-century manuscript in the same library (11–2–7 MS. 444) confirms Vallejo's accounts. And this manuscript was in part based on yet a third manuscript found in the Toledo Public Library (Borbon-Lorenzana ms. 154). Finally, in that same public library was found the Arcayos manuscript itself, which is the basis of all the interest (42.29), together with a 1765 copy. A fifteenth-century manuscript in the library of the University of Madrid and a fourteenth-century breviary complete the laborious reconstruction of the evidence for liturgical drama at Toledo.

Fortunately, the manuscripts from Catalonia are more numerous and more informative. Donovan found a good deal of material in archives and libraries throughout the region. The most important are the following: (1) the Ripoll troper in the Cathedral Library at Vich (MS. 32), a collection of the oldest Catalan tropes and plays that have come down to us; (2) a fourteenth-century *consueto* in the Gerona chapter library; and (3) a manuscript in the collegiate church of Gandia, which contains the only liturgical Easter play preserved with polyphonic music, composed by St. Francis Borgia in the sixteenth century. The text and music were published in 1902 by Mariano Baixauli in *Razon y Fé*, a fortunate circumstance, since the original documents were destroyed in 1936, during the Spanish Civil War.

## England

From the relatively rich collections of Continental Europe we turn to the few relevant manuscripts in England. Foremost among them is, of course, the *Regularis Concordia*, which includes a *Quem Quaeritis*, an *Adoratio*, a *Deposito*, and an *Elevatio Crucis* as well as Bishop Ethelwold's famous instructions on the proper conduct of the *Quem Quaeritis*. From the same cathedral we also have the Winchester Troper, dating from 978–80, now in the Bodleian Library at Oxford. Of some significance too are the so-called Shrewsbury Fragments, preserved in an early fifteenth-century manuscript in the library of Shrewsbury School (MS. VI). This manuscript, first made known in 1890, is important on a couple of counts. In the first place, it makes use of English as well as Latin. And in the second place, it is an actor's "side"; that is, it provides the part of a single actor in each of three plays: *Officium Pastorum*, *Visitatio Sepulchri*, and *Peregrinus*. (The intermingling of the vernacular with Latin occurs as well in several Continental manuscripts, and was taken at one time as evidence for the "secularization" theory of dramatic development.) England has little else to offer the student of the liturgical drama.

## Byzantium

There is some dispute concerning the possibility of a liturgical drama in Byzantium (where the language was, of course, Greek). Those who argue that such a drama is represented in sections of dialogue inserted into homilies dating as early as the fifth century also identify the canticle, or cycle of hymns, as dramatic literature. An example that has been cited consists of a group of twelve hymns on Christ's nativity, written by Sophronius, Patriarch of Jerusalem (560–630), and preserved in the *Codes Dalassinos*, a thirteenth-century manuscript in the National Library of Vienna. More persuasive evidence comes in the form of two Passion plays. Both the famous *Christos Paschon* (ed. J. G. Brambs, 1885) and an unnamed Passion play in the Vatican Library (Palatinus 367) are relatively late (eleventh to thirteenth centuries), although there have been attempts to backdate *Christos Paschon* to the fourth century. On the other hand, there is no evidence that *Christos Paschon*, which mingles Christian and classical elements, was ever staged; and the genesis of Palatinus 367, which may well have been staged, is problematic and obscure.

## The Growth and Dissemination of the Liturgical Drama

The questions prompted by this textual material have not as yet been totally satisfactorily answered, possibly because they were initially asked in the wrong form. Evolutionary assumptions caused scholars to inquire into the development of the liturgical drama from the church service, and into the subsequent development of the vernacular religious drama from the liturgical drama. Since medieval culture was assumed too to be monolithic, it mattered little where in Europe the textual evidence came from, and any inconvenient gaps in the narrative at one place could be filled in with details from another. The picture was further kept orderly by assuming that a simple to complex structural change corresponded with an early-late chronology. Ironically, so deeply embedded was the assumption of evolutionary development that it actually inhibited investigation of primary evidence.

A case in point is Spain, where archives and libraries lay almost totally undisturbed until Donovan's work in the 1950s, because it was assumed that development there would parallel the pattern discovered elsewhere. Thus, J.P.W. Crawford in *Spanish Drama before Lope de Vega* (1922; rev. 1937) notes that material is "almost totally lacking for a study of the liturgical drama in Spain" but argues that "the close relationship that existed between the ritual of the Spanish church and that of other countries of Western Europe, and particularly of France after the eleventh century, allows us to assume that in Spain, as elsewhere, the religious drama developed from the tropes attached to the Introit of the Magna Missa of Easter and Christmas" (p. 1). At the same time, it was usually thought that the liturgical drama was imported into Castile from France in the eleventh century, just as, according to its preface, the *Concordia Regularis* was based, at least in part, on the practices at the Benedictine monasteries of Fleury and Ghent. And behind it all were the prime disseminators of the monasteries of St. Gall and St. Martial.

An early attempt to reconcile these two explanations for the rise of the liturgical drama—parallel development or dissemination—was Edith A. Wright's *The Dissemination of the Liturgical Drama in France* (1936), in which the author attempted to determine the historical, geographical, political, and ecclesiastical considerations that affected the dissemination of the liturgical drama and its "development from the simple Easter trope to the elaborate plays of Fleury and Origny," to establish a *stammbaum* or family tree. Wright, then, introduced the comparative method and, by drawing attention to the particular conditions and initiatives at the various places where the liturgical drama flourished, began inadvertently to undermine the idea of autonomous development which is endemic to the evolutionary theory. No longer can the process of rise and development be viewed as uniform throughout Europe. Donovan points out that Castile and Catalonia must be distinguished from one another, that the latter "contained within its own boundaries the same germ which produced the plays elsewhere" (*The Liturgical Drama in Medieval Spain*, p. 29), but he counters this bow in the direction of parallel development with the observation that at least one Easter trope and play may have originated in the monastery of Santa Maria de Ripoll and thence gone to St. Martial of Limoges rather than the other way around. Indeed, the comparative method is now generally recognized as most appropriate to a theatre so international in character and to a situation in which influences moved back and forth constantly from one country to another.

## FRENCH RELIGIOUS DRAMA

The French religious drama of the Middle Ages surpasses all other vernacular dramas in both quantity and quality. Still the most comprehensive survey of manuscripts and texts is Petit de Julleville's *Mystères*. The standard survey in English is Grace Frank's *Medieval French Drama*.

### Twelfth- and Thirteenth-Century Plays

a. *Le Mystère d'Adam* (1146–74) is found in a manuscript in the Municipal Library of Tours (MS. 927). It is of particular interest to the theatre historian because of its elaborate and comprehensive stage directions (in Latin), which indicate that the play was intended for an outdoor performance, against the side door of a church, and which suggest a fairly complex system of multi-level staging.

b. *La Seinte Resureccion* (ca. 1180) exists in two manuscripts, both incomplete: an early fourteenth-century version of an early thirteenth-century revision of the play (Bibliothèque Nationale ms. fr. 902); and a copy of a mid-thirteenth-century revision from about 1275 (British Museum Add MS. 45103). The prologues to both texts include references to staging, but their cryptic nature, together with the peculiar narrative links between passages of dialogue, suggest that the texts were prepared for readers rather than for actors. At any rate, interpretation of the staging has proved difficult.

c. *Le Courtois d'Arras* (ca. 1200), a dramatization in contemporary terms of the prodigal son story, survives in four manuscripts, three from the thirteenth, and one from the fourteenth, century. The dialogue is not divided; the speakers are not named; and some lines are clearly narrative. In these circumstances, it appears likely that the text was prepared for reading.

d. Jean Bodel's *Le Jeu de Saint Nicholas* (ca. 1200) has come down to us in a manuscript dating from about 1300, now located in the Bibliothèque Nationale (fr. 25556). The text gives little in the way of stage directions; indeed, the rubrics that are there seem to have been added by a different hand from the one that copied the play.

e. *Le Miracle de Theophile*, by a professional writer known only as Rutebeuf, is, like Bodel's play, an early French miracle play. Composed about 1261, it has come down to us in a single late-thirteenth-century manuscript. Once again, the rubrics and stage directions have not proved very helpful.

### Collections of Plays

An important collection of forty later miracle plays, *Les Miracles de Notre Dame*, is preserved in a unique manuscript dating from the late fourteenth century. The manuscript is now in the Bibliothèque Nationale, bound in two volumes (fr. 819, 820). Some of the rubrics preceding each play appear to have been erased, and in 1954, a German scholar, Rudolph Glutz, succeeded in deciphering a good deal of the erased text and discovered the repeated phrase, *joue au pui des orfeures a paris*—"played at the guild of the goldsmiths at Paris." Seven dates were also discerned, and it was therefore possible to establish that the plays were performed annually over a period of approximately forty-three years (ca. 1339–82) and that they appear chronologically in the manuscript. It has been speculated that the reason for the erasures was that the manuscript was adapted as a reading text or, more likely, that it was prepared as an official *registrum* for permanent deposit with the guild. In 1733, the manuscript was presented to the Bibliothèque Royale by the Duke Châtre de Cangé: hence its popular appellation, "manuscrit Cangé." Each play in the collection is preceded by a miniature depicting an important scene from the following Miracle. There is some doubt, however, concerning the value of these miniatures as evidence for staging: They illustrate the texts, but there is nothing in them to provide a connection with performance. *Les Miracles de Notre Dame* has been edited in eight volumes by G. Paris and U. Robert (1876–83).

Another late fourteenth-century manuscript, MS. 1131 of the Bibliothèque Ste. Geneviève, is similarly important for the theatre historian. The collection includes a variety of plays on biblical subjects and on the lives and miracles of saints. It was evidently designed to serve as a repertory, perhaps for the Confrérie de la Passion. The stage-directions are very valuable, indicating not only details of stage presentation, but offering advice on joining or omitting plays at a producer's discretion. The manuscript was published in its entirety in 1837 by Achille Jubinal as *Mystères inédits du quinzième siècle*.

One further collection deserves attention. MS. 617 of the Musée Condé in Chantilly is of uncertain date—perhaps from the fifteenth century—and seems to have been copied by nuns living in the Convent of Saint Michel at Huy near Liège. It contains nativity scenes and three moralities. The nativity scenes, written in a Walloon dialect, are modelled on Latin liturgical plays on the same subject, sometimes using antiphons and tropes from them in translation or even in the original Latin. There are fairly extensive stage-directions. The manuscript was edited by Gustave Cohen (1920; 2d ed. 1953).

## Passion Plays

Elie Konigson remarks that, although production details vary from time to time and from place to place, the Passion plays of the fifteenth century can be considered as variations on a single text, based on the Vulgate, Jacques de Voragine's *Golden Legend*, and other pious works of meditation and saintly lives (*L'Espace théâtral médiéval*, p. 205). The earliest extant French Passion play, the *Passion du Palatinus*, is based on a popular poem, the so-called *Passion des Jongleurs*. The play survives in a single fourteenth-century manuscript, but it is related textually to three other manuscripts containing Passion plays or parts of plays, and it is therefore theorized that all four descend from a lost play that was strongly influenced by the *Passion des Jongleurs*. The other three manuscripts include an eighty-seven line fragment found at Sion and two fifteenth-century manuscripts, called *Biard* and *Roman* after their copyists but known collectively as *La Passion d'Autun*. None of these manuscripts gives any explicit indications of staging practice; and the *Biard* manuscript incorporates so much obvious narrative that the possibility of its use as a stage document is negligible.

Of far more importance for the theatre historian are the later generations of the same family of Passion plays: *La Passion de Semur*, *La Passion d'Arras*, Arnoul Greban's

*Mystère de la Passion*, and Jean Michel's *Passion*—all of which in one form or another served as texts for the great spectacular performances of the fifteenth and sixteenth centuries.

*La Passion de Semur* exists in a unique manuscript dated 1488, but the play itself is probably older. Its 9,582 lines required two days to be performed: At line 4,295 the audience is instructed to go home and return the next day.

*La Passion d'Arras*, MS. 697 of the Bibliothèque d'Arras, also dates from the mid-fifteenth century, and is usually attributed to Eustache Mercadé on the grounds that the play following *La Passion, La Vengeance de Nostre Seigneur Jhesucrist*, is signed by Mercadé. The Passion play's 25,000 lines required four days to perform. The manuscript is adorned with 349 miniatures, but there seems almost universal agreement that the pictures are not useful for the theatre historian, principally because they do not correspond with the stage-directions in the text. The standard edition of *La Passion d'Arras* by Jules-Marie Richard (1891) does not include the miniatures, and they are not even mentioned in Grace Frank's *Medieval French Drama*. For those who wish to make up their own minds, twenty-eight of them are reproduced in the first volume of Cohen's *Théâtre en France au moyen-âge*.

Greban's great play was the most popular Passion of its day. It survives in many manuscripts, although in some of these only portions of its more than 30,000 lines appear. In the Benedictine Abbey of Saint-Vincent at Le Mans, where Greban was born and where he died, there exists a manuscript of the first day's presentation which may be an author's copy. It provides elaborate stage-directions, particularly concerning the use of music. Records indicate that the play was performed in its entirety, in part, or in combination with other texts, in various centres throughout France: It was played at Paris at least three times before 1473, perhaps by the Confrérie de la Passion. As late as 1951, there was a successful performance of Greban's *Passion* before Notre Dame Cathedral. The standard modern edition of the play is that of Omar Jodogne (1965).

Greban made use of Mercadé's outline and some of his original scenes in the composition of his play. Similarly, Jean Michel appropriated much of Greban's play for his *Passion*, which went through at least fifteen editions between 1490 and 1542. The many extant manuscripts are based on these editions. A modern edition is provided by Omar Jodogne (1959). Michel's play, together with Mercadé's and Greban's, formed the basis of numerous performances: They were constantly cut, revised, combined, and adapted to fit local circumstances.

One further play from the fourteenth century, not strictly a Passion play but resembling in some ways the *Passion du Palatinus*, is *Le Jour du Jugement*, which survives in a manuscript in the Bibliothèque de la Ville de Besançon (MS. 579). An indication of the author's attempt at spectacle is the large number of characters listed—over ninety—for a play of only about 2,500 lines.

## Other Late Plays

A single edition from about 1490 provides us with *L'Incarnation et la Nativité*, played at Rouen in 1474. Evidence concerning staging is unusually detailed: We are given information about the number and location of *sedes* and the stationing of the characters; we are told that the entrance to hell was represented by the jaws of a dragon that opened and closed, and that limbo was fashioned to look like a prison. We learn that devils were to make a dreadful din, accompanied by drums and other noises made by "engines,'' and that they were to spit fire and throw serpents. (The play was edited by Pierre le Verdier, 1884–86.)

Two plays from the late fourteenth century, both titled *Le Vengeance de Nostre Seigneur Jhesucrist sur les Juifs par Vespasien et Titus*, survive, one anonymous, the other by Mercadé (included in MS. 697 of the Bibliothèque d'Arras).

The text of *Le Mystère des Trois Doms*, performed at Romans in 1509, was not discovered until the 1880s, by Paul-Emile Giraud. The manuscript is now preserved in the Civic Library at Lyons. It was published by Giraud and Ulysse Chevalier in 1887 in a limited edition of 200 copies. The scarcity of this edition may help to explain the play's neglect by theatre historians until relatively recently. Although Cohen refers to it in *Histoire de la mise en scène*, Grace Frank in 1954 does not mention it. Such neglect is a pity, since the manuscript includes extensive rubrics, together with a list of the parts and the people who played them. Also, as we have seen, various other production documents concerning the 1509 performance have survived to complement the text.

Finally, we must note the tendency of the later medieval French theatre to go to almost any length—quite literally—in order to provide an extended spectacular entertainment. *Le Mystère des Actes des Apôtres*, written between 1452 and 1478 by either Simon and Arnoul Greban or Jean du Prier, runs to no fewer than 62,909 lines and is reported to have taken forty days to perform at Bourges in 1536. The play exists in five printed editions. A full discussion of the text is provided by Raymond Lebègue in *Le Mystère des Actes des Apôtres* (1929). Almost as long is *Le Vieux Testament* (49,386 lines), although it has been reasonably postulated that the three complete editions that have come down to us from the sixteenth century represent a collection of plays by different playwrights, assembled by the printers and probably not intended to be performed as a whole. The standard modern edition is by James de Rothschild (1878–91).

Many more religious plays, particularly saints' plays, survive from the fifteenth and sixteenth centuries. They are surveyed in some detail in Petit de Julleville's *Mystères*. But those noted above have proved of most interest to theatre historians, and the varying states of their preservation illustrate some of the difficulties inherent in any attempt to infer stage practice from them.

## GERMAN RELIGIOUS DRAMA

German drama of the Middle Ages has always been of more interest to theatre historians than to students of literature. Although in some instances the religious theatre developed independently—notably in the processional performances associated with the Feast of Corpus Christi—in general, especially in its later years, it seems to have furnished further examples of the kind of thing we found in France. The most convenient collections of medieval German drama are by R. Froning (1891–92) and Eduard Hartl (1937). An authoritative survey of the drama and the surviving texts is provided by Wolfgang Michael in *Das deutsche Drama des Mittelalters* (1971).

The German plays associated with the Feast of Corpus Christi, which had been instituted in the early years of the fourteenth century, were evidently, like their English counterparts, processional in nature. The earliest extant manuscript (1391) is linked with Innsbruck and consists of a series of monologues in thirty set speeches. The text of a play performed at Zerbst in 1507 provides 399 rhymed couplets, which have been interpreted as explanations for a series of *tableaux vivants* performed in succession. The manuscript of another play, performed in Kunzelsau in 1479, is titled *Registrum processionis corporis christi*, and each scene is introduced by an explanation by the "Rector Processionis." Finally, there exists an *ordnung desvmbgangs*—order or processing—for a performance at Freiburg in 1516. This kind of performance seems not to have been the norm, however; and most of the extant texts suggest staging conditions similar to those of France.

Like France, Germany produced her great Passion plays, and it is these plays, mainly from the late fourteenth and early fifteenth centuries, that we know the most about and that have received most attention from theatre historians. The *Redentin Easter Play* (1464), the manuscript of which is now in the library at Karlsruhe, was probably staged in the market-square of Wismar before a seated audience, but little more can be determined from the text. Much more elaborate are the texts of Passion plays performed in the vicinity of Frankfurt-am-Main, which involved complex staging and required large casts of characters. The most important of these texts, which bear a marked relationship to one another, are: (*a*) the *Saint Gall Passion Play* (early fourteenth century), preserved in a manuscript in the monastery of St. Gall (edited in 1978 by Rudolf Schützeichel); (*b*) the *Alsfeld Passion Play* (1501), preserved in the Landesbibliothek at Kassel; and (*c*) the *Frankfurt Passion Play* of 1493. Of these, the most important for determining staging is the Alsfeld manuscript, which provides extensive rubrics, together with a rudimentary stage-plan (reproduced in Nagler, *Medieval Religious Stage*, p. 33).

Another group of Passion plays are held to have derived from an original *Tirol Passion*, which was reconstructed in 1897 by a German scholar, J. E. Wackernell, on the basis of five manuscripts from the Tirol region, dating between 1486 and 1551. The manuscripts come from Sterzing (1496), Hall (1514), Bozen (1495), Pfarrkirchen (1486), and Brixen (1551).

Two more Passion plays exist in Manuscripts 137 and 138 of the Hofbibliothek of Donaueschingen. The first, referred to as the *Donaueschingen Passion Play*, is dated 1485 and includes some quite precise stage-directions and a list of mansions or houses needed for performance. The second, called the *Villingen Passion Play*, dates from about 1585. Related to these two plays is possibly the best known to theatre historians of all the German Passion plays, that played in the city of Lucerne in Switzerland between 1450 and 1616. The play exists in eight incomplete manuscripts in the Burgerbibliothek of Lucerne, dating between 1545 and 1616. Three manuscripts from 1616 are complete, save for the first half of the first day, which is provided in a 1583 fragment. It is therefore possible to reconstruct pretty much the entire play. (See Chapter 4.)

## ITALIAN AND SPANISH RELIGIOUS DRAMA

In Italy, the vernacular religious drama developed out of a slightly different background from that of France or Germany. In the mid-thirteenth century, as the result of a religious mania, there arose the penitential movement of the Flagellanti (who alternately lashed themselves and lauded God), which manifested itself in great processions of *Disciplinati di Gesu Cristo*. After 1260, the *Disciplinati* formed themselves into religious fraternities and continued their practice of offering *laude* to God. Two *devozioni* of the early fourteenth century, contained in the Codex Palatini in the Vatican Library, illustrate how the original *laude* developed almost chance dialogue into real dramatic pieces. The ultimate stage of such development is supposedly the *Passion of Revello*

(1490), preserved in a manuscript in the Biblioteca Medicea-Laurenziana. In its construction and size, however, the play is reminiscent of the contemporary French theatre.

More than one hundred dramatic *laude* have been preserved in three other codices, the *laudari* of Urbino, Orvieto, and Perugia. Of these, the most important is the Laudario of the Confraternity of St. Andrew in Perugia, which contains the fullest selection of extant dramatic *laude*. It makes up the second part of a fourteenth-century manuscript concerning the confraternity in the Biblioteca Augusta in Perugia (MS. 955) and presents us with a total of 117 different lyric and dramatic *laude*. In addition, we have several sixteenth-century manuscripts containing relatively elaborate *laude* for the districts of Umbria and Abruzzi.

Another kind of drama developed in Florence. The *sacre rappresentazioni* were directly comparable to the French *mystères* and flourished especially between 1450 and 1550. Very little of this drama has been analyzed or discussed by theatre historians outside Italy. The only treatment of it in English, in Joseph Spencer Kennard's *The Italian Theatre* (1932), is sketchy and imprecise, postulating its origins in Roman spectacle and the *devozioni* and noting the relationship of its staging techniques to those of the French theatre.

Although on a smaller scale, this sacred drama approached the French model in its emphasis on spectacle. For those who read Italian, Alessandro D'Ancona's *Origini del teatro italiano* (1891) provides a standard survey of both *laude* and *sacre rappresentazioni*; and the texts of the plays are available in Vincenzo de Bartholomeis' *Laude drammatiche e rappresentazioni sacre* (1943).

All but specialists have similarly neglected the medieval theatre of Spain. Fortunately, the English-speaking world has been well served in recent years through the publication in 1958 of Donovan's book on the liturgical drama of Spain, and in 1967 of N. D. Shergold's *History of the Spanish Stage*. The earliest vernacular dramatic text is the *Auto de los Reyes Magos*, a brief play of the mid-twelfth century found in an early thirteenth-century manuscript of the Chapter Library of Toledo and preserved in the Biblioteca Nacional of Madrid. No further dramatic texts from Castile appear until we find the *Representación del nascimiento de Nuestro señor*, a series of four nativity plays by the fifteenth-century poet Gomez Manrique (1412?–1490?). But a great number of later religious plays are contained in two large codices from the sixteenth century. The first of these, discovered in 1887 and now housed in the Biblioteca Central of Cataluna (MS. 1139), contains forty-nine plays liberally provided with stage directions. The manuscript is a copy of the original, which may have dated from the fifteenth century; the plays seem likely to date from that time. The second is the *Códice de autos viejos*, catalogued as MS. 14.711 in the Biblioteca Nacional in Madrid. Purchased in 1844, the collection's origin and purpose are unknown, as is the original place of performance. The ninety-six plays include plays on biblical subjects, plays on the lives of saints and martyrs, and *farsas sacramentales*, or moralities. Some texts provide staging information concerning the use of floats or carts; and various prologues seem to indicate the presence of municipal officers in the audience. (The collection has been edited by L. Rouanet.) There exists in addition to these a manuscript from 1672, containing three mystery plays from the late fifteenth or early sixteenth century performed at Valencia: *Adam e Eva, Misterio de San Christofol, Misterio de Rey Herodes*.

Finally, the large number of Christmas and Easter plays from the late fifteenth and the sixteenth centuries that have survived in printed form present certain problems of interpretation. There is often nothing to link them with any particular time or place; there are few indications in the texts—either explicit or implicit—to help us reconstruct the original conditions of performance; some plays may have been written to be read rather than performed; and the texts of those that were performed may have been revised for printing.

## ENGLISH AND CORNISH RELIGIOUS DRAMA

The best known of the religious dramas of medieval England are, of course, the four great cycles of Chester, York, Wakefield (Townley), and the so-called *Ludus Coventriae*. But there are individual plays extant from other cycles, together with manuscripts containing saints' lives and moralities. In addition, we have several manuscripts containing plays in the Cornish language.

The Chester Mystery Cycle is preserved in whole or in part in eight manuscripts, five of which are full cyclic versions; the remaining three consist of a fragment of the Resurrection play, the whole of the play on the Antichrist, and the whole of *The Trial and Flagellation*. Of the cyclic versions, three of the manuscripts are in the British Museum, another at Oxford, and the last in the Huntington Library in San Marino, California. The dates and conditions of the manuscripts do not indicate much hope that we are dealing with production documents. The earliest of the complete versions, the Huntington manuscript, dates from 1591, and it and the British Museum manuscripts are judged to have been prepared as reading or presentation copies: Two of them in fact were prepared by the same scribe. The badly executed and battered manuscript at Oxford—clearly *not* a presentation copy—similarly holds little promise for the theatre historian, in that it was prepared by one William Bedford in 1604, a quarter of a century after the cycle had ceased to be performed. The only extant manuscript that is arguably an acting text is that containing the fragment of the Resurrection play, dating from the fifteenth century and preserved in the Manchester Free Library. But for the cycle as a whole we are dependent upon what must be considered to be a synthetic text, amounting to a judicious conflation of the extant versions.

The York Cycle, the Wakefield Cycle, and the *Ludus Coventriae* have come down to us in single manuscripts: the York and *Ludus Coventriae* manuscripts are preserved in the British Museum; the Wakefield manuscript is in the Huntington Library. Their relatively early dates make them of interest, however. The York manuscript dates from about 1430–40; the Wakefield from the second half of the fifteenth century; and the one containing the *Ludus Coventriae* has the year 1478 inscribed on one of its leaves. The first two seem likely to have been prepared as official copies for deposit with municipal authorities; the manuscript of the misnamed *Ludus Coventriae* appears to be partly a copy and partly a compilation of material from other manuscripts. Its attribution to Coventry is based on the mistaken notation written on the manuscript by Richard James, Sir Robert Cotton's librarian, when it was acquired by Cotton, sometime after 1629. One further manuscript, containing the Scrivener's play from the York Cycle, dates from the early sixteenth century and is in the possession of the York Philosophical Society.

The *Ludus Conventriae* differs from the other three cycles in ways other than its misnomer. It consists of three distinguishable groups of plays, and it seems unlikely that they were ever performed as a whole. One group is composed of Old Testament plays; a second consists of plays devoted to the Virgin; and the third is a Passion play in two parts. The stage-directions for the first two parts are few and indicative of the processional staging traditionally associated with pageant wagons. Those accompanying the Passion play, however, are fuller and indicate that the performance may have been stationary and multi-scenic, after the Continental manner. It is this Passion play that gives some credence to the tradition, stemming from another of Richard James' annotations, that the *Ludus Coventriae* was at one time played by "Monachos sive fratres mendicantes"—mendicant monks or brothers. A. M. Nagler goes even further, and on the basis of some similarities between the Passion play of the *Ludus Conventriae* and the *Alsfeld Passion Play*, proposes the sermonizing technique of the Franciscans as the common origin of both plays—and thus, in spite of the non-Coventry dialect, links the English play to the Franciscan house at Coventry (*Medieval Religious Stage*, pp. 12–14). The theory has little support among theatre historians. But even conservative scholars are allowed their speculations.

Individual plays are represented in several extant manuscripts. They include: (1) an *Abraham and Isaac* in the library of Trinity College, Dublin; (2) the Brome *Abraham and Isaac*, in the Yale University Library; (3) *The Play of the Sacrament*, also at Trinity College, Dublin; (4) *Dux Moraud* (one speaker's part) and *Burial and Resurrection*—both in the Bodleian Library at Oxford; (5) the *Coventry Shearmen and Taylor's Pageant*, the manuscript of which was destroyed by fire in 1879, but the text of which was preserved in Thomas Sharpe's *The Pageant of the Company of Sheremen and Taylors* (1817); and (6) the Coventry *Weavers' Pageant*, preserved in the Munement Room, St. Mary's Hall, Coventry. Finally, we have in Bodleian Digby MS. 133 a collection of four plays: *The Conversion of St. Paul*, *Mary Magdalene*, *The Massacre of the Innocents*, and *Purification*. There is in addition a fragment of the morality play *Mind, Will, and Understanding*.

The complete text of this last-named play is included in the important *Macro Collection*, named after an eighteenth-century clergyman in whose possession it once was. The manuscripts are now owned by the Folger Shakespeare Library in Washington, D.C. Besides *Mind, Will, and Understanding*, the collection includes *The Castle of Perseverance* and *Mankind*. *The Castle of Perseverance* (ca. 1420) is accompanied by a stage plan indicating a performance in the round, and a list of characters. The *Macro Plays* are available in facsimile, in John S. Farmer's *Tudor Facsimile Texts* (1907–8), and with facing transcriptions in David Bevington's *The Macro Plays* (1972). The primary corpus of English medieval morality plays is completed with the early *Pride of Life*, whose manuscript, stored in the Public Records Office in Dublin, was destroyed during political disturbances in June 1922, and *Everyman*, which survives in several printed editions from the early sixteenth century.

Two manuscripts from Cornwall complete our survey of religious dramatic texts from England. A Passion play, normally now referred to as *The Cornish Ordinalia* and consisting of three parts—*The Beginning of the World*, *Christ's Passion*, and *The Resurrection of Our Lord*—has come down to us in a unique, early-fifteenth-century manuscript, now found in the Bodleian Library (MS. 791), the gift in 1615 of one James Button. The text is in Middle Cornish, with the stage directions and the names of the characters in Latin. The stage directions exist in relative abundance and indicate that the performance—probably in the round—had a two-level vertical as well as a horizontal dimension. Also included in the manuscript are three schematic drawings, one for each play, locating on a circle the positions of the various stations necessary for its production. The *Ordinalia* has been translated into English by Edwin Norris (1859) and by Markham Harris (1969). Norris includes reproductions of the three drawings. Finally, in the National Library of Wales there exists a late-fifteenth-century manuscript (Peniarth MS. W5) entitled *Ordinale de Vita Sancti Mereadoci Episcopi et Confessoris*— The Life of St. Meriasek—complete with a stage plan similar to those accompanying the *Ordinalia*. The play has been edited and translated by W. Stokes (1872).

## THE SECULAR DRAMA

Non-religious dramatic texts date from as early as the thirteenth century in France, but in the rest of Europe they do not appear on the scene until the late fifteenth or early sixteenth century. By this time medieval dramatic traditions were being challenged by humanistic and academic drama modelled after the practice of Greece and especially Rome. Until the second half of the sixteenth century, however, the medieval influence was strong enough for us to include this admittedly untidy era as part of the medieval period.

When considering the extant non-religious dramatic texts as evidence for theatre history, we must bear several things in mind. In the first place, we should differentiate between those plays that were produced at a time when the religious drama dominated and the increasingly large numbers of interludes and farces that, by the late fifteenth and early sixteenth centuries, formed the repertories of the emerging troupes of professional players. The former are preserved in manuscript; the latter principally, though not exclusively, in printed editions. In the second place, when considering later texts, it is wise to try to differentiate as well between plays intended for the professional repertory and those intended for amateur or occasional performance. This latter distinction is more readily made with respect to English drama than to that of France, where theatrical activity tended sometimes to render meaningless the notions of sacred and secular, professional and amateur. Finally, as always, we must remain wary of the text printed to satisfy the growing appetite for "literature."

The early secular drama of France that is preserved in manuscript is of considerable interest. Two plays by Adam de la Halle, *Le Jeu de la feuillée* (1276–77) and *Le Jeu de Robin et de Marion* (1287–88), may be claimed as the earliest vernacular non-religious plays in any European language. Both are included in a manuscript dating from 1300 (Bibliothèque Nationale fr. 25566), but each also exists—at least in part—in two other manuscripts. Neither text includes stage directions, although both include songs. Indeed, *Robin et Marion* may well be termed a musical comedy. Also, the oldest surviving farce in French dates from the last half of the thirteenth century. *Le Garçon et l'aveugle* survives in a thirteenth-century manuscript, with sparce rubrics added in the fourteenth century. The only stage-direction, which occurs twice, is "they sing together."

Three serious plays on non-religious subjects but clearly related to the *mystères* are also preserved from the late fourteenth and early fifteenth centuries. *L'Estoire de Griseldis*, perhaps by Philippe de Mézières, has come down to us in an illuminated manuscript dated 1395 (Bibliothèque Nationale fr. 2203), which may have been intended as a presentation copy for King Richard II of England. The stage-directions are particularly full. *Le Mystère du Siège d'Orléans*, a long play of over 20,000 lines, survives in a single manuscript, once in the library of Fleury and now in the Regina collection of the Vatican. Finally, Jacques Milet's even longer *L'Histoire de la destruction de Troye la grant* exists in more than a dozen manuscripts and an equal number of printed editions dating between 1484 and 1544.

There is no doubt that the invention of printing in the last quarter of the fifteenth century is largely responsible for the increased numbers of dramatic texts that have survived from the period 1475–1575. In Spain, secular drama tended to be overshadowed by the continuing religious drama, especially the *autos sacrementales* performed annually during the Feast of Corpus Christi. The beginnings of a professional repertory, however, is to be found in the *pasos* of actor-playwright Lope de Rueda (ca. 1505–65). In Italy, the popular theatre that had its roots at least partially in the medieval theatre was similarly overshadowed by the revival of classical learning and the attempts to write plays after classical models. Possibly the best Italian playwright in the popular tradition, Angelo Beolco, called Ruzzante (ca. 1500–42), represents, like Lope de Rueda, the new professionalism. In Germany, interest centres principally on the Nuremburg Shrovetide plays, originally associated with apprentices' revels preceding Lent but culminating in the farces of Hans Sachs (1494–1576). In England, what has become known as the Tudor Interlude developed mainly along the lines established by the medieval morality play, such as *Mankind*, and again served as the basis of a professional repertory. Finally, in France we find the largest number of late medieval dramatic texts, consisting of approximately 400 farces, *sotties*, *moralités*, and monologues.

The bulk of this output exists only in printed form, and the use of these texts to the theatre historian is governed by the uses for which they were intended and to which they were put.

In England the earliest printed texts date from the 1520s and 1530s and come from the press of John Rastell, mostly in single-volume editions. In these and in later printed texts from England, historians are dependent upon textual implication and the information provided by the title-pages. In *From Mankind to Marlowe* (1962), an important study relating the requirements of performance to the structure of the dramatic texts, David Bevington was able, on the basis of internal evidence and explicit indications of casting requirements on title-pages, to distinguish the professional repertory (those plays "offered for acting") from plays intended for amateur or courtly production, and to demonstrate that limited troupe size and the consequent necessity of doubling and versatility on the part of the actors promoted a dramatic structure based on the alternation and suppression of characters.

In France, on the other hand, publishing was undertaken in a different manner, and it is generally agreed that most of the extant editions do not reflect performance practice, were not prepared for the use of actors and producers, and that consequently their value for theatre historians is limited. If, as has been suggested, the printers may have provided the actors with acting copies, there is no indication in the extant texts of their use by actors. The standard survey of the material is Petit de Julleville, *Répértoire du théâtre comique en France au moyen-âge*, and the texts are available to us mainly in a handful of collections. The principal printed collections include the following: the British Museum Collection (C.20d/4) of 64 plays; the *Recueil Trepperal* of thirty-three plays, named after the Parisian printer Jehan Trepperel (the *sotties* edited by Eugénie Droz in 1935, the *farces* by Droz and H. Lewicka in 1961); a collection of fifty-three plays edited by Gustav Cohen in 1949 under the title *Recueil de farces françaises inédites du XVᵉ siècle*; and two smaller collections of seven and nine plays respectively—that of the printer Nicolas Rousset, and the so-called Copenhagen Collection of 1619.

There are in addition several manuscripts containing French plays or fragments of plays, at least two of which are of considerable importance. The Vallière manuscript in the Bibliothèque Nationale (fr. 24341), dating from about 1575, contains 74 plays and is therefore the largest collection extant. And in the Biblioteca Laurenziana in Florence there are manuscripts that represent the only copies of French secular plays that *were* involved in performance. Two of the plays give evidence of having been revised, and, more important, the texts contain numerous marginal notes indicating stage action and musical interludes. These important manuscripts are discussed and partially reproduced in Paul Aebischer, "Moralités et farces des manuscrits Laurenziana-Ashburnham nos. 115 et 116," *Archivium Romanicum* XIII (1929).

## REFERENCES

Aebischer, Paul. "Moralités et farces des manuscrits Laurenziana-Ashburnham nos. 115 et 116." *Archivium Romanicum*, XIII (1929), 448–518.

Baixauli, Mariano. "Las Obras musicales de San Francisco de Borja." *Razon y Fé* IV (1902), 154–170, 237–283.

Bartholomeis, Vincenzo de, ed. *Laude drammatiche e rappresentazioni sacre*. 3 Vols. Florence, 1943.

Bate, Keith, ed. *Three Latin Comedies*. Toronto, 1976.

Bevington, David M. *From Mankind to Marlowe: Growth of Structure in the Popular Drama of Tudor England*. Cambridge, Mass., 1962.

———, ed. *The Macro Plays*. The Folger Facsimiles. New York and Washington, 1972.

———, ed. *Medieval Drama*. Boston, 1975.

Bodel, Jehan. *Le Jeu de Saint Nicolas*. Ed. Albert Henry. Brussels, 1965.

Bogdanos, Theodore. "Liturgical Drama in Byzantine Literature." *Comparative Drama* X (1976), 200–215.

Brambs, J. G., ed. *Christus Patiens [Christos Paschon]*. Leipzig, 1885.

Cohen, Gustave. *Le Théâtre en France au moyen-âge*. 2 Vols. Paris, 1828–31.

———. *L'Histoire de la mise en scène dans le théâtre religieux français du moyen-âge*. 2d ed. Paris, 1926.

Cohen, Gustave, ed. *La "Comedie" latine en France au XII ᵉ siècle*. Paris, 1931.

———, ed. *Mystères et moralités du Manuscrit 617 de Chantilly*. Paris, 1920. [Revised and retitled *Nativité et moralités liégeoises du moyen-âge*. Brussels, 1953.]

———. ed. *Recueil de farces françaises inédites du XVᵉ siècle*. Cambridge, Mass., 1949.

Collins, Fletcher, ed. *Medieval Church Music-Dramas: A Repertory of Complete Plays*. Charlottesville, 1976.

Coussemaker, Edmond de. *Drames liturgiques du moyen âge (texte et musique)*. Rennes, 1860.

Crawford, J.P.W. *Spanish Drama before Lope de Vega*. Rev. ed. Philadelphia, 1937.

D'Ancona, Alessandro. *Origini del teatro italiano*. 2 Vols. Turin, 1891.

Davis, Norman, ed. *Non-Cycle Plays and Fragments*. London, 1970.

Donovan, Richard B. *The Liturgical Drama in Medieval Spain*. Toronto, 1958.

Droz, Eugénie, ed. *Le Recueil Trepperel*. Vol. I: *Les Sotties*. Paris, 1935.

Droz, Eugénie, and H. Lewicka, eds. *La Recueil Trepperel*. Vol. II: *Les Farces*. Paris, 1961.

Falvey, Kathleen. "The First Perugian Passion: Aspects of Structure." *Comparative Drama*. XI (1977), 127–38.

Farmer, John S., ed. *The Castle of Perseverance*. Tudor Facsimile Texts. London and Edinburgh, 1908.

————, ed. *Mankind*. Tudor Facsimile Texts. London and Edinburgh, 1907.

————, ed. *Wisdom or Mind, Will, and Understanding*. Tudor Facsimile Texts. London and Edinburgh, 1907.

Frank, Grace. *The Medieval French Drama*. Oxford, 1954.

Froning, R., ed. *Das Drama des Mittelalters*. 3 Vols. Stuttgart, 1891–92.

Giraud, Paul-Emile, and Ulysse Chevalier, eds. *Le Mystère des Trois Doms, joué à Romans en 1509*. Lyon, 1887.

Girardot, Auguste-Théodore de, ed. *Mystére des Actes des Apôtres représenté à Bourges en avril 1536*. Paris, 1854.

Greenberg, Noah, ed. *The Play of Daniel: A Thirteenth-Century Musical Drama*. New York, 1959.

Greenberg, Noah, and W. L. Smoldon, eds. *The Play of Herod: A Twelfth-Century Music Drama*. New York, 1965.

Haller, Robert S., tr. *Figurative Representation of the Presentation of the Virgin Mary in the Temple*. Lincoln, Nebraska, 1971.

Harris, Markham, tr. *The Cornish Ordinalia: A Medieval Dramatic Trilogy*. Washington, 1969.

Hartl, Eduard, ed. *Das Drama des Mittelalters*. 2 Vols. Leipzig, 1937.

Hunningher, Benjamin. *The Origin of the Theatre*. New York, 1961.

Inguanez, D. M. "Un dramma della Passion del secolo XII." *Miscellanea Cassinese* XII (1936), 7–36.

Jodogne, Omar, ed. *Le Mystère de la Passion (Angers, 1486)*. Gembloux, Belgium, 1959.

————, ed. *Le Mystère de la Passion d'Arnoul Greban*. Brussels, 1965.

Jubinal, Achille, ed. *Mystères inédits du quinzième siècle*. Paris, 1837.

Kennard, Joseph Spencer. *The Italian Theatre from Its Beginning to the Close of the Seventeenth Century*. 2 Vols. New York, 1964 [1932].

Konigson, Elie. *L'Espace théâtral médiéval*. Paris, 1975.

Lazaro Carreter, Fernando. *Teatro medieval*. Valencia, 1958.

Lebègue, Raymond. *Le Mystère des Actes des Apôtres, contribution a l'étude de l'humanisme et du protestantisme français au XVIᵉ siècle*. Paris, 1929.

Le Verdier, Pierre, ed. *Mystère de l'Incarnation et Nativité*. Société des Bibliophiles Normands. Rouen, 1884–86.

Lumiansky, R. M., and David Mills, eds. *The Chester Mystery Cycle*. Vol. I: *Text*. London, 1974.

Michael, Wolfgang F. *Das deutsche Drama des Mittelalters*. Berlin, 1971.

Monaci, Ernesto. "Appunti per la storia del teatro italiano: Uffizi drammatici dei disciplinati dell'Umbria." *Rivista di Filologia Romanza* I (1872), 257–260.

Nagler, A. M. *The Medieval Religious Stage*. New Haven and London, 1976.

Norris, Edwin, tr. *The Ancient Cornish Drama*. 2 Vols. Oxford, 1859.

Paris, G., and U. Robert, eds. *Les Miracles de Nôtre Dame*. 8 Vols. Paris, 1876–83.

Petit de Julleville, L. *Les Mystères*. 2 Vols. Paris, 1880.

————. *Répertoire du théâtre comique en France au moyen-âge*. Paris, 1886.

Picot, E., and C. Nyrop, eds. *Nouveau Recueil de farces françaises des XVᵉ et XVIᵉ siècles, publié d'après un volume unique appartenant à la Bibliothèque royale de Copenhague*. Paris, 1880.

Pinet, Christopher. "French Farce: Printing, Dissemination and Readership from 1500–1560." *Renaissance and Reformation*, n.s., III (1979), 111–131.

Richard, Jules-Marie. *Le Mystère de la Passion: Texte du manuscrit 697 de la Bibliothèque d'Arras*. Geneva, 1976 [1891].

Rothschild, James de, ed. *Le Mistère du Viel Testament*. Paris, 1878–91.

Rouanet, L., ed. *Colección de autos, farsas, y coloquios del siglo XVI*. 4 Vols. Barcelona and Madrid, 1901.

Rousset, Nicolas [Printer]. *Recueil de plusieurs farces, tant anciennes que modernes, lesquelles ont este mises en meilleur ordre et langage qu'auparavant*. Paris, 1612.

Schützeichel, Rudolf, ed. *Das Mittelrheinische Passionspiel der St. Galler Handschrift 919*. Tubingen, 1978.

Sharp, Thomas. *The Pageant of the Company of Sheremen and Taylors in Coventry*. Coventry, 1817.

Shergold, N. D. *A History of the Spanish Stage from Medieval Times until the End of the Seventeenth Century*. Oxford, 1967.

Smoldon, William L. *The Music of the Medieval Church Dramas*. Ed. Cynthia Bourgeault. Oxford, 1980.

———, ed. *Peregrinus: A Twelfth-Century Easter Musical Drama*. London, 1965.

———, ed. *Planctus Mariae: A Fourteenth-Century Passiontide Musical Drama*. London, 1965.

———, ed. *Visitatio Sepulchri: A Twelfth-Century Easter Music Drama*. London, 1963.

Sticca, Sandro. *The Latin Passion Play: Its Origin and Development*. Albany, 1970.

Stokes, Whitley, ed. *The Life of St. Meriasek*. London, 1872.

Symons, Thomas, ed. *The Monastic Agreement of the Monks and Nuns of the English Nation: Regularis Concordia*. New York, 1953.

Tintori, Giampiero, and Raffaello Monterosso, eds. *Sacre rappresentazioni nel manoscritto 201 della bibliothèque municipale di Orléans*. Cremona, 1958.

Wackernell, J. E., ed. *Altdeutsche Passionspiel aus Tirol*. Graz, 1897.

Weiner, Albert B., tr. *Philippe de Mézières' Description of the "Festum Praesentationis Beatae Mariae."* New Haven, 1958.

West, Larry E., tr. *The Saint Gall Passion Play*. Brookline, Mass. and Leiden, 1976.

Wright, Edith A. *The Dissemination of the Liturgical Drama in France*. Bryn Mawr, 1936.

Young, Karl. *The Drama of the Medieval Church*. 2 Vols. Oxford, 1933.

Zucker, A. E., tr. *The Redentin Easter Play*. New York, 1941.

# INDEX

Abraham of Souzdal, Bishop, 102-3, 109
*Abregiés,* 99, 103
Adonis, 14
Adrados, Francisco R., 22-23
Adrastus, 6, 20
Aeschylus, 21; *Agamemnon,* 43, 43-44; dramatic texts, 40
Ailred, Saint, 111
Alsfeld Passion Play, 100
Alsloot, Daniel van, 121
Amalarius of Metz, 24
Ambrosian Palimpsest, 68
Amphitheatres (Roman), 74
Ancient scholarship: Alexandria, 57; Greece, 56-59; Rome, 82-83
Anderson, M. D., 122
Andromeda vase, 50
Anthropology, 7-12, 25-26
Anti, C., 47
Antiquarianism, 90
Apuleius, Lucius, 79
Archaeology: Greek theatres, 44-47; Medieval theatres, 109; Roman theatres, 73-77
Archilochus, 5
Archival documents, 101-2, 112-13
Arion, 5, 19, 20
Aristophanes, dramatic texts, 41

Aristophanes of Byzantium, 39, 42, 57
Aristotle: *Didascaliae,* 49, 54, 57; *Poetics,* 3, 5, 6, 54
Arnobius, 84
Arnott, Peter, 43
Art and theatre, 120-25. *See also* Monuments
Aspendos, theatre at, 75
Athenaeus, 6, 58
*Augustan History,* 82
Augustine, Saint, 84

Balbus, theatre of, 75
Beare, William, 64, 66, 69
Bede, the Venerable, 119
Benedictine monasteries, 23, 24
Bieber, Margarete, 36, 52, 66, 69, 76
Bigongiari, Dino, 114
Borlase, William, 109
Bourges, 1535 performance, 104
Bretex, Jacques, 116
Bulle, Heinrich, 44
Burton, Roger, 102

Cabham, Thomas de, Bishop of Salisbury, 111
Cailleau, Hubert, 105, 106
Calliopian Recension, 69

Cambridge Anthropologists, 12-16, 27, 120
Campanian vase, 50
Carbonares, M., 113
Carew, Richard, 107
*Castle of Perseverance,* 110, 116
Chambers, E. K., 26, 91, 113, 115
Chaumeau, Jean, 104, 106
Choricius of Gaza, 80, 85
*Christian Art, Index of,* 123
Christian Church, 110-12
Christian Writers, on Roman theatre, 83-85
Chronicles, medieval, 114-15, 117-18
*Chronique de Charles V,* 118
Chrysostum, John, 84
Church Fathers, 84
Churches (as places of performance), 108-9
Cicero, Marcus Tullius, 78-79, 85
Clement of Alexandria, 6
Codex Bembinus, 68
Codex Etruscus, 69
Cohen, Gustave, 23, 91-92, 96, 103, 110, 113, 114, 122
Collins, Fletcher, 95, 123
Cologne, 101
Colosseum, 74
Comedy, origins of, 5-6, 15, 22
Comparative anthropology, 7-12, 25-26
*Concordia Regularis.* See *Regularis Concordia*
Confraternity of St. Dominic (Perugia), 112-13
*Contaminatio,* 65
Cornford, Francis, 12, 15
Cornish *Ordinalia,* 100
Cornwall, 109
*Corpus Inscriptionum Graecarum,* 47
*Corpus Inscriptionum Latinarum,* 70
Craig, Hardin, 93
Curio, C., 79
Cyrene, wall-paintings, 72
Cysat, Renward, 105

Davies, R., 113
Dawson, Giles E., 113
*De Amphitheatro liber,* 121
*Décor simultané,* 110

Didascaliae, 48-49, 68
*Didascaliae* (Aristotle), 49, 54, 57
Didymus, 57
Diogenes Laertius, 58
Dionysius of Halicarnassus, 83
Dionysus, 5, 6, 14, 16, 19, 21; Theatre of, 44-46, 47, 75
Diomedes (grammarian), 83
*Dirigierolle,* 99, 103
Disguisings, 115, 118
Dithyramb, 5, 6
Documents of production, 99-108; archival documents, 101-2; eyewitness account, 102-3; play texts, 98-99; promptbooks, 99-100; questionable instances, 105-8; stage plans, 100-101
Donaldson, John William, 34-35
Donatus, Aelius, 68, 83
Donaueschingen Passion Play, 101
Dorians, 5, 6, 19
Dörpfeld, Wilhelm, 35-36, 44
Doué, amphitheatre, 121
Davidson, Clifford, 124
Dramatic texts, 39-44 (Greek), 69-70 (Roman), 96-99 (Medieval); Aeschylus, 40; Aristophanes, 41; Euripides, 40-41; Menander, 41; Plautus, 68; Seneca, 69-70; Sophocles, 40; Terence, 68-69
*Drōmenon,* 13-14, 29
Duckworth, George E., 64, 69
Dugdale, William, 106
*Dyskolos,* 41

*Edfu Drama,* 18
Egypt, theatre of, 16-18
*Ekkeklema,* 43, 56
Else, Gerald F., 15, 16, 20-21
Epidaurus, theatre at, 46-47
Ethelwold, Bishop of Winchester, 24
Etruscan tomb paintings, 71-72
Euripides, 5; *Bacchae,* 14; dramatic texts, 40-41
Eusebius of Caesarea, 84
Evolution, theory of, 7-8

Fabulae Varronianae, 68
Fasti, 48
Favyn, A., 116

Fergusson, Francis, 16
Festus, Sextus Pompeius, 83
Fiechter, Ernst, 44
Flaccus, Marcus Verrius, 83
Flickinger, Roy C., 36
Florence, 102-3
Folk-drama, 26, 27, 119-20
Fouquet, Jean, 106-7, 110
Frazer, Sir James, 7, 12-13
Froissart, Jean, 117-18
Funeral monuments, 72

Gardiner, Harold C., 93-94, 112
Garton, Charles, 79
Gaster, Theodore, 15, 17-18
Gautier, Léon, 24
Gelasius, 84
Gellius, Aulus, 58
Gerald of Wales, 119
Geta, Hosidius, 70
Giraud, Paul-Emile, 103
Gnathia Vase (Taranto), 50
Graeco-Roman theatres, 75
Grande, C. del, 20
Greban, Arnoul, *Passion,* 98
Greek scholarship (ancient), 56-59
Greek theatre: dramatic texts, 39-44; in-
    scriptions, 47-49; monuments (picto-
    rial), 49-53; origins, 4-7, 14-16; schol-
    arship (modern), 33-39; theatres, 44-47;
    written sources, 53-59
Gregory of Nyssa, 84
Groos, Karl, 8
*Grundriss der Romanischen Literaturen des
    Mittelalters,* 96

Haigh, Arthur E., 4-5, 35
Hall, Edward, 117, 118
Hamelin, Jean, 101
Hanson, John Arthur, 76-77
Hardison, O. B., 25, 29, 108-9
Harrison, Jane, 12, 13-14, 29
Havemeyer, Loomis, 8-9
Hécart, G.A.S., 90, 113
Hellenistic theatres, 74-75
Herculaneum, 52, 71
Herodas, 42
Herodes Atticus, Odeon of, 74

Herodotus, 5, 6, 16
*Histoire de Guillaume le Maréchal,* 116
Historians: Christian, 84; Roman, 80-82
*Histriones,* 26-27
Honorius of Autun, 24, 29
Horace, 77-78
Hunningher, Benjamin, 26-27

Iconography. *See* Art; Monuments
Ikhernofret, 18
Impersonation, 21, 25, 29
*Inscriptiones Graecae (IG),* 47
Inscriptions: Greek, 47-49; Roman, 70
*Ioculatores,* 26-27
Isidore of Seville, 111

Jacobus of Coccinobaphus, 121
Jenkins, Linda Walsh, 11
Jerome, Saint, 84
*Joculatores,* 26-27

Kahrl, Stanley J., 113
Kernodle, George, 12
Kirby, E. T., 11-12, 29
Kolve, V. A., 95
Konigson, Elie, 95, 110, 121, 124

Lactantius, Lucius, 84
*Lanercost, Chronicle of,* 119
*Leeds Descriptive Catalogue of Medieval
    Drama,* 96
Lexicons, 57-58, 83
Limoges, 27
*Lives of the Ten Orators,* 39
Livius Andronicus, 64, 81
*Livres de Conduite du régisseurs,* 99
Livy, 71, 80-81, 82, 85
*Logeion,* 56
Lollards, 112
Loomis, R. S., 114
Lucas de Iranzo, Miguel, 115
Lucerne, 1583 performance, 105
Lucian of Samosata, 73, 79, 85
Lydgate, John, 118-19

Macrobius, Amrosius Theodosius, 83
Magnin, Charles, 23
Mahr, August, 21-22

Mâle, Emile, 121-22, 123
Marble Plan (of Rome), 74
Marcellus, theatre of, 75-76
Marmor Parium, 6, 47-48
Martianus Capella, 83
Masks, terracotta, 72-73
Mass, 23, 23-24, 24-25, 25, 26
Maydiston, Richard, 118
*Mechané,* 56
Medieval theatre: art, 120-25; dramatic
    texts, 96-99; folk-drama, 119-20; origins,
    23-27; places of performance, 108-10;
    production documents, 99-108; schol-
    arship (modern), 89-96; written sources,
    110-14
Megarians, 5, 6, 19
*Memphite Drama,* 18
Menander, 39, 63; dramatic texts, 41; re-
    lief of, 51
Mézières, Phillippe de, 118
Mime (Roman), 79-80
Mimes (Medieval), 26-27
*Mimesis,* 11, 29
Moëles, Jacques des, 105
Molinari, Cesare, 12
Monasteries: Benedictine, 23; records, 112-
    13; St. Gall, 23; St. Martial, 23, 27
Mons, 1501 performance, 103
Monstrelet, Enguerrand de, 117-18
Monuments (pictorial): Greek, 49-53; Ro-
    man, 70-73
Mosaics, 51
Mummers' Play, 27
Mummings, 115, 118-19
Municipal records, 113-14
Murray, Gilbert, 12, 14-15, 20
*Mystère de Trois Doms,* 103

Nagler, A. M., 101, 103, 105, 107, 110
Nelson, Alan H., 95, 123
Nicoll, Allardyce, 66-67, 111, 121
Nonius Marcellus, 83

Odeons, 74
Oenochoe vase, 50
Olaus Magnus, 119
Orange, theatre at, 75
*Ordung des vmbgangs,* 102

Origins of theatre: Egypt, 16-18; Greece,
    4-7, 14-16; medieval, 23-27
Osiris, 14, 16
Outreman, Henri d', 105, 106

Pageantry, 114-19
Pageants, street, 117
Pantomime, 79-80
Parfaict, Claude and François, 110
Parian Marble, 6, 47-48
Paris, Matthew, 117
Pas d'armes, 116-17
*Pas d'Armes de la Sauvaige Dame,* 116
*Pas de la Bergière,* 116
Patzer, H., 20
Paul the Deacon, 83
Pausanias, 54
Peiraeus Relief, 51
*Peregrinatio Etheriae,* 24
*Periaktoi,* 55-56
Perrier, Louis, 103-4
Perugia, 112-13
Peterweil, Baldemar von, 100
Petit de Julleville, L., 90-91, 113
Phallic songs, 5
Philostratus, 73
Phlyax vases, 51, 71
Photius, 58
Pickard-Cambridge, A. W., 15-16, 43, 44-
    45, 46, 66; on monuments, 35, 36-37,
    52; on origins, 18-19, 20; on written
    sources, 37
Pictorial Evidence. *See* Art; Monuments
Plato, 5
Plautus, 63; dramatic texts, 68
Plays. *See* Dramatic texts
Play Texts. *See* Dramatic texts
Pliny the Elder, 79
Plutarch, 6, 53
Plutarch (pseudo), 39
Pollux, Julius, 34, 35, 54-56, 85
Pompeii, 52, 71, 74
Pompey, theatre of, 75-76
Pratina, 19
*Procès-verbal,* 102
Procopius, 79
Prompt-Books, 99-100
Pronomos vase, 50

Prosser, Eleanor, 95
*Prothyron,* 50
Prynne, William, 112

*Querolus,* 63, 70
Quintilian, 78

Raber, Vigil, 100
*Ramesseum Drama,* 18
Records, Written: Church, 110-12; medieval, 110-14; monastic, 112-13; municipal, 113-14
*Records of Early English Drama,* 113-14
*Regularis Concordia,* 24, 112
Reliefs, 51
René d'Anjou, 116
*Retractatio,* 67
Rey-Flaud, Henri, 110
Ridgeway, William, 6-7, 9-10
Ritual and theatre, 4, 9, 13-15, 17, 18, 20-21, 22, 23-25, 29
Rogers, David, 106
Rollinger, Wilhelm, 107
Romans, 1509 performance, 103-4
*Romans d'Alixandre,* 121
Roman drama, influence in Renaissance, 64
Roman historians, 80-82
Roman scholarship (ancient), 82-83
Roman theatre: inscriptions, 70; monuments (pictorial), 70-73; popular forms, 66-67; scholarship (modern), 63-67; theatres, 73-77; written sources, 77-85

Salter, F. M., 94
Salvianus, 84
Satyr-play, 5, 19, 22
Scaurus, M. Aemilius, 79
Scholarship (ancient): Alexandria, 57; Greece, 56-59; Rome, 82-83
Scholarship (modern): Greek theatre, 33-39; Roman theatre, 63-67; medieval theatre, 89-96
Scholia, 58-59, 68
*Scriptores Historiae Augustae,* 82
Seneca, Lucius Annaeus, 63; dramatic texts, 69-70
Seneca, Marcus Annaeus, 83

Servius, 83
Shamanism, 11, 12
Sharp, Thomas, 90, 106, 113
Sicyon, 6
*Skene,* 45-46, 56
Sophia, Saint, Cathedral of, 121
Sophocles: dramatic texts, 40; *Oedipus the King,* 43
Southern, Richard, 94, 100
Stage-directions, 43-44, 97-98
Stage-plans, 100-101
Statuettes, 52-53, 72-73
*Statuta Armorum,* 116
Stilo, L. Aelius, 82
Stow, John, 117, 118
Stratman, C. J., 96
Studemond, Wilhelm, 68
*Suda,* 5, 34, 58
Suetonius, 82
Susarian, 6

Tacitus, Publius Cornelius, 80, 82, 119
Taplin, Oliver, 38, 43
Terence, 63; dramatic texts, 68-69; illustrated manuscripts, 69, 121
Tertullian, 76, 81, 84-85
Theatres: Greek, 44-47; Roman, 73-77; medieval, 108-10
Themistius, 5
Theodoret, 84
Thespis, 5, 19, 21, 22
Thiboust, Jacques, 104
Tirol Passion Play, 98, 100-101
Tomb paintings, 71-72
Tournament, 115, 116-17
Tragedy, origins of, 5, 14-15, 22
Tropes, 24-25
Tydeman, William, 109-10, 120

Valenciennes, 1547 performance, 101, 104-5
Valerianus, Flavius, 72
Valerius Maximus, 80
Varro, Marcus Terentius, 68, 82-83
Vase-paintings, 49-51, 71
Vegetation-God, 13, 14, 26-27
Victors-Lists, 48-49
Vienna Passion Play, 107

Vigne, André de la, 102
Villingen Passion Play, 101
Vitruvius Pollio, Marcus, 34, 35, 55-56, 63, 75, 85

Wall-paintings, 52, 71
Walsingham, Thomas, 117
Webster, T.B.L., 20, 37-38, 71
Westminster, Matthew, 117
Wickham, Glynne, 25, 94-95, 100, 115, 117, 119, 120, 125

Wilamowitz-Moellendorff, Ulrich von, 34, 40
Williams, Arnold, 113
Withington, Robert, 115
Woolf, Rosemary, 95, 122-23
Wright, F. Warren, 78
Written sources: Greek theatre, 53-59; Roman theatre, 77-85; medieval theatre, 110-14

Young, Karl, 24-25, 92-93

**About the Author**

RONALD W. VINCE is Associate Professor of English and a member of the Instructional Committee on Dramatic Arts at McMaster University, Canada. He has published articles in *English Studies, Essays in Theatre, Walt Whitman Review,* and *Studies in English Literature.*